30 DAYS IN SPAIN

WALKING THE **CAMINO DE SANTIAGO** AND **RUNNING WITH THE BULLS**

ANDER ETXANOBE

*Forewords by Bobby George
& Aaron Marshall*

This book is dedicated to three special people:

My father. You are the toughest man I know. Many will never comprehend the sacrifices you made. But that has not stopped you from cementing an undeniable legacy of courage, bravery, and strength.

Von George. Thank you for being a model of devout Catholic faith. And for being a continuous example of how to treat others—with kindness, humility, and compassion.

Jeffrey "Thor" Hendricks. May the light of your memory live on forever in our hearts, illuminating the path when life is dark, and warming our spirit when in despair. Rest in peace, little angel.

"I praise you, for I am fearfully and wonderfully made.
Wonderful are your works; that I know very well."

—Psalm 139:14

FOREWORD:

BY BOBBY GEORGE

The Camino de Santiago is more than a mere hike through the Spanish countryside, but rather is a pilgrimage. It is an important distinction; a pilgrim is on a journey to reach something higher than him/herself. Specifically, the pilgrims who walk the Camino enter a spiritual voyage to the burial site of St. James at the Cathedral of Santiago de Compostela. Historically, pilgrims have ranged from the devout Christian laymen to criminals sentenced to walk in The Way of St. James as their penance. And although the Camino has become more of a bucket list activity to many of its participants today, all pilgrims have been bound together through scallop-shell salvation. Pilgrims since the 800s have experienced spiritual transformation while walking on the Camino, and it has therefore become a place for meditation and retreat.

The Camino is filled with interesting characters who all come to Spain for their own reasons, and it is often these unique and fascinating people that draw others to embark on their own pilgrimage. Historically, the Camino has been undertaken by men like Louis VII of France in 1154, St. Francis of Assisi in 1214, Pope John XXIII in 1957, and thousands of others. Ander Etxanobe is one of those pilgrims who has been able to inspire others. As though the near 500-mile trek over 30 days was not daunting enough, Ander decided to complete his Camino in only 20 days. The rush was not an attempt to be among the fastest pilgrims, but simply a result of scheduling; Ander had to complete his pilgrimage in time for the Fiesta of San Fermín in Pamplona for the running of the bulls.

Fiesta, as it is commonly called, is where Ander and my paths first crossed in 2017 when two Americans decided to run with the bulls of Spain.

The encierro (bull run) is a duty. What many fail to realize is that the opportunity to run with bulls is not exclusively a thrill, but a method of transportation for those beautiful and noble creatures. Before we had trains and trucks, bulls were only transported by runners. In Pamplona and various other towns throughout the world, this method is still used. When a runner successfully locks himself/herself on the horns of the bull, s/he has a brief moment of pure euphoria. There is a reason we run with the bulls; we do not run from, against, near, or any other preposition. "With" implies equality between the runner and the bull, where the bull is respected and not treated as a spectacle for just entertainment. The runner is to join the herd, and in that transcend his/her daily life and enter into the primitive mind of the animal.

Our modern lives are filled with constant decision making, stress, and over-thinking. Highways are covered with billboards telling us where to eat, watch strippers, and buy used cars; our homes are painted strategically to give us a new emotion for each room, art and furniture are replaced and reorganized to fit the right Feng Shui. We cannot be alone, and we are constantly seeking an escape. The encierro and the Camino de Santiago truly allow for us to tap into primal states of being so that we can learn about ourselves and grow into better versions. Through the pain of the camino and the intensity of the run, we gain a true appreciation for life and to focus on what is important. Ander has been able to master both forms of these bizarre therapies. As a Basque-American, Ander offers a unique perspective into the history, reasoning, and first-hand experience of his pilgrimage and his incredible skills of herding fighting bulls with nothing more than his agility and rolled newspaper. As Ander's friend and brother-of-the-bull, I have been blessed to learn and grow alongside him in our many travels to Spain. I am honored to have been asked to write this foreword, and hope the reader can find inspiration herein.

Bobby George, Esq., Allentown, 19 November, 2023

FOREWORD:

BY AARON MARSHALL

I went to Spain. A very traumatic thing happened. I thought I was going to die. This guy, Ander, helped get me home and saved my life. A year goes by. I see Ander again; I haven't seen him in the balance of time. We experience the run together once more. He knocks it out of the park, one of the best runs I've ever seen. But, he has a traumatic life-altering experience, and I get the chance to change his life, with my skill and my expertise and my experience, tailormade for this exact situation. I get to repay him for what he once did for me. I am the only one who is in the right place and the right time with the right training to do this, to make sure he gets home, like he did for me. That is what forges a brotherhood. Akin to conflict. The brotherhood, the fraternity, the camaraderie, the esprit de corps, the spirit amongst the two of us. It's the way Pamplona is; it's the spirit of San Fermín.

I've spent a career, a lifetime, in shithole places no-one in their right mind should be in. Disasters, emergencies, crises, humanitarian clusterfucks, and I found beauty amongst the death, destruction and loss. I found the greatest parts of myself, and of others, lurking on the edge of what many people would find to be the worst possible environments imaginable. And I loved every minute of it. It's clear that something is a little different, off you might say, in someone who finds joy amongst such horrible places. But I was taught to look for the helpers; and what I found in Pamplona and San Fermín were many people who were just like me; crazy, not stupid, but damnit, we all have a love for life. Zeal, for all that life could be.

Make no mistake about it. San Fermín and the encierro are combat, just without the bang and boom. It's the "hero's journey" wrapped into minutes if not seconds of life-altering, crippling fear to joyous, Everestsummiting elation, culminating with an unmistakable high, an appreciation and admiration for life, for cheating near-certain death at the hands of six animals destined to kill you if you get in their way.

In 2021, I was damn near dead at the hands of one of these bulls. Innocently, I went right when I should've gone left; I got caught up in a column of inexperienced runners, fell, got rammed by the right hoof of a bull, and severed my arm in half. Transported to the hospital by Spanish doctors and nurses, stabilized and sent on my way, no help, no way home, wandering aimlessly, bleeding all over the place. My brothers, my family of fiesta found me on the street; stopped the bleeding, got medicine so I could be transported home, and got me back to the states and to some of the best American medicine possible, within 14 hours. Make no mistake about it. These men saved my life, they saved me, and they leveled upon me a debt that can never be repaid.

Ander is one of my closest friends, although we've only spent time in the states together seldomly. We've spent the past nine years (with a hiatus for COVID in 2020 and 2021) together between 6 and 14 July in Pamplona. As you'll read throughout this beautiful story, I was able to help him have one of the greatest runs of his life, all the while dealing with devastating injuries and an overwhelming personal story of grit and tenacity in the face of adversity. This story is a testament to whom Ander is, to whom we are when we're aligned with him, and the way he lives his life on the edge. He empowers us to live just the same, and practice that same edgework in what we do, to get back to Pamplona each year. We come each year to continue to push the limits of ourselves, and to participate in the same conflict, against mediocrity, towards immortality enshrined by our collective experience. Ander, my friend, this is for you. Thanks for saving my life, letting me help you, and for allowing me to share some of the greatest experiences alive with you. Viva San Fermín.

Aaron Marshall, Atlanta, 15 November, 2023

CHAPTER ONE:

A MISSION IS BORN

Thump-thump, thump-thump. I could hear my heart throttling inside my chest, each breath steadily pacing my body and 30-pound backpack up the 20% gradient. Click-clack, click-clack, went the sounds of my trekking poles with each stride, sweat dripping down my ghostly-looking face, off my nose, and onto the gravel path below me. At almost 5,000 feet of elevation, the wind whistled by my ears and ruffled my hair. I was roaming above the clouds, surrounded by lush green mountain pastures, sheep resting in the sun, and horses frolicking near the path. I was on the Camino de Santiago. And the suffering had begun.

Before I found myself on the Camino, climbing the famed Napoleon Pass at the foothills of the Pyrenees, my story began at home, in Miami Beach, Florida. It was Friday, April 7, and the last few waves of adolescent Spring-Breakers had made their way to the famous tropical waters on the Atlantic Coast. Most of them dressed scantily in their two-piece bikinis, oiled-up bodies, complete with their silicone implants—no judgment here.

In the evening, as I usually do, I fired up a maduro cigar and took a walk down the boardwalk that runs parallel to Ocean Drive—the epicenter of Miami Beach nightlife. I started off on Ocean Drive and fifth street, slowly traversing the winding path northbound. At seventh street, tourists, still cloaked in their beachy attire, bathed in the neon lights of the Beacon Hotel, the Colony Hotel, and other nearby properties that defined south Florida for much of the 70s and 80s. I took a few puffs of my cigar and continued up to ninth street. There, I found a spot along the two-and-a-half-foot concrete wall that borders the path, took a seat, and gave my cigar a couple more puffs. It was getting good. When you light a cigar, it can take a bit for the fire and smoke to really fill out the cigar and open it up. And it was starting to open up.

I sat there in a gaze along the darkened boardwalk. 50 meters across from me on Ocean Drive was Mango's Tropical Cafe. This staple of Miami Beach opened in 1991, and since then, it has always attracted partygoers with its lively salsa music, exotic bar-top dancers, and colorfully decorated murals on the inside walls. As the salsa music poured out from the large open entrance, I started thinking about my upcoming summer travel plans. It was going to be my fifth year running with the bulls in Pamplona, Spain. If you have read my memoir, *The Basque,* you know that this tradition is near and dear to my heart. It changed my life by reconnecting me to my Basque and Navarran roots. My father is from a town called Mañaria, about 35km outside of Bilbao, the largest city in the Basque Country. My mother's family is from Navarra, as my grandfather was born in a small village called Urdániz, about 16km outside of Pamplona, the site of the running of the bulls. The tradition boasts of 850 meters of morning glory, as each bull run begins at 8am sharp, with bulls and runners alike stampeding their way through the old town of Pamplona and into the bullring. The feeling of running in front of charging bulls is one that is practically impossible to encapsulate with words on a page. But one thing is for sure: running with the bulls keeps me alive. The summer of 2023, though I still planned to run with the bulls, would be a little different.

On previous trips to Pamplona, I would typically travel in early July, as the festival of the running of the bulls goes from July 6 to July 14. However, I had received a wedding invite in the mail from my cousin, Amaia, in Pamplona. Amaia was getting married on June 17, a few weeks before the festival. What was I going to do between the wedding and the festival? "Should I travel back to Miami, then back to Pamplona?" I wondered. "Should I find an Airbnb in Ibiza and sip red wine on the Mediterranean Sea?" Surely, I could not do that. I had another idea in mind.

As I inhaled and exhaled the smoke from the darkened tobacco leaves of my maduro cigar, my phone started ringing. It was Cash Lawless, my best friend from high school. Cash and I had been on several journeys together. After we graduated high school in Oregon, we took our chances and flew across the country to attend American University in Washington, DC. And years before that, Cash accompanied me on a summer visit to the Basque Country, where we experienced our first foray into the Fiesta of San Fermín (Saint Fermín), the official name for the festival of the running of the bulls.

"What's up dude?" I said to Cash, answering the call.

"Are you really going to do it?" he asked. We had been texting about my summer dilemma.

"I would have just enough time to do it."

"20 days doesn't sound like a lot of time. A few years ago, I walked part of the Appalachian Trail, and anytime I walked more than 16km in a day, I wanted to kill myself. It's a grind. And you're talking about walking 800km in the span of 20 days. That's an average of 40km per day—that's insane!"

"Well, you know I'm crazy enough to do it."

"Yeah, I know you are."

The Camino de Santiago, or the "Way of Saint James," dates back to the ninth century as an ancient Christian pilgrimage. It all started around the year 820, when the bishop of Iria Flavia, a municipality in the Galicia province of Spain, sent a letter to Alfonso II, the King of Asturias, a province to the north. This letter informed the king of the discovery of a tomb believed to contain the body of Apostle Saint James. Shortly after, King Alfonso II was the first to make the pilgrimage to Compostela (which would later be called Santiago de Compostela), to be in the presence of the holy remains. Since then, millions of people have strapped on their boots and backpacks to make the ancient trek to the city of Santiago de Compostela.

Today, there are seven major routes to reach Santiago. You can travel from Lisbon or Porto, cities in southern and northern Portugal, or you can travel from A Coruña, Oviedo, or Irun, all cities in northern Spain. However, there is one route called the Camino Frances, or the "French Way," which begins in St. Jean Pied de Port, a small village in France, at the foothills of the Pyrenees. From there, pilgrims make their way across the 800km path to northwest Spain. The French Way has become the most popular of the routes. One of the main reasons for this is because most pilgrims from central Europe chose it as their path. However, a more modern reason for the popularity of the French Camino is likely due to a film called *The Way*. It follows Tom Avery, played by Martin Sheen, an American Ophthalmologist who travels to France to recover the body of his son, Daniel Avery, played by Emilio Estevez. Daniel died during a storm while climbing in the Pyrenees, attempting the Camino de Santiago. Upon arrival, in a last-minute decision, Tom cremates his son's body and walks the French Way in his memory. Another modern depiction of this route is a documentary called *I'll Push You*. This heart-warming film is about two friends and the power of friendship. It follows Patrick, an able-bodied person, and Justin, who has a neuromuscular disease, which has deprived him of the use of his arms and legs. We watch as Patrick pushes Justin in a wheelchair through the entire 800km journey. Much like *The Way*, it is a tearjerker. In the end, these two films helped provide a modern resurgence of the French Way, as well as the Camino in general.

While I have watched these films, my journey was going to be more about the physical nature of the challenge. Particularly the part about walking 800km in 20 days. Over the years, tourism authorities and travel agencies have helped create a standard approach to completing the pilgrimage to Santiago. They organized the walk into stages, and each day you tackle one stage. Typically, these stages land you in a town with sufficient accommodation, places to eat, and things to do. The stages also help pace you throughout the journey, often ensuring you only walk between 15km (a light day) and 25km (a heavy day). My plan to walk the French Way in 20 days was going to require an average walking pace of 40km per day, a blistering pace. But executing that pace would require a bit of planning.

True to my nature of working in finance, I sat down at my computer and opened an Excel spreadsheet to create the stages. After spending some time Googling around on the internet, I found a list of all the villages, towns, and cities along the route of the Camino. The list even had the incremental kilometer distances between the localities, as well as a rough indicator of the availability of lodging. Given the distance between each locality, planning each stage was not as easy as defining the set number of kilometers I would walk each day. For example, if I walked 40km in one day, but there was no lodging at the 40km mark, I might have to walk another 5km to find a place to stay. And as you would expect, larger towns and cities have more options for accommodation compared to the smaller villages, where you might be lucky to find more than one place to sleep (more on that in a bit). Because of this, planning each stage was not a simple task. It took a bit of trial and error.

Further complicating my pilgrimage, I had to factor in my cousin's wedding. For starters, Pamplona is a town on the Camino. However, Pamplona is 68km from St. Jean Pied de Port. Sure, I could start my pilgrimage in Pamplona, after my cousin's wedding, but then I would shortchange myself the 68km—I wanted the full 800km. Instead, by arriving a few days early, I could start in France and time my walking so that I arrive in Pamplona for the wedding, then resume the Camino afterwards. With this in mind, and after some tedious planning, I scheduled all of my stages.

To summarize my summer travel, my first day on the Camino would be June 15, arriving in Santiago on July 4, taking the train back to Pamplona on July 5, and departing Pamplona for Miami on July 15. I would have 30 full days in Spain—20 days to walk the Camino and 10 days in Pamplona to run with the bulls. After creating my own stages and booking the flights, the next pieces of the puzzle were the lodging, gear, and training.

Booking places to sleep was not exactly straightforward. You need some blind faith when sleeping on the Camino. This is because there are several types of accommodations, and it is not common practice to pre-book. The most popular option is called an "albergue," or pilgrim's hostel. As you might have guessed, albergues (in its plural form) are specifically for those who are on the Camino. Upon check-in, you are required to provide your "pilgrim's passport," which serves as evidence that you are indeed a pilgrim. Albergues offer lower nightly rates compared to other places available in the area. However, most of the accommodations from town to town are in the form of albergues. And within this category, there are three types: 1) public or municipal, 2) private, and 3) parochial. Public/municipal albergues are operated by the locality. They are often the cheapest form of accommodation and typically offer only the most basic of necessities—bunk bed (no sheets). Private albergues are a little more expensive than their public counterparts, but they usually offer bed sheets, toiletries, laundry services, Wi-Fi, and maybe even a few meals. Then there are the parochial albergues, which are called "donativos," or donation basis. These are simply albergues operated by a religious institution, such as a convent, monastery, or Catholic charity. You are not required to pay for your nightly stay, but are encouraged to donate what you can, as the donations collected from pilgrims are how these albergues continue to operate. The final few forms of accommodation, which require brief explanation, are hostels and hotels. For these, you are not required to furnish a pilgrim's passport, but they are often significantly more expensive than the albergues.

For my mission, I planned to stay mostly in private albergues, sprinkled in with some public albergues. There were a couple of reasons for this. I wanted an authentic pilgrim's experience (or at least what I envisioned as authentic), and I wanted to avoid bed bugs. From the little research I had done about the Camino, I had read horror stories about pilgrims encountering these pesty, flesh-biting, blood-sucking critters. It appeared the consensus was that pilgrims were more likely to encounter bed bugs when sleeping in the public albergues, as they were rumored to be less cleanly. Again, before I offend anyone, that was a rumor. And as we know, not all rumors are true. However, the consequences of encountering bed bugs on the Camino appeared to be grave. Anecdote after anecdote, I read of people waking up with red, itchy bumps all over their bodies. And worse, as they packed up their sleeping bags and other gear, they would inevitably take the tiny creatures with them to their next destination. And for being an 800km route, word seemed to pass rather quickly among other pilgrims. If an albergue had a case of bed bugs on its hands, the word got out. And right quick. For this reason, if your next albergue realized you came from one with bed bugs, you might be turned away. Ultimately, I made every effort to plan my nightly stays in villages with at least one private albergue. However, there were a handful of nights where I would have to pony up and stay at the municipal albergues. I kind of just threw my hands up in the air and said, "bring it on."

My last note on albergues (for now) is how to book them. The internet told me to book my first couple of nights on the Camino ahead of time, on websites like Booking.com or Priceline.com. So, I did. Previous pilgrims also recommended booking your last night in Santiago, as accommodations get booked weeks in advance and can get incredibly pricey. But not nearly as pricey as the cost of all my gear.

Buying the gear was a challenge. I had little reference for what to buy, due to the never-ending opinions of former pilgrims on the internet. There were very few points of consensus, which made it difficult to home in on what I needed to buy. None of my friends had completed the journey. And although my family was from the Basque Country, not one person had completed the trek from St. Jean Pied de Port in France, all the way to Santiago. I have one cousin, bless her heart, that completed the final 100km of the Camino. She recommended I buy sandals. That is not a dig against anyone who wears sandals on the Way, I just could not imagine walking 800km in sandals. It is also not a dig against anyone who only walked the final 100km of Camino. But there is a big difference between walking 100km and 800km, not to mention the changes in weather and terrain as you walk across the Iberian Peninsula. I needed to be prepared to complete *my* mission, not someone else's. In the end, I did my best to buy what was right for *me*.

The shoes. Where do I begin? In my humble opinion, this might be the most important purchase you will make for the Camino. After all, it is a walk. A very long walk. Over a matter of weeks, I must have bought and tried on at least 10 different shoes before I settled on a pair. I tried various sizes from brands like ALTRA, Nike, Hoka, and New Balance. I will highlight only a few here.

The first shoe I tried was the ALTRA Olympus 5 Trail Running Shoe. Trail runners and Camino enthusiasts alike revere this shoe brand. I liked the wide toe box that allowed my toes to spread out, breathe, and really grip the road as I walked. But the midsole section was narrow for my taste. My feet are on the wider side, and I could not envision myself walking 40 or more kilometers a day with those. The ALTRA shoe was also a "zero-drop" shoe, which refers to the height difference between the heel and the forefoot. In other words, a zero-drop shoe has a completely flat sole. The biggest problem with that style was the fact that I have flat feet. Podiatrists will tell you that zero-drop shoes are a non-starter for people with flat feet, as they might cause musculoskeletal injuries—this book is called 30 Days in "Spain," not 30 Days in "Careless."

The next shoe I ordered was the Nike React SFB Carbon Elite Outdoor Shoe. This shoe sounded badass. The description started out with "Built for special operators and elite outdoor athletes..." OK, well, maybe I am not a special operator, but buying the shoes sort of made me feel like one. The shoe was a blend between a hiking boot and a walking shoe, complete with a low-drop. Former pilgrims cautioned against buying hiking boots for the French Way, as a solid portion of the walk is on flattish terrain, on a mix between dirt, gravel, and pavement. And since hiking boots are on the heavier side and typically wrap high on your ankle, they can make for an uncomfortably long walk, complete with heel blisters. Built for durability and varying terrain, I thought this Nike shoe could be the winner. Sadly, the comfort was awful, as the toe box was narrow, midsole too tight, and my metatarsals felt like someone had handcuffed them. After trying a few different sizes, I realized they would not work.

The next candidate for the Camino de Santiago was the Hoka Speedgoat 5 Trail Running Shoe. The Hoka had great traction for the changing terrain I would face, as well as good cushion support at the base of the foot, which would be a lifesaver for all the excess kilometers I planned to walk each day. But, the Hoka's were too narrow on the midsole and too low on the ankle. Also, the high-drop felt a bit too high, putting lots of pressure on my toes and metatarsal bones.

After weeks of failure to find the right pair, I landed on the New Balance Fresh Foam X 1080v12. This running shoe featured a low/mid drop from the heel, a large toe box to let my toes wander about inside, and enough cushioning to make me feel like I was walking on clouds. But what made this choice unique was the fact that it came in a regular, wide, and extra-wide fit. I went with the extra-wide fit. I had never owned a more comfortable shoe. It had to be the one. Was it waterproof? No. Was it the lightest shoe available? Not really (10.3oz). But the fit was spectacular.

Now, before we move on, some Camino experts might find a glaring omission from my shoe selection above. It is missing a pair of Salomon shoes. Yes, Salomon shoes are one of the most popular choices for the great pilgrimage. However, I had read some posts mentioning that these shoes, especially the Salomon XT-6 GTX, have Gore-Tex material. This material makes the shoes 100% waterproof, which appeared to be a blessing and a curse. Some pilgrims said these shoes would keep your feet dry and blister-free in the event of a downpour, while others stressed that heat and breathability would be your enemy on hot and sunny days. To me, this shoe was more of a cold and wet weather item, versus a shoe more tailored to confront the hot summer heat in Spain. OK, so what about the rest of the gear?

This is not a guidebook, but for those of you who might plan your own Camino, or are simply curious about what I stuffed into my backpack, below is a quick, but complete list of everything that I picked up. However, if you are not curious, skip or gloss over.

Bags and Equipment:
- Osprey Manta 34 Men's Hiking Hydration Backpack
- (2) Osprey UltraLight 20L Dry Sack
- Tri-Fold Carbon Cork Trekking Poles
- "S" Hook

Clothing:
- Columbia Men's Silver Ridge Lite Plaid Long Sleeve
- Eddie Bauer Men's Cirruslite Down Vest

- (3) ExOfficio Men's Give-N-Go Boxer Brief Single Pack
- CQR Men's Convertible Cargo Pants
- (3) Darn Tough Men's Merino Wool Micro Crew Hiker Socks
- PTEROMY Hooded Rain Poncho for Adult with Pocket
- Fox River Wick Dry CoolMax Liner Socks 3-Pack
- Old Cotton T-shirt
- Nike Dri-Fit Running T-shirt
- Nike Dri-Fit Running Sleeveless Shirt

Sleep:
- Get Out Gear Down Camping Blanket 650 Fill
- Sea to Summit Coolmax Sleeping Bag Liner 85 x 36in
- Ear Plugs
- Blindfold

Shoes:
- New Balance Fresh Foam X 1080v12 Shoes
- Superfeet Trailblazer Comfort Carbon Fiber Orthotic Insoles
- Shiwely Silicone Waterproof Shoe Covers with Zippers

Accessories:
- Osprey Ultralight Stuff Waist Pack 1L
- Columbia Unisex Bora Bora Booney Fishing Hat

Electronics:
- BioLite HeadLamp 330 Lumen Rechargeable
- USB C Sacrack 100W 6 Port Charging Station
- Amazon Basics USB-C to Lightning Cable Cord
- Miady 2-Pack 10000mAh Dual USB Portable Charger

Shower:
- Adidas Men's Adilette Comfort Adjustable Slippers
- Sea to Summit Tek Towel Medium 20 x 40in

Laundry:
- Homevative Laundry Detergent Sheets 30-Count
- Sea to Summit Lite Line Camping and Travel Clothesline

Toiletries:
- Right Guard Sport 3D Deodorant Clear Gel
- Body Glide Original Anti-Chafe Balm
- Body Glide Foot Glide Anti Blister Balm
- Half-used Toothpaste Tube 8.2oz

- Hair Comb

Supplements:
- (2) Smart Water Sports Cap 700ml Bottles
- (10) Granola Bars
- GU Energy Original Sports Nutrition Energy Gel 24-Count
- AdvoCare Spark Vitamin & Amino Acid Supplement 14-Count
- (20) One A Day Men's Multivitamin
- (20) Allergy Tablets
- (10) Ibuprofen Tablets

Medical:
- Extra Durable Moleskin
- (5) Large Eye Sewing Needles
- Medpride Alcohol Prep Pad 100 Pack
- KT Tape Kt Tape Classic
- Advanced Blister Care 10-Count Medium Pads
- Fiskars Travel Folding Scissors 4in
- Sewing Thread 24in

I spent just north of $1,000 acquiring the gear above. In my mind, it was going to be worth every penny. But money aside, I had to be smart about what I was going to bring with me. I had limited space. And carrying what I believed to be the bare essentials, my backpack still weighed about 30 pounds when I stuffed everything inside—a bit heavy on the spectrum of Camino backpacks. I thought about training with the backpack so that I could get used to the weight, but I decided against it. The main reason being that I suffer from bone spurs and facet joint issues in my lower back. I also have arthritis in my knees. These issues began about six years before this mission. To care for it, I do lots of stretching, using a bit of self-taught Yoga at home. Weightlifting has always been an obsession of mine, but I avoid lifting too heavy, and instead perform higher reps with lower weight. I will not lie, I am still a bit jacked, but it is a "humble" jacked, of sorts. Enough to carry around my 30-pound backpack, I thought.

My primary training included walking five miles a day, mixing it up between the boardwalk and the sandy beaches of Miami. A typical day was heading out in 90-degree heat, with 80% humidity, and getting scorched by the sun. And I rarely took water on these walks. I wish I could say it was because I did not need it, because I did. It was just annoying walking around with a water bottle—I know, problems of a Miami Beach resident. There were days I was on the verge of heat stroke, but part of me relished that experience. The objective was to toughen myself up for the Camino, particularly "The Meseta," or in English, "The Plateau." This is a 180km

19

stretch of the Way, in central Spain, mainly between the cities of Burgos and León. Often regarded as one of the most troublesome parts of the Camino, given the hot, shadeless path you must walk for kilometers on end. In short, there is no escape from the sun in The Meseta. But there were other elements to train for besides the great desert-like plains of Spain.

In Miami, staying fit is a must if you want to look good at the beach. But to be honest, that mattered little to me. Around the year, I made it a point to stay in shape, for one reason and one reason only—the running of the bulls. Apart from daily walks to prepare for the Camino, every two to three days I went on 3km runs. My target pace was to run at an average speed of five minutes per kilometer, but I often averaged less than four minutes and twenty seconds per kilometer. Running with the bulls is less about distance, and more about speed and agility. It also helps to have a bit of muscle mass, as the streets get crowded with other runners and you must jockey for position. For this reason, I hit the weights in the public weightlifting area in Miami Beach about four times each week. The routine consisted mostly of bench press, incline press, seated arm row, standing bicep curl, and an old-fashioned pull-up bar. But like most fitness plans, if the diet is not locked in, you will not see great results.

My food plan consisted mostly of peanut butter and jelly sandwiches for breakfast, eggs and potatoes for the mid-morning snack, pasta with ground beef and tomato sauce for lunch, and either chicken breast or a couple of beef fillets with green beans for dinner. Rinse and repeat. On days when I felt baked by the hot Miami sun, I made a smoothie using Costco-bought frozen fruit bags containing strawberries, bananas, blueberries, and an assortment of mangos and melons.

As someone once said, success occurs when opportunity meets preparation. And exercise, fitness, and meal choices were all things that could be controlled. I thought of myself as a vehicle. I could be repaired, improved, tweaked, and tuned up. And because of that, I had a supreme amount of confidence going into the Camino and my trip to Spain.

CHAPTER TWO:

ST. JEAN PIED DE PORT

My Basque and Navarran parents raised me as a Catholic. Although I still identify as a Catholic, you could probably describe me better as a lapsed Catholic. I had not been to Mass in years, did not pray daily, or take part in the sacraments. But I admired those who did. Days before I started the Camino, I flew up to Allentown, Pennsylvania, to be a groomsman at my friend's wedding. His name is Bobby George—he has become a brother to me. The day after the wedding, Bobby's father, Von, invited me out to lunch with the family. It would be the last time I would see Bobby for a while, since he could not travel to Pamplona; he was preparing for the Bar Exam. As soon as we sat down, I noticed the waitress bring us the bill.

"Did we already order?" I asked, surprised at the swift pace of things at the restaurant.

"No, it's the other table. He always does that..." said Jane, Bobby's mother, with a smile on her face. Von was paying for the meals of two Catholic Nuns we had passed by inside on our way to the terrace. This little gesture was touching. As well as what happened next, when the two sisters came over.

"God bless you... all of you," said one nun. "At the convent, we have something that we call the 'Box of Good Intentions.' We will place a note inside for all of you at this table." It was a heart-warming moment. And a gesture from Von, Bobby's father, that stuck with me.

On June 13, I said goodbye to my father, jumped inside a Lyft car and headed straight for Miami International Airport, leaving Miami Beach behind. The day had arrived. With my backpack stuffed into the overhead compartment and my legs stretched out in a premium seat aboard Iberia

21

airlines, I remember feeling relaxed. My AirPods were pumping Rat Pack music into my ears, as if I was savoring my last minutes at home. But where was home, really? My father lived with me in the United States after years of family crises. And my mother lived in a suburb of Portland, Oregon. Excluding a few other relatives in the United States, the rest of our family was back in the "Old Country," as my grandfather used to say when he referred to the mountainous and agrarian nature of the Basque Country.

After landing in Madrid, I stopped at an electronics shop inside the airport to pick up a Spain sim card. It was a Vodafone plan with 200gb of data and unlimited phone calls within Spain—a great deal! After all, I was planning to spend hours on end on the Camino each day, and needed to make phone calls to albergues, double check the Camino route, and of course, check Instagram from time to time—I am only half-joking. The prepaid phone plan set me back 45 euros, which was a bargain for 30 days of usage.

At 17:30, I arrived in Pamplona, which was not exactly a breeze. Before I could grab a taxi to St. Jean Pied de Port in France, the start of the Camino, I had to take my suitcase to a friend's house before they left Pamplona for the evening. Since I was attending my cousin's wedding on Day 3 of the Camino (during my stop in Pamplona), I needed to bring acceptable clothing and shoes, as well as my gear for the Fiesta of San Fermín. After grabbing my luggage at the carrousel, I made my way toward the exit, where a line of 25 people had gathered, all waiting for taxis. A medical convention was in town, and a plane full of attendees had followed me in from Madrid—fantastic. Uber and Lyft were not operating in Pamplona, and my friend's flat was a 1 hour and 15-minute walk into Pamplona's city center. Long story short, it was not walkable, given that I had to be there in 30 minutes. If I did not make it in time, I would have had to wait until the next morning, setting my mission back by an entire day. The Camino had not even started, yet I was already having issues with my schedule.

Luckily, small groups of two to three businesspeople began hopping into the same taxis, making the line move a little more quickly. When it was my turn, I leaned into the passenger-side window.

"Hey, I have one stop in Pamplona, then have to go straight to St. Jean Pied de Port. Can you take me?" I asked. The drive to France alone was a 1 hour and 30-minute haul.

"Of course, get in," he said matter-of-factly. It took a weight off my shoulders as I wiped a bit of sweat from my brow. Then we were off.

Bzzz, went the sound of the intercom, as I stood at the street entrance to my friend's building.

When Patxi came down to meet me, he gave me an enormous hug. He was so happy to see me, and I to see him. Patxi is my friend's father-in-law. And he was kind enough to store my belongings for me while I chased my Camino glory.

"Listen, I want you to borrow something," said Patxi, as he revealed what looked like a large, hollowed-out scallop with a red cross painted on it. There was a small hole punched in it, and an old rustic-colored piece of twine looped around.

"What is this?" I asked.

"This is my wife Cristina's scallop from when she completed part of the Camino. The scallop is a symbol of the pilgrimage, since Santiago is just 35km from the Atlantic Ocean. All the pilgrims wear this on the outside of their backpacks. It's a sign to others that you are a pilgrim on the Camino, and that you are part of the community." It was a beautiful gesture. I thanked him, gave him one more hug, then headed back to the taxi. Next stop: St. Jean Pied de Port.

It was about 19:00 when we left Pamplona, the famous city in the foothills of the Pyrenees. It was odd, making the drive over the hills and across the Spanish border. The very stretches of land that we were rushing through to get me to France would take me two days to back track—68km worth. Many people decide to skip the first couple of stages on the Camino, given the extensive climbing and descending that is required just to get to Pamplona. However, the Camino officially started in France, and I was not about to short-change my mission.

About 20km into the drive through Navarra's mountain range, we passed by a town called Zubiri, where the road began snaking back and forth. The driver made a sharp left turn, followed by a sharp right, then left again. I could feel my stomach grumbling with each switchback, as the driver seemed to revel in the winding road, much like a rally car racer. The car quickly decelerated before the turn, then quickly sped up to whip out of it. We had about 45 minutes still to go. It did not help that I was sitting in the back of the taxi, with the front seat blocking my view of the road ahead. So, I stared out of the side window, trying to anticipate the turns as best I could. I was officially car sick. And the driver noticed.

"Are you doing OK back there?" asked Jose, the taxi driver. He was a man in his mid-forties. He was a nice, polite, and conversational man, it turned out.

"Oh yeah, I'm fine."

"Do you get carsick?"

"No, I never get car sick. Is that a thing?" I asked, trying to veer the attention away from my pale face and lying eyes.

"Oh yes, I make this drive from Pamplona to France every week. Many of my passengers get sick on the way. I usually have to pull over." I immediately thought of people puking on the side of the road. What a way to start the Camino.

"Have you ever done the Camino de Santiago?" I was trying desperately to change the subject and pass the time.

"No, I've never done it. But I've lived in these mountains all my life. You see that building right there?" asked Jose, pointing to an old, worn-down structure at the edge of a field.

"What is it?"

"It's an old grain processing facility. I used to work there back in my 20s."

"Do you miss it?"

"Sometimes I do…"

By 20:30, we rolled into St. Jean Pied de Port, stopping in a small parking lot next to a tourism office in the center of town. I thanked Jose for the ride and ponied up 130 euros. I made it there in one piece, and without expelling my ham sandwich from the flight onto the side of the road. There was an instant beauty about this little French town, maybe because it was a French-Basque town. The Basque region extends from northern Spain into southwestern France, with a province called "Iparralde." Street signs and restaurant letter boards were all in Basque, the language predominantly spoken in the area.

Walking from the parking lot, I passed by a bar with an outdoor terrace full of pilgrims. I remember them staring at me as they talked amongst themselves and sipped their beers. It may have been my oddly tanned face, my skintight Nike t-shirt showing off my muscles, or perhaps my bright-green John Deere hat. There was a lot of "American" to take in there. I also could not help but feel there was a competitive vibe about that moment. Maybe it was just me. After all, my mission was about to begin. And I was about to deploy.

Walking up the narrow, cobbled slopes of the old town, it was like I had fallen asleep and woken up in Oz. St. Jean Pied de Port is a small village of about 1,500 residents. It has roots going back to 1177, when it was called Saint-Jean-le-Vieux. After a siege by England's Richard the Lionheart, they rebuilt the village in its present-day location and named it St. Jean Pied de Port. As I walked, there were charming bread and pastry shops, storybook-like candy stores, and a fresh, rejuvenating scent in the air. Green landscapes straddling the Nive River surrounded the village. Above the doorways were flowerpots made of old pilgrim's hiking boots, adorning the facades of the timeless architecture throughout. After a few minutes, I reached my hotel for the night—Hotel Itzalpea.

The manager of the hotel had left a key for me inside a nearby mailbox, since I was arriving after-hours. As I went to enter, I saw a woman approaching from behind, carrying a large pizza box.

"Are you trying to get in?" she asked, with an American accent.

"Yeah, they left me a key, but the lock is finicky," I said as I opened the door.

"Oh, you're American! That's great. I'm Cathy, from Denver. I'm here with my husband."

"My name's Ander. I'm from Miami. By the way, that pizza smells good!"

"They're about to close soon, so if you're hungry, you should probably head over now."

After opening the door for her, I pulled a 180 and walked directly across the street to the pizza parlor called "Pizza Ona Garazi." I stepped inside and ordered a large "meat-lovers" pizza—OK, it was not called that, but it was their pizza with the most meat on it. I had not eaten for the better part of the day and felt famished. As they prepared the pizza, a younger-looking woman asked me if I was a farmer.

"No, I'm not a farmer," I said, confused by the question.

"But you have a tractor?" she asked, pointing to my John Deere hat. It all made sense.

"Oh! Yeah, I just like John Deere. Nothing says 'Americana' quite like a green John Deere hat." The woman giggled.

When the pizza was ready, I hurried back over to the hotel. It was 21:00. I devoured the entire pizza in 10 minutes. I was starving. Then, it was time to prepare my things for tomorrow. My Camino to Santiago would begin in the morning.

My alarm went off at 06:30, to allow me enough time to get ready, pack up, and stop at the Pilgrim's Office, which opened at 07:30. I would have made this visit the day before, but because I arrived late into the evening, it was closed. I woke up tired, jet-lagged, and feeling the exhaustion of my transatlantic travels and rat-race to get to France. It did not take long before I made my first mistake of the Camino—I took a morning shower. This was a big "no-no," as any moisture on your toes or your feet can make you susceptible to blisters. So, I dried my feet with a towel as best I could. Still, I shook my head in disbelief.

As I approached the Pilgrim's Office, I knew I was in the right place when I saw the arched wooden door with the number "39" at the top, and a large scallop plaque placed just below it. Waiting outside the office at 07:15, the minutes passed excruciatingly slowly. Group by group, I watched as other pilgrims made their way down the narrow road, toward the official route of the Camino. Day 1 on the Camino is unanimously considered the hardest day. And that meant I needed to get started ASAP, especially since I was walking double the distance as everyone else. So, I used the borrowed time to stretch.

At 07:30 sharp, the arched door suddenly opened at the Pilgrim's Office. An older woman ushered me over to a long, narrow wooden table. They set six chairs up on each side of the table, allowing new pilgrims to sit one-on-one with a volunteer, helping to get their walk underway. These volunteers were former pilgrims and had a wealth of knowledge about the

Camino. After taking a seat, other volunteers trickled in to help, but I was still the only pilgrim in the office. Meanwhile, the woman across from me asked for my passport and two euros, which was the cost of the pilgrim's passport. It was 5in x 6in, made of thick construction paper, and contained 16 pages. As I mentioned earlier, the passport would be essential for walking the Camino and staying in albergues. The first page was in French, where I had to inscribe the date, my name, home address, where I was starting the Camino from, and finally, a little box to check for the method I was using to tackle the Camino—"à pied" (by foot).

"Do you know where you're going today?" asked the woman. Before I could answer, she pulled out a pamphlet. "Let me show you this detailed list of all the towns and villages on the Camino."

"Oh… OK," I said.

"Here is a list of all the stages along the way… their elevation profiles, a list of all the albergues, phone numbers, whether they serve lunch or dinner…"

"I don't need—"

"Look, this is where you are going today," she said, cutting me off, pointing to Roncesvalles, a village 25km away.

"Actually, I'm going to be Zubiri today," I interjected in a soft, low-key voice. The woman looked like she had seen a ghost.

"Zubiri!?"

"Yes, Zubiri," This time, the other volunteers gasped and looked at me in unison, speaking in French-Basque amongst themselves. They must have thought I was another crazy American.

"Zubiri is 47km from here… it's Stage 2 of the Camino. You understand this, don't you?"

"I know," I said with a little smile and a bit of a chuckle. I was used to reactions like that. After all, when you tell people you run with the bulls every year, it is not like saying you go golfing on the weekends.

"You should probably leave now," she said, looking at her watch, then at the clock on the wall. It was 07:45. "You have a long day ahead."

I quickly stood up from the chair, knocking over my trekking poles. After picking them up, I started stuffing my papers into a clear, Ziplock bag, then into my fanny pack. Before exiting, I noticed a shelf with an array of scallops. These were just like the one Patxi lent to me when I was dropping off my suitcase in Pamplona. I needed one of my own.

"Are these for sale?" I asked the woman.

"They are donation-only. We don't charge for them."

I unzipped my fanny pack and pulled out a two-euro coin, then dropped it into the coin box. Then, I needed to select a scallop. They all varied in size, color, and shape. Some were plain white, others had orangish endings, some were proportionate from end to end, and others had jagged edges. Half of the scallops had a red cross painted on them, while the rest did not. I thought about what other pilgrims might choose. Surely, they picked the most perfect, proportionate, and pretty scallops. I picked up the biggest one I could find. It was white with discolored endings and no red cross. I grabbed a piece of brown twine and tied it to the back of my backpack. With my scallop in tow, I waved goodbye to the woman and the other volunteers before making my way back into the street.

"Buen Camino!" they said.

"Buen Camino!" I said, pumping my fist in the air. This was a popular greeting on the Way. When you saw another pilgrim, you said, "Buen Camino," or when you were parting ways, you also said, "Buen Camino." It means, "Good Way," or "Good Journey."

It was a mild-weather day in St. Jean Pied de Port. It was 66 degrees Fahrenheit, cloudy, with a slight wind passing through. I gripped my carbon-fiber trekking poles and dug them into the cobbles with every couple of steps. Click-clack, click-clack, went the sounds as I traveled down the street. About 80 meters down, the street bent slightly to the left, where the Church of Notre-Dame du Bout du Pont first came into view. Built with stones in the twelfth century, it stood there immaculately, next to the Notre-Dame Gate, a magnificent tower, with a clock at the top and an arched doorway below. This was the beginning of the French Way. I savored those last few moments as I gazed up at the tower, collecting myself before walking through. I was beginning the most difficult climb on the Camino—the Napoleon Pass. This was a 21km climb up the legendary Pyrenees mountains. An ascent of over 1,250 meters, right out of the gate. I felt the nervous confidence of a fighter before he enters the boxing ring, and I felt the naïve hope of a child as they dream away in sleep. I felt the weight of a thousand voices, strapped tightly to my back, of those who thought this mission to be a delusion. "But what remains of a delusion if you can make it a reality?" I wondered. Then, I stepped through the arched doorway, onto the Camino de Santiago, and over the bridge of the Nive River, leaving St. Jean Pied de Port behind. Only 800km left to go.

CHAPTER THREE:

THE NAPOLEON PASS

We were hiking up Eskuagatx. It was a typical Saturday morning. On the weekends, my father and I made our way up the mountain to locate our sheep in the Basque countryside. We needed to bring them down for the winter. At 10 years old, the hikes would seem endless to me, mostly given the pain I felt, climbing the steep gradient. Rocks covered the path, some small and others large, making the surface uneven. As we climbed, it was difficult to see where the summit was, as we were deep in the forest, surrounded by tall trees, shrubs, and a thick layer of fog. "When is this going to end?" I asked myself. I did not bring a watch, and I preferred not to ask my father. If I annoyed my father or impeded with the hike, I might not get to go next time. Herding sheep was not a simple task, and the sheep spooked easily. I had to be on point. But I kept wondering how long we had been on the path. "How much longer do I have to walk?" I kept asking myself. I was tired, hungry, and sweating profusely. My legs felt like Jell-O, yet somehow kept moving. With every step, I took a deep breath, hoping my father would stop for a break, then that way I could take one too. We kept moving up the mountain. It seemed to go on forever. On the Camino, these memories from my childhood came flooding back.

When I began the Camino in St. Jean Pied de Port, I knew I had a rough day ahead. My objective was to climb the Pyrenees, descend rapidly into an old monastery town called Roncesvalles, then walk for several more hours until I reached Zubiri. But staring at me from the start was the infamous Napoleon Pass, named after the nineteenth century French dictator, who had used the route over the mountains to cross from Spain into

France. The route would be an asset during the Napoleonic wars, between 1803-1815. On the outskirts of St. Jean Pied de Port, I saw the first signs for the route. Stopping only for a moment to re-tie my shoes, I turned and began making my way up the mountain. The Pyrenees is a mountain range between France and Spain that spans almost 500km. Serving as a natural border between the Iberian Peninsula and European territory to the north, it reaches an elevation of 3,400 meters. It is not for the faint of heart.

Many people have died climbing in these mountains, attempting the Camino de Santiago. The quick and unpredictable changes in weather can leave pilgrims stranded, lost, injured, or worse. In 2002, a 78-year-old pilgrim disappeared after leaving St. Jean Pied de Port. Days later, searchers found her in Orzanzurieta, a col just before the summit. A snowstorm claimed the life of a 51-year-old Scottish pilgrim in 2007, before he could reach Roncesvalles. In 2016, they found a Spaniard from Salamanca dead after having fallen down a ravine between Val Carlos and Roncesvalles. In 2019, another pilgrim died while taking refuge at a shelter in Roncesvalles. And there are many other pilgrims who have fallen victim to the Camino— strokes, aneurysms, heart attacks, and more causes. In the Middle Ages, Christians believed that if you died on the Camino de Santiago, you bypassed purgatory and went directly to Heaven. This was hardly a comforting thought for someone at the bottom of the mountain and looking up.

On the right-hand side of the road, just a few feet from the pavement, was an arched block of concrete stuck in the ground. It was a white-grayish color, only two and a half feet high. Mounted on it was a blue square plaque with yellow lines—it was the scallop that served as one of the many symbols of the Camino. On top, there was a stone cairn. In ancient times, these signified a landmark or a burial monument. I found it curious. I kneeled down, picked up a small rock from the ground, and placed it on top. Then, I kept moving.

The initial ascent had a paved road leading up the hill. Surrounded by green grass and roadside ditches, I worked feverishly to set my pace, fueled by adrenaline and last night's pizza. The nearest pilgrim in front of or behind me was about 50 meters away. It helped me to look ahead and keep my eyes fixed on the people in front, as if they were my prey. It gave me a little extra motivation to keep a good pace. In doing so, it was not long before I would catch them. It proved to be awkward, as the people you passed looked surprised that they were being passed up. Surely, they thought I was walking fast. I was in the fucking zone.

After about 30 minutes, my shirt became soaked, and my face dripped with sweat. There is something animalistic about sweating. It brings out the ferociousness in a person; it throttles the beating heart and gives you a little reminder that you are in suffer mode. I was passing people up left and right, and flying up the mountain.

Before I left St. Jean Pied de Port, I filled up my two Smartwater bottles and packed them on the sides of my backpack. It made for an easy reach when I needed a quick drink. I filled one with water, while the other was a mixture of Spark Energy drink. On the Camino, it was key to be conservative when drinking liquids, as you did not always know how many water fountains (if any) you might pass. Another resource that came in handy was my protein granola bars. I had one before I left the hotel earlier in the morning. The GU Energy Gels were solid aids as well, but it was better to save those for the second part of the day, when I needed a pick-me-up, or if I bonked on the Camino, due to low blood sugar. Between the granola bars and my Spark Energy drink, I was really flying.

As I marched up the French mountainside, I remembered a conversation I had with Paula, Patxi's daughter.

"Ander, you are doing something militaristic. You must be careful. Do not hurt yourself," said Paula. I could tell she was worried about me. And I knew she was used to danger, which elevated her concern to another level.

One year before, Paula married my friend, Bill Hillmann. Bill and I both run with the bulls in Pamplona. Bill alone has been doing it for the better part of two decades. He is a former Golden Gloves Boxing Champion from Chicago, Illinois. The Los Angeles Times dubbed him as the best young bull runner from the United States. He has provided expert commentary surrounding the bulls to the likes of BBC, CBS, CNN, and more. Bill has been the recipient of three gorings on the streets of Pamplona. On two separate occasions, the gorings left baseball-sized wounds that took months to recover from. Yet, he still runs the bulls with me. Some might say he is crazy, but I think he is just a tough dude, and he loves the culture. After all, the older runners in Pamplona will tell you it is just a matter of time before you get hurt. And Paula knew this. Yet she loved how Bill continued to run with the bulls. Born and raised in Pamplona, it was in her blood. Since she carried around a pacifier, her family gathered around the TV at 08:00 sharp every July to watch the bulls stampede through the old town. She watched as people took their chances "running on the horns"—running just inches or a few feet directly in front of a bull. In short, danger was familiar to Paula. But her heed of caution only served to fuel my drive and give flight to my feet.

Further up the mountain, the first opportunity to stop and refuel would be in a village called Orisson. About an 8km trek from the bottom, the Orisson Refuge was a place to eat, sleep, drink, and pee. After walking for about two hours, I reached the refuge. People had gathered in front of the large, stone-built, two-story structure, scattered across some tables next to a lengthy railing. The railing protected people from the cliff on the other side. The panoramic views of the valleys of the Pyrenees were breathtaking. My line of sight was just below the sprawling white clouds, but above the morning fog that still lingered in the air. After having a quick look, I stepped into the entrance of the bar and restaurant. The cooler interior of the shaded entrance sent a few shivers down my sweaty spine. At the front of the bar, I tried placing my trekking poles against the neatly polished wooden counters. They immediately slid to the sides and fell to the ground. I groaned as I bent down to pick them up, then ordered my first true meal of the day: a "cortado" and "pintxo" of "tortilla." A cortado is an espresso mixed with a little warm milk—it is delicious. Pintxos are small snacks served at bars. They are well prepared, individual portions that come in a variety of choices, typically served on a piece of bread. The most popular pintxos comprise jamon (ham), chorizo (sausage), croquetas (croquettes—meat, fish, cheese, and more varieties), and, of course, perhaps the most desired pintxo, tortilla (omelet).

"Let me heat up the tortilla for you," said the bartender. I took my backpack off for the first time since the beginning of the arduous hike, placing it on the stool next to me. People say never to place your backpack on the ground. You had to take your bag with you everywhere, and you did not want to risk the chance of a creeper crawler finding its way inside.

"Is there a bathroom?"

"Yes, but it's outside." He pointed to the window, toward the terrace out front. I asked for some aluminum foil to wrap the half-eaten pintxo and stuffed it into my backpack for later.

Leaving the bar, I started looking around for the bathroom, then realized it was an outhouse swarmed by groups of pilgrims. "Fuck that," I thought. Then, I moved along. I had climbed 600 meters since the start of the day, and there were 650 left to go, just to summit the Pyrenees. The crowd thinned out after leaving the Orisson Refuge. This was because many pilgrims broke up the epic climb into two pieces. But I continued marching forward up the mountain.

I could see more of the mountain range as the paved road twisted and turned its way up. There were no more bushes and trees along the road. On one side, it was the mountain, and on the other, a dangerous cliff that would lead to death if one was not careful. It now made sense that people had died up there. It would only take a bit of fog and precipitation to lead you off the edge. And people often walked along those grassy edges. After walking on the paved road, I could feel the pressure of the unforgiving asphalt on my knees and ankles. The grassy edges next to the road provided a bit of bouncy comfort, but I preferred to stay on the road. I tried the grass twice, heading up to the Orisson Refuge, but the unevenness of the grassy, mountainous terrain made me constantly have to adjust my feet for different pressure points with each step. It also slowed me down.

On my left, I noticed a white van parked on the embankment. It had a canopy extended out from the van, covering what looked like snacks for sale. When I was at the Orisson Refuge, I completely forgot to fill up my water bottles—they were nearly empty—and I had been conserving water ever since. But have no fear. What I did not have, the white mountain van could provide. There were a few other pilgrims sitting on a bench next to it, eating muffins and bananas. An old man was in charge. I asked him for a bottle of water. He looked like an old French-Basque shepherd. I paid the man, took a quick chug of the water, and carried on.

The mountain sounded different as I worked my way toward the summit. There was a slight whistle in the air as I looked around and realized I was above the clouds. It was wide-open up there. Nothing but mountains and valleys as far as the eyes could see. It was as if I could move them with a twist of the neck or the boldness of a stare, as if I had my finger on the world. It was God-like. That is the best way I could describe it. And yet, I needed more, like I had tasted the blood of an animal. And there were many animals. Ponies frolicked in the green pastures with their golden manes and tan hides, with a few patches of white throughout. They were used to seeing people and did not spook easily. Herds of white sheep with full coats of wool were picking away at the grass, as were the off-white-colored cows. Animals often climb up to high elevations near the summit. This is to avoid the wrath of storms and other unpredictable weather, and also to find grass. And as I prepared to approach the summit, there was supposedly a statue of the Virgin Mary built in her honor. I never saw the statue.

The paved road soon gave way to a terribly steep dirt path, cluttered with an assortment of devilish rocks. Surely, the summit had to be close. Cyclists, who biked the Camino instead of walking, were off their bikes and slowly pushing them up the hill and through the valley of two peaks. Up and over, the path continued toward a section of gravel road next to a barbed wire fence with rotted wooden posts, protecting us from a trip down the treacherous ravine. The route leveled out as the path became even narrower, decorated with a slew of trees on the right-hand side. A few minutes later, I stumbled upon the Roland Fountain, 17km into the march. It was not the summit, but it was indeed the entry into Spain. There were no guards, no security checks, and no passport stamps required. Separating me from Spain was a small wooden gate with yellow arrows painted on it. After filling up my two Smartwater bottles, I packed them in my bag, and took my first steps into Navarra, the northern province of Spain, leaving French territory behind. There was a temporary reprieve from all the climbing, with a gentle downhill stroll through a forest with beech trees. The climb began yet again, as I reached for a protein granola bar to muster up the energy needed. My mouth remained open as I sucked in the thinned-out air of the Pyrenees. In and out of shade, the path continued to twist around the mountain. Only one thing was for sure: I was still going up. Finally, 5km from the fountain, at 12:15, I reached the Col de Lepoeder, the highest point on the Napoleon Pass. Thank God.

At the top of the col was a monument-like structure, with a solar panel on top, and what looked like a small wind turbine. To the right, there was a trail with a little drop that would mark the official start of the descent into Roncesvalles. There was only one problem. A few meters down, the trail split into two. The wooden signs above had two arrows. One that would take 1 hour and 15 minutes, and the other 1 hour and 30 minutes. When waiting in the Pilgrim's Office, the volunteer had strongly urged me to take the longer path. It added 15 minutes to my day, but the trail would not be nearly as steep and dangerous as the alternative. The shorter path, which dropped off a cliff (well, kind of), is a steep descent through a minefield of rocks and fallen timber. Local authorities in the area were at their limits with careless hikers and out-of-shape pilgrims. So much so that they urged all pilgrims to take the longer, safer trail. I stood there looking at the sign, wondering what to do. "I did not summit over 1,250 meters just to take the easy option," I thought to myself. As I stood there, a woman, probably in her late 40s, was catching up to me.

"Buen Camino," I said to her. She mumbled a few words back, as she was out of breath. She looked up at the two signs, then started speaking in Russian. I did not understand a word.

"What this is?" said the woman in broken English.

"One is short and dangerous. The other is long and easy. I'm taking the shorter one," I said as I slowly turned toward the path.

"Oh yes. I take short road."

Within a few seconds, I was racing down the mountain, toward the ancient monastery town of Roncesvalles. Growing up in the hills of the Basque Country, my father used to say that I descended mountains like a goat—violently leaping from rock to rock, making quick lateral moves, each step with an oddly choreographed precision. Hustling my way down, the trail led into the Irati Forest, the second largest beech and fir tree forest in Europe. When I looked back, the woman was gone. I was descending at a thundering pace. And my legs were beat. During the strenuous hike up the Napoleon Pass, most of the pressure was being put on my glutes, quads, hamstrings, and calves; they hurt and felt drained of energy. My back felt relatively good. My lats (the flat broad muscles of the back) were the keys to carrying my backpack, which relieved much of the pressure from my lower back. But on the downhill, it felt like I was performing the entire effort with my knees. Even with my trekking poles, my knees constantly tensed up in order to support my weight with each drop or step. This is part of the reason I descended so rapidly. My knees could rest every time I was momentarily in the air, dropping down to the next surface.

After I lost the Russian woman behind me, I walked through most of the forest alone. It was deafeningly quiet. The only noises I heard were the ones I was making, as if I was disturbing the quiet slumber of the Irati Forest. Halfway down the 7km descent, I ran into a Korean couple. The man was out in front, while the woman trailed by a few meters. They did not have trekking poles, which made the descent even more difficult and dangerous. One minor slip and you would fall forward, risking the chance of cracking your head open on a fallen tree or trail-side rock. As I got closer to the man walking ahead, I noticed he picked up his pace, so I followed (animalistic mentality). He did not even look back. It went like this for a few minutes until he finally turned his head and saw me. The look on his face was priceless. He must have realized I was not his wife, but another dude on the Camino. The man stopped, giggling a little as I passed him up.

"Sorry!" the man said to his wife, 20 meters behind us.

Next, I passed an older couple. This time, they were walking side-by-side, in unison.

"Buen Camino," I said to them.

"Buen Camino! Where are you from?" asked the older man.

"Miami, Florida. I'm a long way from home. What about you?"

"Well, we're from California. Just trying to get through this damn forest to Roncesvalles," said the man, with an exacerbated look on his face. His wife laughed. "Say, did you feel like dying when you went over the Napoleon Pass back there?"

"Oh, for sure. More than once!" I said in jest. They were a sweet couple, likely in their late 60s, but I kept on keeping on.

At 13:30, I stepped out of the forest and into the sun, crossing a wooden panel bridge that extended over a small stream. Exhausted, the ancient monastery in Roncesvalles came into view, which served as a momentary distraction. Built in the thirteenth century, this Gothic-style complex houses the tomb of King Sancho VII, the former King of Navarra. However, the oldest relic of this town was the Romanesque church called Chapel of Sancti Spiritus, or "Charlemagne's Silo." Charlemagne was King of the Franks and went on to become the Holy Roman Emperor. According to legend, Roland, Charlemagne's nephew, and one of his twelve Paladin knights, died in 778 at the Battle of Roncevaux Pass. During this battle, Basque forces ambushed Charlemagne's army atop the Pyrenees, following the destruction of the city walls of Pamplona. It was an act of retribution. But history needed to wait, as I was tired, hungry, and wanted to stop for lunch.

Following the road from the forest and into town, there was a restaurant called La Posada de Roncesvalles. It was a large, two-story building that I later found out was also an albergue. It would be a reoccurring theme throughout the Camino. Most restaurants along the Camino were albergues, and most albergues were also restaurants. And La Posada was no different. Entering through the doorway, I made a beeline for the bar, only to be redirected to the dining room area. There must have been 30 tables set up, with only a handful of people inside. I ordered a filet of beef with some fries and a can of Coca-Cola. This was the first time I had a regular, sugar-filled Coke in over 10 years. But my body craved the sugar, and I figured I was burning untold amounts of calories with all the walking and hiking. Within 10 minutes, the food came out hot and ready. The people at the table next to me marveled at how quickly I devoured the meat, as their conversation would pause for a moment or two, as their eyes fixated on me and my plate. I knew I still had another 22km to finish out the day, and I was risking feeling bloated, but I also knew I needed the proper fuel. 25 minutes after sitting down, I was up and out of my chair, moving gingerly as the soreness had set in. Before leaving, I stopped at the bar and whipped out my pilgrim's passport to get my first stamp of the day. Pilgrims are required to get at least one stamp per day in order to earn the Compostela (Camino certificate) after reaching Santiago. The stamp was pretty, but I also noticed that I had pages and pages of white space to fill up. It was a reminder of all the kilometers I had left to hike.

Outside La Posada, I set down my things to stretch out. First my calves, then my hamstrings. I tried stretching my quad by bending my knee and grabbing my ankle from behind, but my knees were so swollen that I could not bend my knee enough. As I stretched, I saw the Russian woman arriving after her descent from the mountain. Most pilgrims stopped at Roncesvalles, checked into the albergue, and began their relaxation and recovery. But not me. I gave a quick wave to the Russian girl, finished stretching, and strapped on my 30-pound backpack. The day was only halfway over, and my body was already a bit of a wreck.

By 14:00, I was back on the Camino, following the signs out of Roncesvalles, en route to Zubiri. One caught my eye. It read, "790km to Santiago de Compostela." It was odd, since I had already walked for 25km. Surely, there had to be less than 790km remaining of the 800km pilgrimage. I shook my head and kept moving down the path. It was a small and narrow dirt trail that ran parallel to the highway. The tall trees made of pine, birch, and oak arched their way over the trail, providing a natural barrier against the sun. The skies had cleared, and the temperature was heating up. My sleeveless shirt helped, but the straps of my backpack had been rubbing against my shoulders for six hours. The skin at the seam of my armpit had developed a slight rash. My feet felt good, other than a bit of pressure I was feeling having been on them for so long. That was good news. So, I kept moving.

30 minutes later, I entered the first of a handful of towns I would pass on the way to Zubiri. Auritz is a lovely little village of about 200 people. The Camino takes you straight down the center. The stone-built sidewalks were narrow, not even wide enough to use my trekking poles. At one point, I just stepped out into the street and took my chances with traffic. I remember thinking it was strange that I was the only person outside. There were no kids playing, couples pushing their strollers, or any people walking

their dog. It was a bit of a ghost town. Then, I realized people were likely taking the famous "siesta," or post-lunch nap. It made perfect sense.

As I turned off the road and back into the Navarran countryside, I remember wondering where all the other pilgrims were. It was an odd feeling being alone like that. After a while, I assumed that most people had probably done what I did that morning. They woke up early and started their walk. Once that sunk in, it felt like the world had passed me by. But then, something blocked my path. There was a herd of sheep mixed in with some goats that bottlenecked the trail. We were moving in opposite directions. To get them to clear, I needed them to come closer, but naturally, they were jumpy. I reached into my backpack and pulled out the leftover tortilla pintxo I had brought from the Orisson Refuge. Then, I scattered little pieces about 10 meters in front of me, then 5 meters, then just a few feet, until the herd formed a line and rushed by me. The path was clear again. For the first 5km or so, the terrain was mostly level with a slight descent. After all, I had just hiked 1,250 meters up the Pyrenees, so I knew the Camino would eventually have to descend. Roncesvalles sits at an elevation of 950 meters, while Zubiri, by comparison, sits at just above 500 meters. But after Auritz, the path to Zubiri became hilly.

Two respectable mountain passes separated me from the final descent into Zubiri: Alto de Mezkiritz and Alto de Erro. Before I started, I stopped in Espinal to fill up my water bottles. Across the street from an old farmhouse, there was a fountain made of large rocks with a spout at the very top. Covered in green moss, the water flowed from the spout down into a small pool of water. I had doubts about whether it was drinkable, but against my better judgement, I figured I would try it anyway. When I was in college, I studied abroad in Monterrey, Mexico. Everyone told us not to drink the water because the parasites gave you diarrhea. But there was one exchange student from Australia who refused to buy water at the store. They spent several days on the toilet. Not a good time. But I was thirsty, and it looked like clean and clear water. And I needed it for the mountain passes to come.

The day moved on, and so did the sun, as it moved from one side of the sky to the other. I had climbed the Alto de Mezkiritz and now found myself in Lintzoain. My body was reeling from the effort. First, I started feeling my calves locking up. Then, my right hip was aching, almost as if it was slightly out of place and scraping the socket. I had no choice but to keep walking. I made a sharp right turn up an old and steep village road. There was a gray sheepdog resting in the shade, just in front of the entrance to a farmhouse. After walking past the dog, I looked back to find the dog following me at his own gentle pace. When I called for it to come closer, it stopped, abandoning the Camino after just a few meters, sending me away on my own. The dog was smarter than it looked.

The descent that followed the Alto de Erro into Zubiri was no joke.

It was probably the worst way to end a day's hike. It was a steep descent down the mountain, filled with long, thin layers of jagged rock that left no place to plant your feet. You had to take your chances stepping on the pointy ledges, hoping your ankles would not give out and send you crashing to the ground. And good thing it was not raining, because that truly would have been a mess. Fatigue was really setting in at that point, after having been walking for over 10 hours, not to mention having started from another country. As quickly as I could, I planted my toes between the layers of jagged rock, trying to get enough of a grip to swing the rest of my body and plant the other foot somewhere. It was like you had to twist and contort your body all the way down. Given the terrain, I seriously questioned whether I was on the right path. Stopping for a moment, I pulled out my phone, opened the Buen Camino App, and turned-on location services. Sure enough, I was on the Camino.

Passing through the jagged rocks of death, the town of Zubiri was in my sight. It was 19:15. As I walked, I cradled both trekking poles underneath my left armpit, using my right hand to reach for some water and a granola bar. I walked and snacked for about a minute, wiping the sweat from my forehead. When I finished, I placed the wrapper in my pocket and switched my trekking pole back to the other hand. But as I went to plow it into the ground, there was no stick. I looked down and realized I was holding the grip without its pole. When cradling it, I must have flipped the metal tightening lever, which released the pole from the grip. I was furious. I turned around and retraced my steps back up the jagged rocks of death. After 50 meters, I found the pole laying in the crevice of the rocks. I could not believe I did not notice the sound of it falling to the ground. After a few "fucks" and "pieces of shit," I continued from where I had left off.

The trail led me to a fork in the road, where I hooked a right-hand turn over the Puente de la Rabia, or in English, "Bridge of the Rage." And I was feeling some that evening. Legend has it that the bridge cures the anger in people. Those infected with it have to go down to the river and take three turns around the central pillar. I would have, but it was time for me to find my albergue for the night. Still, it was impossible not to notice the majestic nature of the bridge and how it extended over the Arga River flowing beneath it. Halfway over the bridge, I noticed a few pilgrims down below, sitting on the edge of the riverbank, soaking their feet in the water, laughing and having a good time.

Albergue Segunda Etapa, or "Albergue Second Stage," was the name of my lodging for the night. After the bridge, I asked a few local teenagers where I could find it, and where I might grab some food. They pointed me down the street, not more than a couple of blocks away. The host of the albergue had left me a sticky note with a brief message, saying he emailed me the passcode for the door. After retrieving the code, I entered. It was quiet inside as I shut the door. To the left, I saw a tiny 10-foot by 10-foot garage that someone had converted into a makeshift washroom. It had a sink for washing clothes and plenty of wire and clothespins for hanging them to dry. On the far side was a tall shoe rack, filled with shoes from top to bottom. They were a mix of hiking boots, trail-running shoes, and sandals. Next to the rack was a small open barrel to hold trekking poles and hiking sticks, along with a metal bench, like the ones you would see in a park. After placing my poles in the barrel, I unclipped my backpack, starting with the magnetic chest strap, then the waist strap, and set it on the bench. My heart was still pounding as I panted. After placing my shoes on the rack, I took off my thick wool socks that felt like they were suffocating my feet, then removed the thin synthetic socks that were supposed to keep my feet dry—they did. My Adidas flip flops felt great to slip into, but my feet had been in such a fixed position inside my shoes, that I felt the pains in my feet with every flexible bend of my flimsy flip flops. Before leaving the washroom, I noticed a stamp with a tin can of ink near the sink. I took out my pilgrim's passport, stamped it, then wrote the date of my arrival. "June 15, 2023." I had walked 47km from St. Jean Pied de Port. It took me 11 hours. Now I needed to shower, change clothes, wash the dirty ones, and eat.

The albergue had three stories. Downstairs was the washroom, kitchen, and a bathroom. The coed dormitories were on the second and third floors, each floor having their own bathroom. The host wrote to me saying I could choose any bed on the second floor. Gingerly climbing up the staircase, I entered the room to find four bunks, making eight beds—each bunk had a lower and upper bed. The host prepped them with a mattress, one white fitted sheet, and a pillow. Nobody was in the room, but it looked like four people had arrived long before I did. The beds had sleeping bags rolled out on top, along with dry clothes neatly folded and ready for tomorrow's hike, and electronic cables plugged into the bedside outlets. There was an open bed that was one bunk away from the window, so I chose the lower bed to be mine for the night. I set my backpack down on a folding chair at the foot of the bed, then began rifling through it. I pulled out my shower towel, a thin sheet of travel-sized laundry detergent, and my dry sack, which had two changes of clean clothes.

The bathroom down the hall had a small shower inside, complete with a sliding glass door. I stripped down and carefully stepped inside. This shower was the genuine pleasure of the entire day for me. I set the temperature on cold and stood there idly with my eyes closed, letting the cool water flow from my head to my toes, washing away all the sweat and grime that I had collected on the 47km hike from France. Luckily, I had no blisters on my feet. After the shower, I threw my clothes in the sink, along with the laundry sheet, and started massaging my clothes together. I was a true pilgrim now. But honestly, I did not know what the hell I was doing. After hanging up the clothes in the washroom, I stepped outside to grab some food.

It was 20:00, and the sun was setting in the western sky. It was warm outside, but there was a pleasant breeze in the air. Down the street was a sporting complex with one of the few bars with food, so I hobbled my sore body down there. Outside on the terrace was a group of English speakers, probably American, eating chocolate almond ice-cream. It looked delicious. Inside the bar, I took a seat on a stool at the counter and ordered a chorizo sandwich. I wanted something quick and easy, as I knew I needed to get back to the albergue to rest up for the next day. After devouring the sandwich, I ordered another, and then a sandwich with jamon as well. And to wash it all down, I ordered a Coke-Zero and a chocolate almond ice-cream bar—it was absolutely everything I hoped it would be. Then, there was a problem. When I got off the stool to leave, I could barely move. I was sitting at the bar for 15 minutes, and during that time my body had locked up. My calves felt like rocks and my feet felt like swollen hoofs, giving me shooting pains every time I bent my foot with each step. I looked injured as I walked out.

Back inside the albergue, I walked up the stairs the way a senior citizen would, one foot at a time, as I held onto the railings for dear life. At the top, I heard some other pilgrims in the room. There were three men, probably in their late 50s. They were from Mallorca, the Mediterranean island off the eastern coast of Spain. Their bunk beds were across from mine. We introduced ourselves and shared a few laughs together.

"You came all the way from St. Jean Pied de Port? Are you crazy!?" asked one of them, in shock. His name was Alberto.

"Maybe a little," I said with a smile.

"I have a lot of respect for you. That's really quite amazing."

"Thank you. But maybe it wasn't the best thing to do. Now I'm suffering like a dog."

"Here, take some of this," said Alberto, pulling a small plastic jar out of his backpack and handing it to me.

"What is it?"

"It's gel for your muscles. Rub some of that on and it will help reduce muscle spasms."

"Hey, that's really nice of you! Thank you!" I said, as I applied a little to my calves.

"My body hurts, but if I had done what you just did, I wouldn't be standing upright. I would be dead in the bed," said Alberto.

I laid down and started doing a few stretches to loosen up my muscles. To ease the pressure on my feet, I tried elevating them using the metal bar at the foot of my bed, reducing the blood flow. But my right hip was so jacked up that I did not have the strength to raise my right leg. Using my hands, I grabbed my leg, picked it up, and set my foot on the bar. As I moved around, there was an older woman in the bed next to me, next to the window. She was probably in her early 70s.

"I love the Camino," said the woman. Her name was Gloria, and she was from Spain.

"Is this your first time?" I asked, wincing from the pain in my legs.

"No, this is my seventh time doing the Camino."

"Why do you keep doing it?"

"It's beautiful. I'm not a very religious person, but I have time to think and enjoy nature," said Gloria.

I laid there thinking about the reason I was on the Camino. For some it was a religious experience, and for others it was a chance to get away from society, to live a simpler life, albeit temporarily. I was doing the Camino to "destroy" it. But that night, it was destroying me. Yet somehow I had "earned" that pain, and I took great pride in that. Still, I had doubts about whether my 36-year-old body could handle the punishment of the 800km hike in only 20 days. I knew this first day was going to be the hardest, but I also knew there were still more than 750km to go. And truth be told, I was not sure my body was going to hold up. But it was nothing compared to how I was going to feel at 06:00 the next morning.

CHAPTER FOUR:

WHAT JUST HAPPENED?

Before we moved to the Basque Country, my parents owned a fast-food restaurant near Portland, Oregon. I was around 10 years old. During summer vacations, if I behaved well enough, they would let me go to work with them. My mother helped manage the front of the restaurant, taking orders at the counter, the drive-thru, bussing tables, and supervising a few other ladies. My father worked in the back, grilling and preparing burgers as the orders came through on the paper tickets. Dressed in a white-buttoned up dress shirt, I would grab a red apron from the back, and stand next to my father. Most of the time, I was not a big help in that capacity. He quickly sent me away to the front to help deliver food trays and pick up garbage after customers left the restaurant. However, one day I was behind the grill with my father, and he tasked me with fryer duty. When an order of chicken strips came up, I grabbed four strips from the walk-in freezer, dropped them in, and lowered the basket. When I did that, the metal tongs slipped out of my hand and fell into the pool of oil. Without contemplating the consequences, I reached for the tongs, sticking my hand and most of my forearm into the 360-degree hot, burning oil. I let out a scream that reverberated around the restaurant. As I braced my burned arm from the elbow, holding it upright, my father rushed me over to the ice machine and dunked my entire arm into the mountain of ice. Stunned by the shock of what had just unfolded, I had not even started crying yet. The severe burns would heal, but the smell of burned, sizzling flesh would stick with me.

On Day 2 of the Camino, I felt like I got hit by a train, twice. I still could not lift my right leg, and I was more immobile than the night before. Part of me thought I understood the consequences of what I had signed up

41

for. And the other part of me thought my body just needed some time to adjust. After all, Day 1 on the Camino was unanimously the most physically challenging day on the entire pilgrimage. "This will surely be the worst I will feel," I thought. What also helped that morning was the fact that it was a short day to Pamplona. In contrast to the 47km hike the day before, I only had to walk 21km to reach Pamplona. I had timed it just right so that I could attend my cousin's wedding the next day, then resume my mission the day after that. So, I felt I would have a bit of a reprieve to get my body back in shape to continue on. But I would be lying if I said I did not have a glimmer of fear about my body's ability to withstand the accumulation of punishment. Nonetheless, I stayed focused on the present. And the present sucked.

I had the worst night of sleep imaginable. Once the lights went out at the albergue, I fell asleep for about an hour, and then woke up to the sound of a tractor. One of the Mallorca guys was snoring so loud you could probably hear him from Santiago. I was in too much pain to get out of bed and rifle through my backpack to get my earplugs, and I did not have the heart to wake the guy up. I just kept thinking, "How hard is it to sleep on your stomach?" And to make matters worse, I could not sit still. I had an aching pain in my legs, from my glutes down to my thighs, quads, calves, ankles, and feet. The aches were deep and throbbed every few seconds. It felt like I was a kid going through growing pains. I just kept tossing and turning throughout the whole night. And every time I did, the ruffling sound of my synthetic sleeping liner made almost enough noise to match the snoring tractor from Mallorca. Then there was the heat.

There were five of us packed in one small room, generating enough body heat and sweat to survive the Pyrenees in the dead of winter. And I was wearing my long convertible cargo pants. Before hopping into bed, I had not zipped off the lower legs to turn them into shorts. And doing so within my cocoon of a sleeping liner was going to cause a ruckus. After stewing about it for a few hours, I realized it would be easier to just take off my pants, rather than fuss with the zippers on each pant leg. But then I looked over and saw Gloria in the bed next to me. She was sleeping on her side, face toward me, eyes still closed. I thought about it for a few more minutes. "What if she sees me in my boxer briefs? My package hanging out for all to see?" I dreadfully wondered. "Well, it probably isn't anything she hasn't seen before in her 70 years," I concluded. So, I took off my pants. And my sweat-soaked shirt too. Finally, I dozed off for a couple of hours of sleep.

At 06:00, our alarms went off as we all groaned about the disturbance. I quickly threw my pants back on before exposing Gloria, then tried to get out of bed. Grasping at the metal bars on the bunk above me, I pulled my body to the side of the bed, taking a few deep breaths, mentally preparing myself to stand up on my feet. It took a few tries, but I stood up, sort of. At first, I could not fully extend my legs as my knees buckled. Biting my lip, I got the full extension and hobbled over to my backpack. My mind was trying to process how I was going to walk in that condition. I must have looked like an old man, groaning and grunting with every movement. Part of me wondered if my blazing fast effort up the Napoleon Pass was to blame for how I felt. Maybe, if I had just toned it down a little, I would have been in better shape. But that is not how I roll.

One lesson I took from my first night at an albergue was to put on my hiking clothes before going to bed, which would eliminate my need to wait for the bathroom. The bathroom on my floor was already in use, so I collected my belongings and tried the bathroom downstairs. Someone was using it. Waiting outside the door, I used the time to fill my water bottles in the kitchen. When the bathroom door swung open, a girl in her 20s quickly whisked her way up the stairs and out of sight. As I entered, I realized why. The bathroom smelled like the bowels of hell. It was paralyzingly bad. But I took a deep breath and maneuvered my way in, like a soldier entering a tear gas chamber. I survived, barely. Next stop: washroom. I threw on my dirty, mud-crusted, and smelly New Balance shoes; I loosened up the laces because of the swelling in my feet. My clothes on the clothesline had not fully dried, so I tied them to a few hooks on the outside of my backpack, hoping they would finish drying on the Camino. The weather outside was much cooler than the night before, having dropped from 75 to 52 degrees. I was wearing my long sleeve windbreaker with a light puffy vest. Besides the warmth, it helped protect my skin from my armpit rash caused by the straps on my backpack.

Outside on the Camino, the route retraced my steps over Puente de la Rabia, hooking right and up a steep paved road. It was parallel to a 15-foot stone-built wall, with overgrown ivy sprawling out from the top. The guys from Mallorca had started 15 minutes before me, and Gloria had stayed in Zubiri to grab an early morning breakfast. I set my sights on Pamplona and looked to settle into a groove. It felt like no time had passed since I had stopped walking the day before. There I was, already back on the trail. 21km or not, the walk to Pamplona would still be a considerable distance to cover, with many short, but steep, climbs along the way. As I exited the village, the paved street led to a trail, with the surroundings covered almost entirely by vegetation. I climbed up a few steps and over a narrow slab of concrete, passing a small creek, and leaving Zubiri behind.

Down the trail, I caught up with the Mallorca guys one last time. We exchanged pleasantries about the Camino and our similar lifestyles on the beaches of Mallorca and Miami Beach. The guys were only going as far as Pamplona, then flying back home to Mallorca. Their walking speed was slower than mine, and we kept getting passed by people, one person in particular. On the Camino, you develop a sixth sense about people approaching from behind. Without hearing them coming, you know they are close. That morning, there was a girl walking at a devilish pace. Let us call her, "Speed Demon." We paused on the side of the dirt trail and let her continue on. I marveled at her speed. She was about 5-feet 6-inches tall, and could not have weighed more than 100 pounds. Strapped with a full-size backpack and no trekking poles, she smiled and waved and said, "Buen Camino!" with an English accent. Speed Demon was quickly down the trail and out of sight. Shortly after, I think my competitive spirit kicked back in, so after 20 minutes, I pulled ahead of the Mallorca group and continued the Camino at my own pace. That is what people frequently said about the pilgrimage, "You must make it your own." So, I did.

At 08:30, my first stop on the day was a place called La Parada de Zuriain. Across a bridge and over the Arga River once again, the small, but lively cafe was full of pilgrims. Seating was outside-only, as the river-side terrace had plenty of open tables. I grabbed a stool near the ordering window. I took a few minutes to myself, sipping my cortado and munching on my chocolate chip cookies, but it was difficult not to notice how virtually everyone there was in a group. Some of them talked about dinner the night before, other places they had traveled to in Europe, or how good the coffee was. These were the makings of what many called their "Camino Family." The term refers to pilgrims who form a bond with others walking the Camino. The bond typically begins at or near their starting point, where the people cross paths with one another. After developing this bond, they often walk together, eat together, and sleep at the same albergues, all the way to Santiago de Compostela. After watching the crowd, I took a few last gulps of my cortado, grabbed my poles, and left the cafe. My plan was to eat lunch with my family in Pamplona. It was a 5-hour and 30-minute walk from Zubiri, which had me arriving in Pamplona by about 12:00.

6km from Pamplona, at the entrance to Villaba, I sat on the ledge of a medieval bridge that was built over the Ultzama River. My feet were giving me problems. I felt a tremendous amount of pressure, starting just below my ankles. As soon as I sat down, there was an immediate relief. On the ledge of the bridge, with my head held low, I saw another pilgrim approaching. He looked like a man in his 50s, wearing a tiny CamelBak water reservoir on his back. He was not carrying a large backpack like most other pilgrims. I would later find out that some pilgrims use a "send-ahead" courier service. For about six euros, you could send your belongings to the next town or albergue you were staying at. It was a handy convenience, but I could not shake the feeling that somehow it was cheating. The man looked over at me as he crossed the bridge.

"Is everything OK?" he asked.

"Yep, just taking a breather," I said. But I imagine my face told a different story.

The town of Villaba is an ancient town formed in the twelfth century. Pilgrims adore Villaba because of the Iglesia de la Trinidad, a basilica that is at the end of the bridge and borders a village called Arre. However, I adored Villaba for another reason. It is the hometown of Navarran cyclist Miguel Indurain. He is one of the all-time great cyclists, winning five Tour de France titles in a row in the 90s. Indurain was also my grandfather's favorite cyclist. Unfortunately, my grandfather died in 2017 at the age of 93. I miss him.

When I left Zubiri, I knew the day would be bittersweet. But it had nothing to do with the walking. It was the fact that I would pass by my grandfather's birthplace—Urdániz. The Camino slightly veered around the village as the path remained tucked away on the opposite end of the Arga River. And as I walked, I thought about how many times my grandfather must have been on the Camino, with a knapsack in tow, walking along the same trail en route to Pamplona. When he was alive, he often spoke of the running of the bulls, but we never talked about the Camino de Santiago. However, I am sure he would have had a story to tell about the times he had walked the path. I really, really miss my grandfather.

As I stepped off the bridge, the pain and pressure in my feet returned almost immediately. It sucked, but I kept going. The final 6km leading into Pamplona was night and day compared to the previous 15km. The Camino transformed itself into an urban metropolis, complete with apartment buildings, traffic, and plenty of crosswalks. Crosswalks were a bit of a pain when you had to wait for the walk signal, as they taunted you with how many seconds remained until you could walk again. The worst part of the urban setting was the surface. Going from dirt to pavement did not help my feet at all. The dirt trail at least gave a little bounce as you walked. But through the city, each step felt like I was walking with weights attached to my feet, as if gravity was 10 times its usual pulling force.

Midway through the town of Burlada, I stumbled upon a bus stop with an empty bench. With my backpack still on, I took a seat sideways, leaning back just enough so that the weight of my backpack was mostly on the bench. The pain was becoming intolerable. Five minutes later, I found another bench and did the same thing. 4km separated me from Pamplona, but those kilometers would prove arduous. My pace had slowed considerably as fatigue set in and the swelling in my feet became worse. What should have been a lovely stroll through the neighboring town of Pamplona was now a true suffer fest. In order to help relieve the pain in my feet, I tried reducing the time I was on each foot, in between steps. I started walking faster. I could feel the burn in my calves as my pace had suddenly doubled. Although I am not sure it did anything to my feet, my burning calves took some of the attention away. I kept that quick pace through Burlada and into the outskirts of Pamplona.

In all my years of going to Pamplona, I had never entered the city from the northeastern side, as the airport and bus stations are on the south side of the city. The Magdalena Bridge took me over the Arga River once more, as I neared the "casco viejo," or "old town." The Magdalena, along with other historical structures in the vicinity, dates back to the twelfth century. It underwent Gothic renovations in 1963. It has three original large and pointy arches, as well as a stone cross that shows the "Pilgrims' Way." For centuries, millions of pilgrims crossed the bridge on the Camino de Santiago, hoping for their first true rest of the pilgrimage, after having overcome almost 70 physically grueling kilometers from France, over the Pyrenees and into Pamplona.

The Magdalena Bridge led me to what many call the "Ancient Fortress," a 5km perimeter wall built in the sixteenth century. Built to fortify Pamplona, the wall warded off potential enemies who might seek to overtake the city, particularly the French. The entrance through the wall, after the Magdalena, was one of the six ancient entrances into Pamplona. They dubbed it the "French Gate," not because of the enemy, but because of the influx of travelers who made their way from France. A carving of a renaissance coat of arms, showcasing a double-headed eagle and the imperial arms, is still present on the gate today. A few centuries after its construction, Pamplona added a drawbridge just below the French Gate, further strengthening its fortification.

The pain in my feet was even worse as I climbed the steep entrance through the French Gate and into the old town. I needed to get off them. It felt like I was carrying two people up the hill. It was 12:15 as I passed through Navarrería, which was its own town in ancient times. I then followed the blue and yellow signs to Santiago. Sometimes, I came across a blue metal sign with a yellow scallop and arrow below it, showing the way. Other times, they marked the Camino with a yellow arrow spray-painted on the side of a building, or even on the pavement as you walked through a town. I was heading in the right direction.

The streets were already buzzing with the anticipation of the Fiesta of San Fermín kicking off in three weeks. The energy of the townsfolk was palpable, and the smiles on their faces basked in the Navarran sunlight. Entering the Plaza Consistorial, or the Town Hall Square, I gazed up at the façade of the town hall. Built in the 1423 by King Charles III, the square united three neighboring jurisdictions: Navarrería, San Cernin, and San Nicolás. The construction of the building took place on the site of a former moat. Today, the four-story building still stands in all its glory. Flags adorn the town hall, which is crowned with ocher sandstone. Lions and shields flank the top, with a trumpet-playing angel in the middle. I was very familiar with this building and its location, as the running of the bulls passes through the square for eight straight days during the festival.

Stepping away from the Town Hall Square, I tried to check-in to my accommodation, but I was early. I needed to wait another hour. The place I chose for two nights in Pamplona was the Europa Hotel. Yes, a hotel. There were two reasons for this. First, on the Camino de Santiago, albergues only allow you to stay with them for one night at a time, so that would not work. Second, I wanted a proper place to clean up my grungy, filthy, smelly self before I showed up at my cousin's wedding. So, the modest hotel did just that. And since I had one hour before I could check-in, I used the time to stop by Patxi's flat a few blocks away. He was holding my suitcase with the tuxedo and dress shoes inside.

"Ander! How are you, man!?" asked Patxi, as he gave me one of his signature big hugs.

"I'm still standing!" I said.

"Would you like a beer?" asked Patxi, grabbing a bottle of Voll-Damm from the kitchen fridge. It was a double-malt beer with 7.2% alcohol.

"Sure, but how about we split it? I haven't eaten much today, so it might send me over the edge," I said.

"So, how did it go over the Pyrenees? More difficult than you thought?"

"It was tough. I think today's effort was more painful than yesterday's, but maybe because I was paying the price for yesterday."

"I love those mountains. I love the Camino. If I didn't have to work, I would've come along for the walk," said Patxi, half-joking. He was an outdoorsman with tons of energy. But the conversation took a somber turn.

"Any plans to go hiking soon?"

"Well, sort of. Next weekend I'll be riding my bike up to Saioa and Erga, two mountains nearby." Then he paused for a moment. "Ander, come here for a second," he said, whisking me away to the outdoor terrace. His wife, Cristina, was outside hanging clothes to dry. The terrace had a beautiful view of the city, as well as the mountains in the distance. "Do you see that peak to the west, and that one to the east?" asked Patxi.

"Yeah, I see it," I said, using my hand as a brim to shade my eyes from the sun.

"That's where I'm going to lay my father's ashes," said Patxi. My heart sank and my stomach dropped.

"I didn't know he passed. I'm really sorry to hear that. But why those mountains?"

"He loved it up there. And so did I. We spent a lot of time there when I was little. It'll be a nice thing, you know? On weekends or when I'm not working, I'll be able to ride my bike up there and talk to my dad," he said with a little smile, wiping his mouth of the beer. "People might say it's strange, but these are *my* things." Patxi, the cheerful spirit he was, I could tell he was trying to keep it together. A few minutes later, I gave him and Cristina a hug and a kiss, took my suitcase, and left for the hotel.

After lugging the suitcase back to my room, I had to lie down. My body was exhausted and stricken with aches and pains. I tried to clear my mind and get some rest. I thought about the time I stuck my arm in the burning fryer oil at my parents' restaurant. The Camino was sort of like that. I instantly regretted the fryer incident, and part of me wondered if I had gotten myself into a similar snafu on the Camino. Part of me wanted to see how much pain I could take, and yet still conquer the ancient pilgrimage. But one thing was for sure: there would be nobody there to save me this time. There would be no magical escape, no freezer full of ice, and no shortcuts. Still, I was happy to be in Pamplona for my cousin's wedding, even if it coincided with some misery.

CHAPTER FIVE:

A NAVARRAN WEDDING

There were black specks up and down on each page. The typed letters appeared slanted to the right, as though the person who scanned it carelessly tossed it over the glass, threw down the plastic lid, and pressed the copy button. "Judgement of Dissolution of Marriage," read the old document. And it marked the end of my childhood as I knew it. I was collecting documents to petition for my father's Green Card so that he could travel to the United States. These included birth certificates, criminal records, and, of course, the dissolution of marriage to my mother. I flipped through the pages for the first time as an adult, reflecting on the chaos that had led to my parents' divorce. My memories were still vivid. It was like a time-machine to the past, but unlike *Back to the Future*, I could change nothing, and I knew how the movie ended.

As I woke up from my nap in Pamplona, I discovered a surprise waiting for me: my first blister on the Camino. It was on my right foot. A blister-free pilgrimage was the "holy grail" of the Camino. Most new pilgrims hope they do not get blisters. They carry jars of oily Vaseline and rub it all over their toes and feet, hoping to ease any friction. I did not subscribe to this approach, since I had tried Vaseline back in Miami, and I actually felt like it caused more friction since my feet started sliding around everywhere. There I was, dealing with a blister the size of a nickel on my second toe, also called the long toe. It was just to the left of my toenail. It was strange, since I did not feel its pain on the way over from Zubiri. But I did now. Just lightly touching or rubbing the skin sent shooting pains through my foot. I contemplated popping it with my needle kit, but I thought it would be best to wait until after lunch with my family. So, I carefully showered, changed my shirt, and went to have lunch.

My younger cousin, Amaia, who was getting married, is the daughter of my older cousin, named Javier. Javier was pivotal to my renewed sense of belonging in Pamplona. At 12 years old, I left the Basque Country with my mother and two sisters to return to the US. I left with some bitter feelings about my experience growing up in the Basque Country. But, years later, with the help of Javier, I made Pamplona my own, and engrained myself in its culture of family, friendship, and, of course, bull running.

Lunch was at the oldest gastronomic society in Pamplona—Napardi. Besides being a member, my cousin Javier was also on the board of directors of the social club. Napardi traces its roots back to 1953, when a group of men visited the San Sebastián social club, Istingorrak. The group came away so impressed by their visit that they started their own club in Pamplona. For decades, Napardi has served as a place where members and their family and friends can gather to bond over food, wine, and the occasional sounds of an accordion player. Or, as Napardi likes to put it, the locale is a "temple of friendship, gastronomy, traditions and good humor."

One by one, the plates began landing on the table. Navarran meals are a feast with multiple courses. First, it was a mixed salad with lettuce, tomato, and tuna, topped with oil, vinegar, and a touch of sea salt. Then came the shrimp, perfectly grilled and full of tasty juices. After that came the cod fish, smothered in a sauce of garlic and parsley. It was a typical dish in Spain. Then came Javier, with an enormous dish of lamb. Javier was wearing the iconic white Napardi apron, bearing the symbol of the social club—a plate with a crossed fork and spoon perched on it.

"Ander, how is the Camino going?" asked Amaia, sitting across from me.

"I'm killing it. They should rename it the 'Camino de Ander,'" I said in jest, soaking up the juices left over from the lamb with a piece of French bread. The table laughed.

"You're not trying to walk the whole thing, are you?" asked Mikel, Amaia's fiancé, sitting next to me.

"Yes, the whole thing,"

"But how?" asked Amaia.

"Whatever it takes."

"Listen, return to Pamplona in good conditions, so that you can run with the bulls. Especially how you run…" warned Javier. He was referring to my desire to get close to the bulls. I love to run on the horns, just a few feet or even inches away. It is not enough for me to be in the street. I have to be front and center, leading those bulls up the street with a newspaper.

Trying to ease the tension and seriousness of the conversation, I took a hard left with a change of topic.

"So, Amaia and Mikel, when can we expect the baby?" I asked

brazenly, with a big grin.

"Oh, shit!" shouted Mikel, putting his hand to his mouth. "I just bit my tongue," he said, dabbing his tongue with his finger, checking for blood.

"Are you OK?" Amaia asked, giggling.

"No, seriously. I bit my tongue at that exact moment," said Mikel.

I remember little after that, as Javier busted out many bottles of Cava (Spain's champagne). All I remember from that afternoon was showing up at a pharmacy after lunch, asking for advice on popping blisters. They hooked me up with a bottle of iodine and a box of bandages, in case I popped the blister on my toe. When I showed the pharmacist a photo, she had mixed thoughts on whether I should pop it. This is because when you pop blisters, you risk infection. Since I had an extra night in Pamplona, I thought I would wait and see how it was the next day, then decide if I wanted to pop it.

The morning of the wedding, I still felt banged up. The pressure on my feet had eased only somewhat, and the blister was still about the same size as the previous day. I figured it would be best not to pop it until I returned from the wedding, since I was going to be there all day, and my feet were going to be trapped inside snug, feet-crushing dress shoes. For the wedding, I did not bring a traditional suit. Before I left Miami, I realized that I no longer fit into any of the ones in my closet. My arms, back and chest had gotten bigger in recent months, since I delved more into weightlifting. The only other respectable attire I had in my closet was a black tuxedo that I had just worn to Bobby George's wedding in Pennsylvania a few weeks back. I had no choice but to take it to Spain.

Amaia and Mikel had arranged for a shuttle bus to pick up everyone in Pamplona, then drive us over to the venue about 15 minutes away in a town called Olloqui. If I am being completely honest, when I showed up on the shuttle and greeted folks, I felt like a complete imbecile. I mean, who wears a tuxedo to a wedding, when they are not even a groomsman? Me, that is who. Not even Mikel, the groom, was wearing a tuxedo. Just me. I looked and felt like a butler. At the venue, whenever I used the restroom, I expected to be asked for a mint or maybe a few paper towels. Still, I sucked it up and enjoyed the wedding.

The venue was spectacular, a total dream. The ceremony was outside on the carefully landscaped lawn, with only a few clouds overhead, and plenty of sunshine to warm the hearts of everyone there. My cousin rented an old palace that had belonged to a noble family. It was one of the original plots in the Kingdom of Navarra, which the old monarchy founded in 824. I watched as Amaia's father, Javier, helped her step out of a 1979 Rolls-Royce Silver Wraith II. It was white, with a brown top, and exuded every bit of opulence and royalty that Amaia deserved on her wedding day. As they walked down the aisle together, Javier was in tears, bringing her to the altar. The scenery was stunning. Amaia looked radiant in her white wedding gown. In the distance, we were surrounded by the Navarran mountains; the town of Huarte to the south and Irotz to the north. It was difficult to hold in the tears. Amaia and I had grown closer over the years, as I became more attached to Pamplona and the running of the bulls. She attended the book signing I held in Pamplona when I published my memoir. And we always sit together at the family lunch every 7th of July during the Fiesta of San Fermín. I was also the only member of the American family she invited to be there for her special day. She even mailed me a wedding invitation with a little hand-drawn bull on the inside of the envelope. I felt blessed to be there that day.

The ceremony had limited seating, so most of us younger guests ended up standing in the back. Every few seconds, I would shift my weight from one leg to the other. My feet were so swollen and those dress shoes were so tight, I thought I was developing bunions in real-time. Once the ceremony was over, we snapped some photos with family and friends, and then went up the elegant steps to the large, covered tent area. Oh, and there was a bar too.

"Ander, what do you want to drink?" asked my cousin, Fermín. Until a few years ago, he played professional handball in Spain. A tall, well-built hombre, Fermín's hands were the size of a bear's—huge!

"Do they have non-alcoholic beer?" I asked, sheepishly.

"No. That is unacceptable. No Camino tomorrow. Today, we are going to drink heavily. Tomorrow you will rest, and then you can continue the Camino," he said, joking. I lamented the fact that I could not let loose with Fermín. He is a party animal. But also, a tremendous athlete with a promising career ahead of him. In recent years, he joined the coaching staff of Spain's national handball team, specializing in video analysis. In 2020, the team won the bronze medal at the 2020 Summer Olympics in Tokyo, and then took home the gold medal at the 2020 European Championships held in Austria, Norway and Sweden.

I stood in the grass next to the tent, sipping my non-alcoholic beer and enjoying the beauty of the party after the ceremony. It was so magical. I watched as Amaia and Mikel made their way around the terrace, greeting and thanking everyone for being there. I watched as one of my cousins lost his balance standing next to a table and collapsed on top of it. He was drinking, eating, and talking, all at the same time. I think he smushed a few of our shrimp hors d'oeuvres. He was holding a strategic position next to the staircase, flagging down servers with food trays to stop for him before emptying the trays underneath the tent—the hors d'oeuvres were absolutely delicious. They brought us garlic prawns, chistorra (Navarran sausage), meatballs, and even some tasty beef sliders. The atmosphere was nothing short of jovial. I love watching people laugh and tell stories, especially family. I thought about how special it was to be back in Spain, attending Amaia's wedding, a 10-minute drive from where my grandfather was born. I thought about how he, like my father, immigrated to the United States as a sheepherder, and what must have gone through his mind when he passed through Ellis Island in New York, circa 1950s. I wondered if he ever thought that the wedding and those precious moments would be possible. It was a special feeling.

As we danced and drank the afternoon away, the sun faded, the clouds moved in, and the sky darkened. As the raindrops fell, we moved inside the palace for an early dinner. After we took our seats, Amaia and Mikel danced to their table as we stood up and applauded the newly wedded couple. Next, in honor of Pamplona and the Fiesta of San Fermín, they unveiled red pañuelos, the traditional handkerchief that is worn by festivalgoers. Friends and family cheered and twirled their napkin cloths around in the air, as Javier tied the pañuelos around their necks, in true San Fermín fashion. At the table, I was never happier to be sitting down, taking some of the pressure off my feet. The first few plates served were raw tuna and octopus, followed up by a rare steak—one of the best I have ever had. For dessert, we had mint-flavored sorbets with Cava. But the night was just getting started.

We went around the dinner table, getting caught up on what everyone was doing in life. My cousin Beatriz and her boyfriend were getting ready to travel to Havana, Cuba, for their first time. They were flying over in August. We joked it was close enough to Miami that they could swim over for a visit if they like. Gradually, the conversation steered its way toward the Camino. Fermín's girlfriend, María, is from a town called Estella, 44km from Pamplona. It was also my destination for Day 4 of the Camino (Day 3 being the wedding day, of course).

"Estella is wonderful. My family still lives there," said María.

"I can't wait to see it tomorrow," I said.

"But you're not going to Estella tomorrow, are you?" asked Beatriz, as everyone looked over.

"Yeah, I leave Pamplona first thing in the morning."

"Ander, the stage from Pamplona is only until Puente la Reina. The one after that is to Estella," said Beatriz.

"I know, but I have to walk two stages a day if I want to make it Santiago before the running of the bulls."

"You're going to walk the whole thing? All the way to Santiago?" asked Beatriz.

"Yeah…" I said, biting my lip a little, acknowledging that it would not be easy.

"Ander, if something happens to you or you can't make it to Estella, call us and we will pick you up," said María.

When dinner was over and the reception began, I called a taxi. It was

21:00. I wanted to get back to the hotel, pop my blister, and get a good night's sleep before I resumed the Camino. From there forward, it was going to be a long walk to Santiago.

The taxi picked me up at about 21:30. It was pouring down rain. Inside, I meditated as the sounds of raindrops hit the windshield while the wipers frantically worked to clear them. I stared out of the window as we rolled along the highway, red brake lights illuminating the dimly lit road. I thought of Amaia's smile as she walked down the aisle to marry Mikel. It was wonderful to witness the happiest day of someone's life. It made my eyes water to see her father, Javier, visibly shaken as he walked her to the altar. But in all the blissful euphoria of that day, I could not help but remember how things had ended for my parents, and how their union was now a distant memory. I started thinking about something Patxi had said to me when I picked up my suitcase. "It might not make sense to other people, but these are *my* things," he said, referencing his intent to scatter his father's ashes across two mountaintops. I was not sure what he meant by that. What did he mean by "my" things? And if he had his, then what were mine? My mind drifted as I continued staring out of the taxi, raindrops sliding down the window next to me.

CHAPTER SIX:

HILL OF FORGIVENESS

I was standing in the middle of my room, crying. Within minutes, I had to pack my life into a small bag, zip it up, and leave the country. My mother was yelling at me to hurry. I was 12 years old when my mother, my three sisters and I finally left the Basque Country for the United States. Only there was one catch: we were leaving my father behind. He was at work at the factory and did not know we were leaving. The violence between my parents, both verbal and physical, had become so intense that my mother saw no other option besides making a run for the United States. We had been living in the Basque Country for two terrifying years. I watched as the dinner table comments turned into screaming matches, the scattering of broken glass across the living room floor, clothes being tossed out of the window, and my parents putting their hands on each other. They say that when you die, you pass on to eternity. But as a kid, eternity seemed like nothing compared to those two years in the Basque Country. Yet, when we packed up to leave, I struggled to leave my father behind. That escape would lead to five long, painful years away from him.

As I made the pilgrimage to Santiago, my father was back home in Miami. It was a strange feeling to be in Spain and not see my father. Before he came to stay with me in Miami, he had been residing in the Basque Country, ever since we moved there when I was 10 years old. And every year I went to run with the bulls, I visited him in his hometown of Mañaria. I would help on the ranch, herd the sheep, and harvest our 10 acres of grass to stock up for the wintertime. But this time in Spain, I was on my own.

When I returned from Amaia's wedding, I opened my backpack, retrieved my medical supplies, and stabbed a sharp needle through my nickel-sized blister. The smelly fluid leaked out onto my toes, dripping onto a piece of scrunched up toilet paper I grabbed from the bathroom. The puncture did not hurt, but I could feel the tingly and sensitive skin underneath each time I squeezed the bubble to empty more fluid. After squeezing it all out, I added a few drops of iodine from the pharmacy and let it dry for a bit, then wrapped it with a bandage.

In the morning, I stuffed my tuxedo, my torturous dress shoes, and everything else non-Camino related into my suitcase. The day before, I hand-washed my clothes in the bathroom sink, then hung them up on a wire in the hotel room—the travel clothesline was well worth the $15 spent. At 06:00, I stepped out of the hotel, dropped the suitcase off at Patxi's, then made my way back to the Camino. It was cooler in the morning, as there was a breeze in the air, following the rainfall from the night before. Still somewhat dark outside, I passed by the glorious town hall, looked at it for a moment, then continued down the cobblestone street. "See you in a few weeks," I said to myself. Destination: Estella, 46km away. I felt significantly better than when I arrived. I did not feel as much pressure in my feet, nor was my body as locked up as it once was. Physically, it was like a new start, but mentally, my mind had never really left the Camino, and it was almost a relief to be back on it.

Leaving Pamplona, heading westbound, one of the more notable landmarks was the famous Citadel. It was an old military renaissance fort built in 1689, comprising 69 acres. In 1808, Napoleon's army successfully sacked the Citadel. However, it was largely intact and did not suffer major damage. In more recent times, the Citadel has been the center of controversy, when during the Spanish Civil War, pro-Franco rebels executed 298 Republicans at the Socorro Gate, which faces the path of the Camino. Today, the Citadel is a public park with landscaped gardens, as the military discontinued its use in 1964. It was silent over there as I passed by.

After Pamplona, the Camino took me through Zizur Mayor, over the Sadar River and the Elortz River, eventually overlooking the town of Zizur Menor. In contrast to the lush and beautifully green landscapes near the Pyrenees, there was a visible change in the scenery. The grass fields were yellow and dry and scattered with hay bales, the wheat fields were a dullish brown, and the dirt path appeared arid. But the occasional field with gorgeous sunflowers was a sight to see. Perhaps one of the more noteworthy (or bizarre) experiences along the way was passing by Guenduláin. In the distance laid the ruins of this abandoned village. The fifteenth-century castle that marks its location still stands, but it is only a shade of its former glory, now covered in overgrown ivy and marred by vandalism. Still, it had a majestic creepiness to it. A church and cemetery also remained, adding to its supernatural feel.

Up the road began the ascent to the Alto del Perdón, or "Hill of

Forgiveness." This was the most strenuous climb of the day. At a height of 735 meters, the mountain sits 13km from Pamplona. As I began the climb, I noticed I was moving my trekking poles in one long stride, the way a skier would propel themselves forward. After a while, this movement started giving me pains in my right hip, as I had less leverage and support when I stuck the poles so far away from my body. Instead, I tried using opposite strokes with each stride, the way your arms naturally swing from side to side with each step. When I did this, my right hip felt better, but it also felt like there was a lot of unnecessary movement, as odd as it may sound. Maybe it was the conscious effort of trying to time my strokes in such a tedious manner. It took me a bit to get used to, but I kept that tactic on my way up the hill.

The wind picked up as I walked further. In the distance, I could see some of the wind turbines atop the Hill of Forgiveness, of which there were almost 40. The trail became narrower, cluttered with rocks and stones, and lined with bushes on both sides. The 2km hike was not a long one, but steep and tricky, because of the large puddles of water that had amassed during the previous night's downpour. These puddles blocked several points of the trail, causing me to have to climb into thorny bushes and maneuver my way around the water. Still, the thorny pokes and slight tears of my clothing were not as bad as if I dunked my feet in water. Legend has it that the devil once tempted a thirsty pilgrim while climbing the Alto del Perdón. The devil told the pilgrim they would reveal the location of a water fountain in exchange for the pilgrim's soul. The pilgrim refused. St. James later rewarded the pilgrim after they arrived in Santiago.

On the Camino, I was not sure why other people made the pilgrimage. It seemed like a personal question to ask. I was not interacting much, which made it a little more difficult to get a sense. The conversation with Patxi about his father had stirred up thoughts regarding the meaning of the Camino, and just the overall purpose of it all. "Was the Camino about penance?" I wondered. "Was it like that thirsty pilgrim tempted by the devil, where sacrifice was necessary on the Camino? Did I owe penance for my sins or for my transgressions?" I kept asking myself. When the Camino started a thousand years ago, people believed that if you reached the cathedral in Santiago, you received a reward—purgatory cut in half. In Roman Catholic doctrine, purgatory is a place or state of suffering where the souls of sinners must atone for their sins before entering the Kingdom of Heaven. These things swirled around in my head as I neared the top of the hill.

As I summited the Hill of Forgiveness, the wind was blowing ferociously now, as my sweaty hair flew all over the place. I was eye-level with the base of the wind turbine towers. The large revolving rotor blades went around and around, producing a whooshing noise that overtook the sound of the wind. The valley below was in plain view. Though the heights paled compared to the Napoleon Pass, I remember marveling at how high I was, with such pristine views out into the distance. At the top of the hill were the brown and rusty-colored metal sculptures that lined the cliff with the view of the valley. Installed in 1996, they pay tribute to the history of the pilgrimage in an exhibit-like fashion. At first glance, the sculptures are simply a group of pilgrims en route to Santiago. Upon closer examination, the sculptures tell several stories. The first pilgrim looks to be searching for Santiago, symbolizing some of the very first pilgrimages that took place. Next, there are three more pilgrims en route to Santiago, showing the increasing popularity of the Camino. Afterwards is a group of merchants on horseback and donkey that symbolize the commercial trends, where tradesmen try to sell things to pilgrims. Next to last is a pilgrim that appears alone, giving light to the fact that religious, political, and social matters caused a decline in the popularity of the Camino. The final sculptures depict a couple of pilgrims walking to Santiago, showing a renewed interest in the pilgrimage in modern years.

After passing the sculptures, I began the steep descent down the Hill of Forgiveness. It was a 4km stretch to a village called Uterga. Similar to the climb up, it was a dirt path with a random scattering of rocks. Nothing too complicated. Then, after about 150 meters, rocks covered the trail from end to end. It was as if a dump truck had backed up and dumped rocks everywhere. This is where the trekking poles really came in handy. I stopped momentarily to re-tie my shoes, which I tried to do before every ascent or descent. I could feel my feet sliding around in my shoes, giving me a slight burning sensation. That was not a good sign. But I kept going.

Coming down the hill, there were only a handful of spots to escape the sun for some shade. In the few that I passed, there was always a pilgrim or two loitering there with their backpacks off, taking a break. To guard my face from the scorching sun, I reached into my backpack and pulled out my hiking hat. This was an essential purchase for the Camino. The wide circular brim extended enough to keep the sun out of my face, and the top layer that covered my head came with a mesh vent panel, helping to provide some relief from the sweaty heat. My feet kept bothering me, almost to where I stopped and took my shoes off. I was afraid that removing my wool socks would worsen the swelling in my feet and make it difficult to put them back on. So, I carried on, and figured I would address it later.

Approaching Uterga, the path leveled out, as I walked next to a brown wheat field that remained unharvested. The strands of wheat moved slightly with the occasional blowing of the wind. After passing the small town of Uterga, I crossed through small towns such as Legarda, Muruzábal, and Óbanos, giving way to Puente la Reina. I was 24km from Pamplona and was ready for my first rest of the day.

Making my way through the narrow cobblestone street of Calle

Mayor, I found a bar and restaurant with a few tables and chairs out front. I claimed a table and set my backpack down on a chair beside me. Although I was still technically in the Basque region of Navarra, I ordered some tapas—small savory dishes or appetizers. Along with my Coke Zero, I enjoyed the sliced pieces of chorizo, patatas bravas (fried diced potatoes in a warm spicy sauce), and ensaladilla Rusa (potato salad). Any time you sit down for a meal in Spain, you can always count on a breadbasket filled with 3-inch slices of French bread. Tourists always complain about how much bread they have to eat in Spain. What gets lost is the reason people in Spain use the bread. First, the reason they have so much bread is because wheat is one of the most cultivated food sources in all of Spain. The wheat tolerates the hard, dry climate of the interior parts of the country. Second, people in Spain typically use the bread to move and position food, a salad, for example. It also works great to mop up egg yolk, oils, and other juices. But I think some tourists have it stuck in their heads that they are supposed to eat all the bread. In reality, you just eat what you need. Anyway, at the restaurant, I grabbed the chair opposite of mine and dragged it over to rest my legs on it as I ate. There was a fly that kept buzzing around my food. No matter how many times I swatted it away, it was hellbent on staying.

After eating, it was time to examine my feet. Earlier, I had kept my shoes on, despite the constant burning sensation. After gently removing my sock, I noticed my blister had returned. It was like I had never popped it. And I was not about to pop it sitting there at the restaurant. There were large groups of pilgrims walking by in the busy street, and I would not give them a show. More importantly, I was afraid that with all the sweat, dirt, dust, and grime, it might get infected. So, I pulled out the iodine bottle and some medical tape, added a few drops, then applied the tape around the blister. Whatever was causing the blister, it had to be some type of friction. My toenails were all cut short, but I figured it was just the rubbing from my big toe. I thought the tape might help. While I was at it, I also placed small strips of tape on the pads of my feet, just before the toes. I figured that might help the burning I felt there, even though they looked fine. Before I got up from the chair to continue the walk, I saw a familiar face pass me by. It was the Russian woman from the Napoleon Pass. I politely waved and smiled, almost as if I knew her. I mean, I barely knew her, but it was like she was a friend. And after walking so many kilometers alone, a familiar face helped brighten up my spirit.

I left the restaurant at 12:30 and followed Calle Mayor toward the edge of town, then stopped at a fountain to refill my water bottles. There was an older couple sitting on a bench to the right of the fountain. They seemed to be doing some people watching. This was common in smaller towns and villages. They probably marveled at all the different pilgrims that wandered through their streets. I could see the older couple staring at me out of the corner of my eye as I pressed the water-release valve on the fountain. I smiled, then chugged about half a bottle of water before filling it up one last time.

"You are thirsty," said the older woman, likely in her 80s. Her husband looked on, wearing a black beret, and holding his cane between his legs.

"Yes, I need some water before walking to Estella."

"To go to Estella, you must cross that bridge," said the older woman, pointing to the Romanesque bridge to the left of the fountain, adorned with a tall medieval archway. It was obvious I had to cross the bridge, since there was no other place to go, but the gesture was a kindhearted one, and I thanked her for it.

I stepped through the ancient archway and climbed over the steep bridge, measuring 110 meters, with six stunning arches. Puente la Reina's bridge, built in the eleventh century under King Sancho III's order, is one of its most iconic elements. It was to help pilgrims cross over the Arga River that flows below. But it lost a bit of its charm when I found out they used to charge pilgrims to cross it. However, there was more to this story. Centuries ago, the bridge had three watch towers: one on each end and one in the center. It was in the center tower where they had placed a renaissance carving of the Virgen del Puy (the Virgin Mary), the patron saint of the town. Since 1824, the locals say that a "txori" (bird in Basque) would periodically visit the carving, using its wings to clean the cobwebs from the sculpture. They even said the bird made quick passes over the Arga River to wet its beak, so that it could clean the face of the Virgen del Puy. As word spread, the people of the town came to expect these visits, and even rang church bells and launched fireworks in celebration of the bird's arrival. Authorities, particularly Cristobal Manuel de Villena, the 6th Count of Via Manuel, and the Brigade of the Royal Army, took exception to these "miraculous" events, even calling them "superstitions." Eventually, authorities demolished the central tower that housed the image. But the townspeople rescued the carving and placed it where it remains today—the Church of Saint Peter.

When I heard these stories, I did not spend too much time thinking about them. It seemed like every town had a story like this, possibly to attract more pilgrims and make more money. A few years back, I traveled to New Orleans to visit my friend Bill Hillmann. We walked around the French Quarter, listening to tour groups embellish tales of ghosts and other various hauntings around town. Were they spooky? Sure. Were they believable? Not so much. But on a more serious note, even before the Camino de Santiago, I had always wondered why "miracles" do not seem to happen anymore. "When was the last time a majestic bird tended to an image of the Virgin Mary?" I thought. "When was the last time the Devil tempted a pilgrim to trade their soul for water?" Not that I refused to believe these things could happen, I just think part of me wanted to experience something like that for myself; something holy.

When I left Puente la Reina, the afternoon weather was heating up. It was nearly 85 degrees. After the bridge, the Camino took me back into the grass and wheat fields, offering little shade to escape from the sun. The next eight kilometers were a mix of rolling hills, sprinkled in with some of the first olive groves I had seen on the Way. Unsurprisingly, Spain is one of the world's top olive exporters. They have even made their way to Costco. Believe me, I buy them. These green olive groves along the walk to Estella were a reminder that I was approaching the La Rioja region, world famous for its highly sought-after wine. The dirt trail I was on was one of the few remaining and well-preserved Roman roads on the Camino. But after eight hours of walking, the novelty wore off.

History aside, these rolling hills were deceptively difficult. The altitude was not anything crazy, but the constant walking up and down was enough to send my body reeling. My feet swelled up again, which probably became worse when I removed my shoes and socks to gawk at them. Playing soccer and basketball in high school, when we sprained an ankle or had a foot injury, the coaches always told us to leave our shoes on. If we removed them, the lack of structure would allow the ankle and foot to swell even more. But on the trail, there was nothing I could do at that point. I just had to keep going. A difficult stretch of the walk to Estella was reaching the hilltop town of Cirauqui, surrounded by vineyards. Slowly, but surely, I was finding out that the kilometers walked in the morning were much easier than those walked in the afternoon. After all, from Puente la Reina to Estella, I was the only pilgrim on the path. Everyone else walking to Estella had left in the early morning hours.

Entering Cirauqui, I found it tough to imagine living there. Calle Portal was so steep that my face could have touched the ground. The street was also extremely narrow and felt more like an alleyway. There were even cats roaming around as I huffed and puffed my way up. The Camino led me underneath the arch of a building connected to the town hall, out the back to another street. Seconds later, I was back on the old Roman road, with six kilometers to the next town of Lorca. I thought about refilling my water, since I only had a few sips left, but I was so annoyed with the hilly terrain of Cirauqui that I just kept pushing.

100 meters down the hill, I went over an eight-meter Romanesque bridge, still in good condition, considering its age. Back up another hill, the path ran parallel to a major highway, then took me across an overpass and next to a couple of vineyards. Then, the trail veered off to the width of a bike path, taking me through a dried-out valley. I was now completely out of water. I was clinging to the hope that I would come across a convenience store or one of those big white vans that sold food and drinks, like I had seen

in the Pyrenees. In the distance, I saw a great big house next to the highway. I thought maybe that was a good sign. As I got closer, the house had broken windows and spray paint everywhere, along with a chain locking the front door. Then, the path took me back into the sweltering hot countryside. I was going to have to wait until I arrived in Lorca to find some water.

My mouth was dry, my lips chapped, and everything hurt. It was 14:30, and I was about 2km from Lorca. I passed under another bridge, this time filled with cool air. I took off my hat and slowed my pace a little, just so that I could enjoy this natural air conditioning phenomenon. The air whipped through my sweaty hair, blowing it around freely. I closed my eyes as I walked through the tunnel, taking a couple of deep breaths. Coming out of the tunnel, I put my hat back on and braced myself for the heat again. Along the dirt path, I came across a table, two chairs, and a container of water that was left out for pilgrims. I was so happy. But the container was bone dry. Next to it was a basket that said "free water" with water bottles inside. They, too, were empty. All that remained was a plate on the small plastic table with 3 pieces of oily garlic bread and a couple of flies buzzing around. In my head, I tried to contain my fury. "Why would anyone need fucking garlic bread on this hot, desolate trail?" I asked myself. Still, it was an act of generosity, and I quickly put it behind me. I had to.

Arriving in Lorca, a small village of less than 100 people, everything was closed. The few bars and restaurants in town all had their shutters drawn. It royally sucked. Just before exiting the village, I saw a small convenience store with a couple of pilgrims sitting on a bench drinking beer. Before I stepped in, I stopped to take my hat off and catch my breath.

"Buen Camino," I said to the two pilgrims with Rastafarian dreadlocks. I think they were smoking weed. They looked high.

"Are you American?" they asked.

"Yeah, but my family is Basque."

"Oh, Basque! That's cool. Can you teach us something in Basque?"

"ETA!" said a woman with a snarly look on her face. She was the manager of the store. She was referring to the armed Basque separatist group that operated for about 60 years until its ceasefire in 2018.

"No!" said the pilgrims. They knew she was trying to stoke the fire. After that, I put my hat on and kept walking. I did not care how thirsty I was. I was not about to give my money to that woman.

"Wait, do you want something to drink?" she asked.

"No, eskerrik asko," I said, which means "thank you" in Basque.

Approaching Estella, dark and stormy clouds started moving in above me. I was about 15 minutes away from the albergue. The first few raindrops did not phase me. In fact, I welcomed it. I was hot, thirsty, and my body fried. Once the rain picked up, I knew I had to pull out my poncho, as well as my silicone waterproof shoe covers. It was really pouring now. The darkened sky and dumping of rain made my vision a little blurry. Then, just ahead, I discovered a water fountain. As the water gushed out from the faucet, I stuck my head under it and drank as much as I could. I loitered there for a few minutes, refilling and drinking my water bottles, then made my way to the albergue.

In the heart of Estella, the Agora Hostel was up a short hill, near plenty of bars and restaurants. It was 19:00. Inside, the manager asked me to remove my shoes and place them in the locker at the entrance to the lobby. He showed me up to the third story, where there was a large room with about 12 beds. The place looked remodeled. The beds were like pods in the wall, with privacy curtains, electrical outlets, and a personal light to flicker on and off. I settled into the place, collected my shower gear, and went to the stalls. My feet looked OK, other than the blister on my toe, which looked like it was ready to pop. I figured I would hold off on performing "surgery" until after dinner. After all, I had eaten nothing since stopping for tapas in Puente la Reina.

Back down the hill, there was a busy bar toward the end of the street. It was called Bar Alday. After ordering some jamon, eggs, and fries to-go, I found a seat at a table and drank an ice-cold beer. When the beer was gone, I took my food back to the albergue. The lobby had tables, chairs, and a little kitchen in the back that had extra plates and silverware. As I ate, I said hello to a Japanese kid at the table next to me. He said his name was "Tony." But after that, he could not speak any English. "Well, nice knowing you, Tony," I said to myself. After dinner, I hobbled up the two flights of stairs to reach my room. A few more people had arrived for the night. Matt was a 21-year-old kid from New Jersey. A little shy, but very kind. Lara, probably in her 40s, was a New Yorker who had just quit her job. Megan was also in her 40s, and she was from Seattle, part of the great Pacific Northwest. Sitting on my bunk, with a needle in hand, I struck up a conversation with Megan as she stretched on the floor below.

"Where did you walk from today?" I asked, sticking the needle through the blister on my toe.

"From Puente la Reina," said Megan. "What about you?"

"I came from Pamplona. I have to walk more than normal so I can finish in time."

"What do you mean?"

"The Fiesta of San Fermín starts on July 6, so I need to finish the Camino in time to return to Pamplona."

"Do you do the bull run thing?"

"Yeah, I'm obsessed. I do it every year," I said, dabbing my puss-like fluid with a paper towel from the bathroom. Lara poked her head out of the bunk below me.

"Wait, you do the running of the bulls!?" asked Lara in amusement.

I handed her my phone with some photos of me in the bull run. Megan went over to have a look, too.

"So why are you doing the Camino, anyway?" asked Megan. This was the first time anyone had asked me that question.

"I'd heard about it as a kid, and then I watched *The Way* with Martin Sheen. Plus, I had the time to do it, since I had to be here for a wedding in Pamplona. What about you?" I asked, moving the attention away from myself.

"My dad died a few months ago. I felt like I just needed to get away. I just needed some time alone to myself so I could process," said Megan. We offered our condolences. Then, it got quiet, until Lara pepped up the conversation again.

"Ander, you're crazy," said Lara, looking at my photos. We all started laughing at my bovine obsession. Matt heard the commotion and joined us, taking a seat on the floor next to Megan. His feet had several bandages on them.

"Oh my God, are your feet OK?" asked Megan.

"Yeah, I don't have any blisters. This is just preventative," said Matt. He was wearing Compeed blister pads that stick to your feet. I had brought some with me as well, but I had yet to use them.

"Do those work?" I asked.

"They're supposed to. I think you just put them on spots where you feel friction, like where a blister might start," said Matt. After wrapping up my toe, I noticed a few light purple circles forming on the bottom of my foot. I threw on a few Compeed bandages, hoping that would do the trick.

"I wish we could stick these on people who snore at night," I said to the group, striking a chord with them.

"You're telling me…" said a guy from another bunk. His name was Stuart. He was from the United Kingdom. "I slept next to a train last night," said Stuart, as we erupted in laughter. We all knew what he was talking about.

"I've been on the Camino for five days, but I can't wait for it to end," said Matt. A few of us nodded our heads in agreement.

"Ander, what are you doing up there?" asked Lara.

"Popping blisters, wrapping my feet, no big deal," I said, cheekily.

"We just started the Camino and you're already getting blisters?"

"It's all good. The body will adjust." Blisters made people nervous. Nothing sucks the enthusiasm out of a room on the Camino like talking about blisters.

"Do you guys know about the three parts to the Camino?" asked Lara, as we looked at her, confused.

"Three parts? You mean 35?" asked Megan, referencing the 35 traditional stages of the Camino.

"No, it's basically the phases you experience on the Way. The first phase is physical, there's lots of climbing and it shocks your body. The second phase is mental, especially when you start The Meseta. Then, the third phase is spiritual, as you get closer and closer to Santiago," said Lara. It was incredibly insightful, but the conversation came to a halt. We went to bed moments later, as another pilgrim ripped open his privacy curtain and yelled at us for being loud. At the albergues, quiet hours usually begin at 22:00, and it was already 22:30. We each climbed into our beds, pulled the curtains, and turned off the lights.

Laying in bed, I thought about what Lara had said about the three phases of the Camino. Prior to embarking on the pilgrimage in Spain, I understood its religious connection. But aside from that, it was a bit jarring to think about the rehabilitative nature of it, as if every pilgrim undergoes a spiritual transformation of sorts. And it was apparent that reflecting on one's past was part of that transformation. My childhood was rough, and there were events in my life where I wondered, had they gone differently, what my life would be like today. Like sweat leaving the body on a hot day's hike, those thoughts from the past bubbled up to the surface.

Walking the Camino alone presented an opportunity to cleanse my mind, which would be more difficult while walking with others. I also felt a lonely romanticism in it. "But why did so many people choose to walk the Camino in a group?" I asked myself. "If this was such a personal and spiritual journey, what was the deal with the groups?" Around 22:45, I laid my head on my pillow, closed my eyes, and said goodnight to Estella.

CHAPTER SEVEN:

MY CAMINO FAMILY

Moving slowly through the brambles, the rough, tangled, and prickly shrubs would rip through our clothes and scratch up our skin. But we did not care. Only a few more meters and we would be there. It was like our own little oasis in the foothills of the Eskuagatx mountain. We were heading for the pool of water that flowed naturally from the mountain springs. Overgrown with vegetation, it was difficult to access, and rarely visited. But once you did, it was magic. We would ride our bikes up there after lunch on hot summer days. After surviving the prickly thorns, it opened up with a flat, grassy plain, big enough for us to lay out our towels. There was a 15-foot drop at the edge of the pool. You had to jump in, as it was difficult and dangerous to climb down. The pool had a circular shape to it, with water flowing down from the creek like a waterfall. The pool had a mysterious way about it. There were darker patches where the water was deepest, sometimes as deep as 12 feet. Still, you could see clear to the bottom. These natural pools were also famous for inhabiting snakes, some as long as four feet. When we approached the pool at the edge, we were all afraid to jump in. "You go!" or "No, you go!" were typical shouting matches amongst us. Other times we just waited there, quietly, waiting to glimpse a snake racing across the bed of the pool in a wavy motion. When we saw one, it would send shivers down our spines. At some point, we knew we had to jump in. And we always did it as a group.

I was still getting used to sleeping in albergues, in rooms full of other people. Although sleeping in Estella was a more pleasant experience (less noise), I still woke up throughout the night. Maybe it was a nervous energy. Maybe it was the aching pains I felt at night from all the walking. Either way, it was part of the experience, and I had to get used to it. The nice thing about the constant waking up was that I knew I would not miss my alarm. On Day 5 of the Camino, I woke up around 05:45. Being a light sleeper, I heard the guy who yelled at us the night before rummaging through his backpack, getting ready to leave. So, I got up too.

Lara, Megan, Matt, and the others were sound asleep. They were in no rush to wake up as they were walking the normal 15-25km stages each day. It seemed rare for anymore to start their day before 06:00. Most people started between 06:30 and 07:30. Not only was it too early for people to wake up, particularly if they had stayed out a little later, but it was also pitch black before 06:00. Most people did not carry a headlamp. In fact, I had not even used mine yet. When I stepped out of the dorm room, I tried to be as quiet as possible. The constant raddling and clunking around of the scallop tied to my backpack had to have woken someone up. Outside on the street, it was still dark, with a faint light coming from the east; enough to walk. My destination for Day 5 of the Camino was a town called Viana, about 40km away.

Back on the route, the streets were still slick with the rain from the night before. I followed the signs out of Estella, which seemed a little like leaving Pamplona—an urban setting with apartment buildings, sidewalks, medians, and parks. After 30 minutes, I was climbing the asphalt slopes into the hilly town of Ayegui, next door to Estella. This town is famous for the wine fountain that is at the entrance to Bodegas Irache, a winery on the Camino. The winery, which has been in business since 1891, is famous among pilgrims for the "free" wine that is just steps away from the Camino. There are two faucets at the fountain: one for red wine and another for water. Each day, the winery fills up the fountain with 100 liters of seasonal red wine. And when it runs out, it runs out. So pilgrims typically take a mouthful or two and carry on with the walk. The story goes that back in the eleventh century, they used to make wine in the Irache Monastery, which used to be a hospital for pilgrims. And during the 1990s, to honor this cultural legacy, Irache Bodegas installed the wine fountain to offer pilgrims a drink along the Camino. I passed right by this fountain. Sadly, I did not stop for a drink, since the gate did not open until 08:00. However, if I am honest, I would not have stopped if it were open, anyway. I had one beer while waiting for my dinner the night before, and I was buzzing badly. Drinking was not exactly conducive to a 40km-plus daily hike through Spain.

After Ayegui, I encountered an Asian girl that looked lost. 99% of the time, the Camino markers were clear and visible. But that 1% could really throw you off if you were not careful. Plus, not all Camino markers were official markers, as helpful pilgrims painted many of them. So, in those rare times of uncertainty, I pulled out my phone, launched the Buen Camino App, and verified the path forward. I did not catch the girl's name or much about her, since her English was not great. In fact, the only thing I remember her saying was that she was Christian. And after helping her, we walked together for about an hour. As it became lighter outside, I noticed it was going to be a rough day. Above us, the clouds were dark and stormy. Eventually, the raindrops started. Only a few at first, but it became gradually worse. We found a tree along the Camino and stopped. As quickly as we could, we pulled out our ponchos and threw them on over our backpacks. And again, I took out my silicone shoe covers. Then, from the asphalt surfaces of the quiet roads, we entered a forest with a dirt trail, steadily climbing over the rolling hills. As we walked, I tried a few more times to make conversation with the girl, but to no avail. The girl, probably in her early 30s, was silent, but I think most of it had to do with the language barrier. Along the path, I stumbled across a couple of rocks, where I slid violently and almost ate dirt. The silicone shoe covers had terrible traction. I had also slipped several times entering Estella the day before. The girl giggled each time I slid. I thought it was funny as well. At one point, we crested a hill-top in the middle of nowhere, where the skies had cleared some. The girl suddenly stopped, staring out into the abyss. The sun was in full view, lighting up a picturesque scene of beauty. I slowed down, almost to a halt. But she just kept looking off toward the sun. I figured maybe she just needed a couple of moments to herself. Or maybe she just wanted to walk alone. Either way, I gave her space and kept on walking.

Once I reached Azqueta, I was 7km into the day's hike. It was also nearing 08:30, and I was starving. I had officially run out of granola bars, and only had a handful of GU Energy gels left. There was a cafe 20 meters from the Camino, so I stopped in and grabbed a cortado with a couple of napolitanas—a buttery, flaky tart filled with chocolate. After breakfast, I headed down the hill, passing a few agricultural warehouses, toward the big climb of Villamayor de Monjardín. Well, the climb was only 1km, but it was super steep, and the trail sucked—narrow and badly preserved. And I still had that cortado and those napolitanas sloshing around in my stomach. However, the acres of Navarran vineyards helped to soothe the pain with some nice scenery.

Approaching Villamayor de Monjardín, I was panting, but my feet were holding up OK so far. It might have been the sugar and caffeine that eventually kicked in, but I felt good. Just before entering the town, I passed by a thirteenth century well called the Fuente de Moros, or "Fountain of Moors." With its double-arched façade, you could walk down the steep staircase, where the water flows out below ground-level. Pilgrims used the water to wash and cleanup on their way to Santiago de Compostela. In town, I veered off the path to look for drinkable water. About 25 meters up the road, I found a fountain that looked like a birdbath. Most fountains along the Camino had small blue plaques that read "potable," if drinkable, and "no potable," if it was not. There was no plaque, but this fountain had a white pilgrim's scallop on it, so I figured it would not kill me.

As I stuffed the bottles into my backpack, I heard voices further up the hill. They were American voices. Four girls were coming down with a peppy step, as if they had just had their morning coffees.

"Hey, maybe this guy knows where we have to go," said one girl. Her name was Noelle, and she was a New York-based chef.

"Uh oh. Are you lost? You can follow me. The Camino is just down the hill, this way," I said, smiling, leading the group forward.

There were three other girls with Noelle. All four of them were in their early to mid-twenties. One girl caught my eye. I kept looking back at her. I felt like I had seen her somewhere before.

"Don't I know you?" I asked, looking back. She was short, thin, and quick on her feet.

"Umm, I don't know. You do look familiar," said the girl.

"It's you! You're the super-fast girl from Zubiri—the 'Speed Demon!'" I said, smiling. "You passed me up!"

"Oh, that's right! That was you!" said the girl, giggling. Her name was Neha. She was a recent graduate of the University of Cambridge.

"How did you all meet?" I asked.

"We met at an albergue in Puente la Reina," said Neha. The two other girls were Sarah and Lily. Sarah, like Noelle, was an American from New York. She worked in marketing. And Lily had just completed her studies at the University of Chicago.

"OK, cool. So, now you're one big happy family?"

"Pretty much!" said Noelle, as we stepped back onto the Camino and toward the next town of Los Arcos, 12km away.

The road from Villamayor de Monjardín included a sharp descent at first, which leveled out and took us over scattered rolling hills. There were patches of mud in certain spots, forcing me to jump over them with my 30-pound backpack. I could feel my facet joints getting twisted out of position. My back was tightening up. Neha, "Speed Demon," was leading the way with me at the front of the group. It gave us a chance to get to know each other a little. Neha was originally from India but was living in London.

"I'm moving to the Netherlands soon to study for my masters," said Neha. "I'm a bit nervous."

"Why are you nervous?" I asked.

"I've lived in London pretty much my whole life. I guess I just don't know how things will go in the Netherlands."

"Think you'll ever move back to India?"

"My brother lives there, but I don't know. I mean, London is home. At least for a few more months until I move to the Netherlands."

Sarah, from New York, was not saying much on the way to Los

Arcos. I think the rolling hills were giving her problems. She had her suffer face on. I let "Speed Demon" bounce along ahead of me and dropped back to chat with Sarah, who was also of Indian descent, but was born and raised in the US.

"Are you doing OK?" I asked. It was a stupid question. None of this was easy. Whether you were walking 20km or 40km, there were going to be elements of suffering.

"Yeah, it's just my foot," said Sarah.

"Blisters?"

"No, it's just a really deep pain on the top of my foot, right below my ankle. I'll be fine." I tried to change the subject.

"So, what brings you to Spain? Why the Camino?"

"Well, I was working in marketing at a tech company. And when the tech company went under, I lost my job. Yeah, that's how I ended up here. I just needed some time to reset and think about what I'm going to do. I still don't know what I'm going to do," she said. Sarah, like Noelle, used to play soccer in college. They were both in fantastic shape—toned, vibrant, and just had a healthy look about them. But even Noelle had her own reasons for doing the Camino.

"I went to Catholic middle school and high school. That's when I first watched *The Way*," said Noelle.

"Oh man, I love that movie!"

"It's honestly one of my most cherished memories. They showed it to us when I was 12 years old," said Noelle. "Ever since then, I've felt a pull to go do the Camino."

"Any big epiphanies yet?"

"I mean, I don't know… I'm just trying to love myself more. It took me years to understand I don't have to believe the harsh things I lived through as a child," said Noelle. Her words hit close to home.

A few kilometers outside of Los Arcos, we felt raindrops. In true pilgrim style, we waited until the downpour was imminent before we went through the hassle of pulling out our ponchos, which always seemed to be stuffed down at the very bottom of the backpack.

"OK guys," I said, "don't laugh at me, but I'm going to put on my shoe covers."

"Where did you get those!?" asked Noelle.

"Amazon! $17.99. They're made of silicone," I said, zipping the shoe covers up and over my shoes.

"Oh, no!" said Sarah.

"What happened?" I asked.

"I just set my backpack down on a massive ant hill!" she said in agony, swatting away at her backpack like it had done something wrong. At that moment, I learned again why not to put your backpack down on the ground. If you had to, at least place your foot under the backpack to keep it just a few inches off the ground. These were the rural lands of Spain, and just about anything could crawl into it. Still, Sarah was a trooper, and we all carried on in the rain.

Luckily, the wet weather did not last long; maybe 20 minutes. But the trail was as monotonous as ever. We were in the middle of the agricultural landscape. There were no homes, houses, barns, or any structures, really. The only thing we found was a panel that said there was a big battle in 1873. The conservative Carlist troops beat General Domingo Moriones and his liberal army during the Third Carlist War. But me and the girls were facing our own battle out on the Camino—one of hunger and exhaustion. We had been walking for 2.5 hours without stopping until we finally reached Los Arcos.

Los Arcos was a popular town to stay in for most pilgrims, especially since the official stage ended there. But I think it was the wineries that convinced most pilgrims to stay the night. Strolling through town, we kept our eyes open for a place to relax and grab a bite to eat. The Plaza of Santa María was a wide-open space next to a church of the same name, surrounded by a few bars and a convenience store. We grabbed two tables in the plaza that were sheltered by umbrellas, as we were still cautious of the rain. The five of us took turns leaving our bags at the tables and wandering inside the bar called Cafeteria Buen Camino. It was becoming clear that many businesses and localities survived by the very existence of the pilgrimage. And we were starving. Gazing at the pintxos stored in the glass cases, everything looked wonderful. I ordered two jamon pintxos, topped with a spread of crawfish. They were delightful. We really needed a relaxing break, especially since the day was not over.

The girls wanted to go 8km further to a town called Torres del Río. And since I was going 11km beyond that, I did not mind at all. I enjoyed the company. Noelle was quick to get up and start walking, as the rest of us lagged getting our gear ready again. That was the spirit of the Camino. Everyone was heading in the same direction. Eventually, most people would catch up. Before I left, I made a quick stop inside a convenience store and bought a bar of Nestle chocolate—the crunchy kind. Chocolate turned out to be a great, but tasty, blast of sugar and energy. I estimated to be burning around 5,000 to 6,000 calories a day. And I had little time to eat throughout the day, so I had to find foods and drinks that were easily digestible, yet packed with a punch. Things like chocolate bars, almond chocolate ice-cream bars, napolitanas, cans of Coca-Cola or Aquarius, and then proper foods, like jamon and chorizo sandwiches, and one of my favorites, servings of tortilla. Calories aside, I needed to change my shirt for the rest of the walk. The wind picked up, and I could feel the chill in the air, especially with my sweat-drenched t-shirt. I threw on the windbreaker, grabbed my backpack, and I was ready to roll. Next to leave were Neha and Lily, so I joined. Sarah went back inside the bar and said she would meet the rest in Torres del Río. And we were off.

Through the archway of the Plaza of Santa María, we crossed the highway, then over a bridge, passing by several apartment buildings. The road kicked up a little as we neared the countryside again. But 10 minutes into the walk, I felt I was missing something. Then I realized I forgot my trekking poles at the table! I was gutted. This was the second time I had to walk the Camino in reverse to find my poles—I was not happy. Neha and Lily offered to wait, but I ushered them along and said I would meet them up the road. So, I ran (yes, I ran) back down the slope to the plaza, grabbed my poles, and double-timed it back into the countryside.

The afternoon rain created piles of mud everywhere. It was a delicate business, trying to find the best footing to avoid the mud and puddles of water. Far off in the distance, I could see Neha, "Speed Demon," blazing the trail as usual. About 100 meters back was Lily. She was a slower walker. After all, we were all slower than Neha. Behind me, I heard the grunt of a woman. I looked back, and about 20 meters out, a woman biking the Camino had slid in the mud and tipped her bike over. She got up quickly, then slowly powered forward. People biking the Camino usually carried small cargo bags on both sides of their bike. It was probably a nightmare riding through the mud with that cargo. But I stopped short of feeling sorry for them. They still arrived at their destinations hours before the walkers did. And let us be honest, it was easier to bike than it was to walk. My shoes were already a mess, and I was still 4km from Torres del Río and 15km from my destination of Viana.

Eventually, I caught up with Lily, just as the rain picked up again. It would not stop. We looked at each other with the fatigue of bewildered pilgrims, then pulled out our ponchos. And my shoe covers too. Walking with Lily gave us a chance to connect. She had been so quiet the whole day, but once we started talking, she really came to life.

"We're going to have to wash our clothes after this," I said to Lily, our legs covered in mud up to our knees.

"You mean hand wash?" asked Lily.

"Yeah?"

"Not me. I'm not doing that anymore. I mean, it's not that it's beneath me or anything like that. I just did it for two years in Africa while I was in the Peace Corps. I had enough."

"Yeah, well, I wasn't in the Peace Corps, but I hand-washed my clothes twice and I'm officially done," I said as Lily laughed. She was finally opening up.

"I heard it's only five or six euros to have an albergue wash and dry your clothes, so I'll just do that."

"So, now that you've graduated, what's your plan?" I asked, changing topics.

"I got a job in Virginia doing consulting. I'm nervous about it though."

"Why are you nervous? Is it the hours?"

"I don't really care about the hours. I mean, I know I'll have to work like 60-70-hour weeks, but the money is good. I think it's just the people I'll be around. I don't know if I'll fit in with them. The culture is just different," said Lily. It was heartwarmingly honest.

"You know, look at it this way. You'll get in there, make a little money, and if you want out, get out. I've had tons of jobs in my career. Don't feel like you're going to be pinned down forever. Plus, you're super smart, and I know you'll kickass."

The weather did not get any better as we walked the trail together. The storm turned into a massive downpour. My poncho was holding up well, but I felt moisture in my shoes. At first, I could feel it at the tips of my toes. Minutes later, it was like I was walking in puddles inside of my shoe covers. It blew my mind. Made of silicone, the shoe covers zipped up tight up to my ankles.

"The covers are probably keeping all the heat inside. It's probably all the moisture that can't get out," said Lily.

We were smack in the middle of deserted country roads. If I took off my shoe covers or messed with my shoes at all, it would make the problem worse. The rain was really dumping now. I just had to suck it up until we arrived in Torres del Río. After a bit, the wet, muddy trail led us to a highway about 2km from town. The road steepened as we clung to the right side, hoping cars would see us and not plow us over. The rainfall was so loud that we could not hear the cars approaching from behind. Still, we moved forward, my feet squishing with every step. Wet feet were the breeding grounds for blisters. The dampness creates friction, which leads to blisters, or even worse, infections. This happens when troops get trench foot in the military. The tissue of the feet begins to breakdown, because of prolonged exposure to moisture. In short, wet feet are the destroyer of pilgrims' dreams of reaching Santiago. Finally, in the distance up the hill, Lily and I could see Torres del Río.

"I might just stay here for the night," I said. "If it keeps raining like this, I'm not sure how I'm going to make it 11km further to Viana."

"I'm sure there's room if you want to stay."

"Yeah, maybe, as long as they have a dryer, they can toss my shoes in there."

Entering town, we sought immediate shelter at Albergue Casa Mariela. This is where the girls were staying for the night, Lily included. Before going inside, I unzipped my shoe covers and noticed there were large, gaping holes underneath. No wonder my feet got soaked. I remember asking Lily if her feet were wet. Ironically, she said, "No, my shoes are made of

Gore-Tex," the shoes I was specifically advised not to buy, because of the summer heat. Anyway, we left our ponchos and trekking poles outside under the covered terrace, then went inside the albergue. We found Noelle and Neha rummaging around for snacks near the check-in counter. They had checked in 20 minutes earlier. I was so excited to see them. Plus, we were finally out of the rain.

"Do you have a dryer?" I asked the host impatiently.

"Yes, it's 6 euros," said the host.

"Is there a bed available?"

"Yes."

"OK, I'm staying," I said with a sigh of relief.

"You're staying!?" asked Neha.

"Yup!"

The host then escorted us upstairs to the dorm room where we would spend the night. An older man was napping in one of the beds. He was probably in his 70s. There were cuts and dried up blood all over his legs, and some white bandages on his knees.

"What happened to that guy?" I asked the host, quietly, so as not to wake the man.

"Apparently, he slipped in the mud on the way here and hit some rocks. He can't see very well, I guess."

After they assigned us beds for the night, I grabbed a plastic laundry container and filled it with all of my wet and dirty clothes, along with my shoes. I took the container back downstairs to have it all washed and dried, but the host said they could not take the shoes, since they would damage their machines. That was not good. The host told me to leave my shoes downstairs on a rack with everyone else's shoes, tucked into a corner, where it was cold and humid, with very little airflow. So, against the host's instructions, I took my shoes upstairs to the dorm, where it was warmer—I needed them to dry.

Up in the room, we greeted Sarah as she arrived from Los Arcos. We were all back together again. One big happy family.

"Wait!" said Sarah, pointing at me as I sat on my bed. "How did you get a lower bunk!?"

"They just said it was mine," I said with a smirk.

"No fair. I want a lower bunk," said Sarah, laboring over to the bunk above me.

"We all got upper bunks," said Neha, looking around. "Except for Ander."

"Yeah, the lower bunks are for us old people. That's how it works," I said, laughing.

It was 13:30 in the afternoon. While the girls went to go shower and change, I sat on the bed for a few minutes. The decision to stay the night at the albergue was already eating away at me. If the rain would let up, and my shoes were dry enough, I could continue on. Looking outside the window, the rain kept dumping. The next day I was planning to walk 45km. To make up for the detour through Torres del Río, I would have to add 11km to that, making it 56km in one day—not a good idea. It was Day 5 of the Camino, and my schedule was already getting thrown out the window. As I pondered my next move, the girls returned from the showers and went to grab a drink down the street. So, I joined them.

Down the hill from the albergue, we stopped inside a place called El Mesón. It was a private club, but they took pity on us foreigners and invited us in. Everyone ordered beer except for me. I ordered Cola-Cao, which is the Spanish brand of hot chocolate. After getting soaked in the rain, it was a nice way to warm up. Also, I was still contemplating whether to continue to Viana that afternoon, so I was not about to drink.

"So, wait, Ander, you're thinking of doing some more walking today?" asked Neha.

"I want to, but it's still raining. If it wasn't a 2-hour walk, I could risk the chance of getting blisters and just go for it."

"Why do you have to get to Viana today, anyway?" asked Lily.

"Because of this…" I said, unzipping my fanny pack and handing Lily a folded-up piece of paper.

"What's this?"

"That's my itinerary that I typed up in Excel."

"Ander…" said Lily, holding the paper in one hand and palming her face with the other.

"Could you imagine having to re-route that entire schedule, shifting around all of my stops from here to Santiago? It would be a nightmare," I said.

"That's why you don't do this!" said Lily, holding the paper up in the air. The entire table was laughing, including me. It seemed a little crazy to plan a mission so meticulously rigid, especially when there were so many variables—one being the weather.

Before we could order another round of drinks, the owner of the bar ushered us out as they were closing up. It was still raining outside, but not so ferociously. Walking back toward the albergue, I stuck my hand out in the air, feeling the drizzling rain. It was not so bad now.

Inside the albergue, we huddled together in the dorm room. I pulled out a bag of candy, to the delight of the group. They were little red sour bricks—so good! I then made the rounds, offering pieces to the girls—their eyes lit up. Sugar and the Camino went hand in hand. Noelle was resting on her bed, Neha was on the floor, Lily was sitting in a chair by her bed, and Sarah was on the verge of passing out on the bunk above me. I sat on the edge of my bed, still battling with my inner demons.

"What are you going to do?" asked Lily. I looked up at her and shrugged my shoulders.

"If I stay the night, I'll have to make up those 11km later on. And today it rained. What happens tomorrow? What if I have to stop because of blisters, an infection, or something worse?" At that moment, I decided. If something was going to take me off of the Camino, it was going to have to be something more than rain. Then, there must have been a break in the clouds, as sunlight poured through the window, lighting up the room. It had finally stopped raining.

"I'm going to walk," I said to Lily. My shoes were about 75% dry by then, which was good enough for me. When my laundry was ready, I packed it into my backpack, then waved goodbye to the girls.

"Be safe, and Buen Camino," I said.

At the check-in counter, I tried to get a refund for the 14 euros I paid, but all I could salvage was four euros. The guy was unwilling to give me back anything else. I had bought snacks, paid for laundry, and now I had paid about 10 euros for a two-hour shelter break. It was worth it. I was not upset. I took my money and got the hell out of there.

As I stepped outside of the albergue, the sky had cleared above me. But out in the distance, in the direction I was moving, I could see darker clouds gathering. I was going to be rolling the dice on whether it would rain. But I was not thinking much about that. When I left Torres del Río, I felt a mix of emotions. In one respect, I felt an overwhelming sense of joy, almost as if I had broken a spell and could continue my mission on the Camino. Still, I felt sadness wallowing up inside. The concept of a "Camino Family" had not really made much sense to me until that point. But then it clicked. I felt I finally understood why so many people walked the Camino alongside others. It was not just out of fear, like the fear of us kids jumping into the snake-filled pool in Urkuletas. Sure, the Camino is a great unknown to those who embark on its paths. It may be daunting to climb solo over a thousand meters in the Pyrenees, or even spend a day alone with your own thoughts on an abandoned Roman road. All of that is true. But you walk with others to form a community, a sense of purpose. You walk with others so that you can inspire confidence in them, and so that they can inspire confidence in you. We had only spent seven hours together, yet I felt a special bond with those girls. It felt like a little family. And it was sad to part ways. I learned that some pains along the Camino were not entirely physical, but also emotional.

Two hours later, I made it to the town of Viana. It did not rain one drop. My feet arrived as dry as the Navarran grass in the heat of summer. And as I laid in bed that night, I thought about how that day had evolved. How I had met such a wonderful group of people. But then, how I had almost quit on myself by staying in Torres del Río, after one obstacle. That night, I made a promise that I would be stronger from that point forward.

Yet, I had a feeling it was not about to get any easier.

CHAPTER EIGHT:

47 REASONS TO QUIT

The Navy SEALs are some of the baddest men on the planet. These special operators are the crown jewels of the United States military. The Sea, Air, and Land Teams (or SEALs) are an elite maritime force, established by President John F. Kennedy, back in 1962. Their missions, though not always in the spotlight, have etched their place in history. They captured former Panamanian military leader Manuel Noriega in 1989, saved Captain Phillips from Somali pirates in 2009, and killed terrorist Osama Bin Laden in 2011. With the SEALS, there is no shortage of courage and valor. However, what I find most fascinating about these warriors is their selection process. To become a Navy SEAL, one must undergo a 24-week training course called "BUD/S," which stands for Basic Underwater Demolition/SEAL Training. This training tests mental and physical stamina, as well as the ability to be a leader. But it is the third week of this program that is most notorious. Most people refer to it as "Hell Week."

Before the United States Navy invests millions of dollars into training special operators, candidates must first successfully complete Hell Week. It is a five-and-a-half-day stretch, where candidates run over 200 miles, carry boats over their heads, experience hypothermic conditions in the chilly waters of the Pacific Ocean, and more. All with about four hours of sleep. But for me, the most fascinating part is the story of people quitting. On average, only 25% of candidates make it through Hell Week, which means 75% quit. In the center of the training compound, there is a shiny brass bell. If a candidate wants to quit, if they want the pain to go away, all they have to do is ring the bell. And most do. They go over, one by one, remove their helmets and set them down on the ground, next to the bell, then ring it three times. By the end of Hell Week, there are typically over a hundred helmets lined up next to the bell. Navy SEALs often talk about how quitting is "an option" or "a choice" that we make as humans. "Just don't quit," they say. Yet, each time a new class of SEAL candidates rolls through BUD/S Training, 75% of the class ends up quitting. Were they not serious about their dreams of becoming a special operator? Did they lack the physical toughness required of these elite commandos? Or did they simply get overwhelmed by all of it?

My desire to finish the Camino de Santiago was a manifesto. It was like I drove a stake into the ground and committed myself to the dream. Quitting might be an option for others, but it was not an option for me. Like a Navy SEAL candidate carrying their helmet, I carried my white scallop on the back of my backpack. Carrying it meant I was still in the game, in the hunt for glory. When I sadly left the girls at Torres del Río, I tightened another notch on my belt and clung tighter to the mission.

The 11km stretch from Torres del Río to Viana was difficult. But thankfully, I did not get caught in the rain. It stayed dry the whole way there. The afternoon heat, combined with the steep climbs and descents, was a punishing way to end the day. Frequent changes in surfaces kept me on my toes. The dirt trail led me out of town, passing by a grim-looking cemetery. Its eight-foot walls created a shadowy interior which was visible through the iron gate at the front. The dirt gave way to a carefully constructed stone surface as I made my first descent into an area with vineyards. The ground changed again to a clunky and uneven gravel trail, where I rolled up and down a few hills in the countryside. Then, the slopes really kicked up, where the well-placed stones returned to provide a better grip to climb the steep hill. The sun was burning my face, so I reached for my long-brimmed hat. Winding left and right, the Camino crossed over major highways, passed through mini-forests and wooded areas.

The exhaustion was mounting as I neared Viana, yet I had to remain focused. After crossing the highway, the path took a few sharp turns around vegetation, where if I were not careful, I would have broken my ankle falling into a natural crevice. It was in the middle of the trail, about 10 inches wide, snaking its way along the path. And just when I thought it was over, a sharp descent appeared out of nowhere, where now the crevice had widened to about two feet. One slip up there and it might have been game over. The steepest climb came just before entering Viana. This time, it was all gravel. I clutched and gripped my trekking poles as hard as I could, digging them as deep into the ground as they would go. The sharp metallic ends of the poles had completely pierced through a set of rubber caps I had placed on them. I hoisted myself up the treacherous hill, one leg at a time, gritting my teeth, sweat dripping from my nose and onto the dusty gravel below. At the top, I stretched my legs for a few seconds, gathered myself, and continued. And just before I reached the Izar Albergue, I heard the stormy sounds of thunder and lightning. The roll of the dice had paid off. I had made it just in time.

My evening shower was the most satisfying shower I had ever had in my life. Night after night, they just kept getting better (or my days kept getting worse, depending on how you looked at it). Those first few drops of cold water were something to savor. From my hair to my face, I felt all of my pores opening up. The showers gave my muscles a small reprieve, from my shoulders, down to my thighs, and then my calves. My feet were a different story. Toward the end of my days, my feet would swell up like watermelons, suffocating inside of my thick wool socks, which were now doubly tight after the albergue washed them in hot water and stuck them in the dryer for an hour. The Compeed pads that were glued to my feet made it impossible to gauge the blister situation on the soles of my feet. But judging by the pain, they were getting a little bigger. Blisters along my toes started springing up. First, the long toes, then the pinky toes, then I had blisters in between my toes. I popped them and drained the fluid, but they would return, even if I wrapped them in medical tape to prevent further friction. 10 to 12-hour walks on the Camino will do that to you.

The next day, I woke up a little earlier than normal. It was now Day 6 of the Camino. Having left Navarra behind, I was officially in the La Rioja region, one of Spain's 17 autonomous communities. The destination for the day was a small village called Azofra, 45km away. I left Viana at 05:30, about an hour before sunrise. I tried to be quiet, closing the front door to the albergue so as not to wake the other pilgrims. It was the first time that I pulled out my headlamp. Putting that thing on made me feel like I was heading into a mine. It had been raining all night, leaving behind puddles of water, particularly at the entrances of small roadway tunnels I had to cross under. At one point, I was hopping from stone to stone along the water, trying to stay above the waterline and keep my feet dry. The terrain was mostly flat after that, in and out of wooded areas, with small stones scattered up and down the trails.

Halfway down the road to Azofra was a city called Logroño. Famous for its city parks and lush rural landscapes, filled with vineyards and wineries, it is the capital of La Rioja. Approaching Logroño, the path turned to asphalt as I passed agricultural and industrial facilities next to the highway. It was cloudy that morning, but unlikely to rain, which was nice. Walking through cities on the Camino was both good and bad. The solid asphalt gave zero bounce or comfort to your feet, but the charming sights and influx of pedestrians provided a welcomed distraction from the long and lonely trails of the Way. One of these comforting sights was the Puente de Piedra, or "Stone Bridge," built in 1884, after the previous bridge collapsed in 1871. Measuring 200 meters, it is one of the four bridges that cross the Ebro River, and it provides the entrance to Logroño on the Way of Saint James.

Mid-way through the city, I stopped off at a bar for some breakfast. I ordered coffee with milk, and to eat, jamon on thinly sliced French bread, with a light spread of olive oil. As soon as the coffee hit me, I rushed downstairs to use the services. It was like something out of the movie *Saw*. The walls of the restroom were white, grimy, and rusty all over. It was eerie. I was in such a hurry to leave that mess that I accidentally left my trekking poles behind, so I had to walk back down the stairs of horror once more. But I quickly forgot about it once my food arrived—it was spectacular. Still hungry, I ordered two napolitanas. Then it was time to move on. I stepped through the majestic arches of the Puerta del Camino, built in the twelfth century, and previously used to defend the city with its massive stone walls. With 10km in the bag, I had 35km left to go.

It took me about 30-45 minutes to get out of the city, passing by a few parks, where a red clay-colored walking path led me to the outskirts. It seemed to go on forever, as joggers and cyclists passed me in both directions. The path led to a lake, and from there to a narrow-paved road up to the top of a hill. The paved surface was flat, which was good for my blisters, but it felt like my Achilles tendons were about to snap off the heels of my feet. In my scenic view were countless vineyards over the rolling hills. I thought about how often I would drink a bottle of wine from Logroño; Marques de Murrieta and Bodegas Campo Viejo, just to name a few of my favorite wineries in the region. I thought about how the very grapes I was walking by would end up in a bottle of red wine I would drink someday. Someday, long after the Camino, and long after the suffering was over.

Nearing Navarrete, I descended from atop the hill, where I spotted a silhouette of the "Osbourne Bull". What began as a method to advertise Brandy soon became a national symbol of pride in Spain. The silhouettes are now scattered across Spanish hilltops. Seeing that bull made me think of Pamplona and the Fiesta of San Fermín. I wondered what condition my body would be in at the end of the Camino, and what that would mean for my runs with the bulls. On the one hand, I wanted desperately to finish the Camino de Santiago. I was hellbent on doing that. Yet, I knew it might put my physical preparedness in jeopardy. Then, in true Camino irony, I walked by the ruins of an ancient hospital called Ruinas Hospital de San Jaun de Acre. It looked decimated, as very little remained of its stone structure. It was a shadow of its former self. I kept walking.

Later in the day, the temperature was nearing 90 degrees, with very few pockets of shade. In typical Camino fashion, I ran out of water again. This time, on my way to Nájera. It was almost 11km from my last stop in the town of Ventosa. Tired, hot, and out of water, I could hear someone catching up to me. It rarely happened because I walked faster than most. I could hear the guy singing in a high-pitched voice. It was annoying. Desperately waiting for him to pass me by and keep going, I slowed down ever so slightly, then pulled off to the side of the road, giving him a nod of the head to go on forward. He took a few quick steps and passed me up, whistling dixie or whatever he was doing. He was prancing around like the Camino was a joke, like he was having a good time. I was not having a good time. In the holster of his backpack, I saw a half-full bottle of Powerade sloshing around. It was the blue kind—Mountain Berry. Nearly salivating, I could almost taste it. Most people would think a drink like Powerade would be terrible for the Camino, given the sugar and calories. But that is precisely the reason it is beneficial. After all the sweat you pour out on the Camino, you need the sugar, calories, and electrolytes it replenishes.

The "whistling man" did not get very far ahead of me after that. I am not sure if I stepped up my pace, given my competitive nature, or if he had overcooked his own pace. He took a few moments to stretch his calves before we arrived in Nájera; perhaps a sign of the latter. I became distracted when I passed a girl walking alone. I recognized her. She had stopped at the same cafe in Ventosa a few hours earlier. She reminded me of Neha. Sure, she was of Indian descent, but she was also thin, short, and walked at a quicker pace than most.

"Buen Camino," I said to her.

"Buen Camino…"

"Where are you from?"

"Switzerland," said the Swiss girl, "but I lived in the US for a while."

"No way! What took you to the states?"

"Well, I was studying abroad in Boston, and then I met someone. We stayed together, and eventually, I moved to the US to be with him in New York. He was getting his master's degree at NYU."

"Aww, it's like a little love story."

"It didn't work out," said the Swiss girl with a soft voice. "After it ended, I was stuck in New York, all by myself. I was lucky enough to get a job at a clothing boutique in Brooklyn, enough to pay rent with some roommates," she said. I was not sure if I should keep probing about her US experience, so I did not.

"What are you doing now?"

"When my US visa expired, I moved back to Switzerland and started my master's degree."

"That's awesome! I'm happy for you. What's your focus?"

"Biochemical engineering," she said casually.

"Umm, OK, that works too," I said, laughing. "So, you're a genius?"

"We'll see. I still have to finish the degree," said the Swiss girl. She had a warm way about her. The Swiss girl ended up walking as far as Nájera, where she planned to stay the night. After we parted ways, I refueled with some Coke Zero, tortilla, and more water, and then continued on toward Azofra, 6km away.

By far the most miserable part of the day on the Camino was the afternoon, after 14:00. I had been walking for about eight hours by that point. It was hot, I was tired, my muscles hurt, and my feet ached with the swelling of the 40km I had already walked. There was absolutely nobody on the Camino. It was a solo journey to the destination.

Leaving Nájera, I passed by the Church of Santa María la Real. King García III, the son of King Sancho III, founded the monastery church in 1052. As the locals will tell you, they say that one day, the king was hunting in the area with his falcon. The falcon was chasing around a dove, which then disappeared into a cave, taking the falcon with it. When the falcon did not return, the king himself entered the cave. Inside, he found the falcon resting beside the dove, under a rustic altar. The altar had an image of the Virgin Mary carrying a child in her arms. On the ground was a bright lamp, a jar of fresh white lilies, and a bell. After that discovery, they built the Church of Santa María near the cave, and dedicated it to the Virgin Mary. And in the centuries that followed, they used the church as a monastery and hospital for pilgrims on the Camino.

Meters away from the Church of Santa María, I began climbing a steep hill toward Azofra. Once again, I abandoned an urban setting for a clay-like mountain trail that was arid and rocky. Trees initially covered the landscape, but the vineyards quickly took over. There were giant piles of dirt every few hundred meters lining the sides of the road. Recent rainfall had flooded many of the vineyards, in some rows up to six inches. To save the grapes, farmers packed the trenches with dirt to soak up the rainwater left behind. But the farmers must have been sleeping, since I did not see anyone out there in the sweltering heat. It was just me out there, sweating, heaving, and suffering. I was stopping every five minutes to lean over my two trekking poles to relieve my feet of the pressure of my body weight. When I did, I stared at the ground below, unsure how much further I could go. I remember having a feeling like I was being watched, like I was there with someone. Nobody was in the area, but I had this strange sixth sense that someone was out there. My eyes wandered obsessively, but I spotted no one. I just chalked it up to being delirious. At one point, I looked back toward the hills I had climbed over. The sky was dark as black. And every time I stopped, I looked back to see which way the clouds were moving. It was like the clouds were following me, moving ever closer in my direction. I did not want to deal with the rain again. And I knew I was only about 20 minutes away from Azofra, so I grinded my teeth and pushed forward, pledging not to stop until I arrived. Then, finally, I hobbled into Azofra, physically at my limit.

The most recommended albergue in Azofra was the municipal albergue. It looked like a little fortress, the way the 10-foot walls guarded it from outsiders. After paying 12 euros for the night, I took my stuff upstairs to my room. The format was different there. There were three floors, including the ground floor, with each having 10 small rooms, and each room having two small single beds. It resembled a renovated convent of some sort, with one significant perk: the pools for your feet in the courtyard. Pilgrims sat on the edge of the pools, soaking their feet in cool water after a long day's hike. Lucky for them, and for me I guess, the rain held off until later that evening, so folks were out enjoying themselves for the moment. I did not soak my feet in the pool for a couple of reasons. One, I had more blister bubbles on my toes than the day before, and two, I did not want to get them infected, since I had open punctures from stabbing them with needles. Instead, I retreated to my room after picking up some food.

My roommate was a 22-year-old kid from Belgium, who walked in with a huge backpack, an entire loaf of French bread, and a bag of sliced deli meat. At first, I was trying to relate to him and his Belgian roots, and the only way I could do that was through my love of cycling. The sport is huge in Belgium, having produced some of the biggest name out there. Names like Eddy Merckx, Tadej Pogačar, Wout van Aert, and Remco Evenepoel. But every time I mentioned a name, or even a Belgian cycling event like the Tour of Flanders or Liège–Bastogne–Liège, his eyes would glaze over with disinterest. Instead, I asked him about the Camino.

"How's your Camino been so far? Are you meeting a lot of people?" I asked.

"Not too many. Most nights I sleep in the fields, or, if I'm lucky, a campsite for pilgrims," said the Belgian. "I've been camping almost every day."

"Are you getting tired of camping?" I asked. After all, he was getting ready to sleep inside of an albergue.

"Not at all. I love camping. It's the best. But I couldn't find a place to set up my tent in Azofra, so I paid 12 euros to stay here."

"Does anyone ever disturb you or bother you?" I asked.

"Not really. There was this one time someone set up their tent next to mine, and they were telling me all these stories."

"What kind of stories?"

"He said he saw God on the Camino."

"He saw God? Was he being serious?" I asked in disbelief.

"Totally serious. That's what he said. He said he saw God along the Camino." I thought about that as I dabbed drops of iodine onto my newly popped and fluid-drained blisters. I snickered at first when he told me the story, thinking the guy was probably crazy. But eventually, I set aside my pontification of the unknown pilgrim who had seen God, and drifted into sleep. A couple of tablets of ibuprofen helped take some of the edge off. My feet were killing me.

On Day 7, I was downstairs by 05:30. The headlamp proved to be useful in the dark, early morning hours. The itinerary for Day 7 had me walking to Villambistia, 45km away. The rain from the night before blocked off passages along the trail. Deep, muddy puddles forced me into the tall, unharvested grass, then back onto the trail. I passed through the small towns of Cirueña and Santo Domingo de la Calzada, stopping in the latter for some pastries and coffee with milk. The switch from cortados to coffee with milk was simply a way to increase my calorie intake. It was a bit of self-imposed suffering to start early in the morning with no food, but I enjoyed the convenience of being able to stop at a bar. It was a novelty of sorts, and perhaps, an opportunity to interact with someone other than myself. When you are on the Camino, alone and with your own thoughts, it is nice to try something different. The town of Grañón was an unsuspecting opportunity for that.

Grañón was the last stop in the La Rioja region, and the beginning of Castilla y León. The yellow Camino arrows and stone markers pointed me toward open pastures. At the edge of town, there was an observation deck with magnificent views of the Spanish rolling hills. The hills varied in colors, from bright green to olive, brown, and dried-out yellow. The peaks and valleys looked undisturbed. There was a natural beauty about that. I thought it was strange that the Camino led me to the observation deck, but then I noticed a staircase attached to it, leading down to the pastures. There was a heavyset man, probably in his 70s, sitting on a bench, taking in the wonderful views.

"Am I going the right way on the Camino?" I asked the man.

"Yes, just follow the stairs and you'll get to where you're going," he said, with a hint of wisdom.

"How far is the next village?"

"It's about an hour away. Just go up and down the hills, and you'll be there soon."

"Is it a nice walk?" I asked, making conversation as I stretched my calve muscles, trying to shake off the spasms.

"A nice walk? Sure. But when I need to go, I just clip on my wings and fly down," he said with a twinkle in his eye. I laughed, but he did not. It was weird. He mumbled a few other words to me, but I started down the staircase and left Grañón for the hills.

The deep pain in my legs was manifesting itself earlier and earlier in the day. But my feet remained the worst. It was 14:00, and I felt like I could not walk anymore. I filled my water bottles at a fountain in Castildelgado, then immediately sought the refuge of an empty bench across the street from an old Catholic church. I took off my backpack, placed it at the end of the bench, then laid down for a few minutes. My hip was bothering me that day. I stared up at the sky, watching the gray clouds move from north to south. The place was a ghost town. Before I got too comfortable, I clipped on my backpack and left town.

The next several kilometers included long stretches of straight walking paths, with few turns, trees, or vegetation. It was a hallmark of Castilla y León, the region I had just entered. Much of the walk ran parallel to a highway, where cars and oversized semi-trucks passed me in the opposite direction. I wondered what those drivers must have thought of me. Did they pity me and my beat-up look, as they enjoyed their air-conditioned ride at high speeds, or did they envy me and my privilege to walk the Camino? Probably the former. The lack of other towns made those long, straight stretches even more monotonous. All you could see was more of the trail. It had no end in sight.

By 17:30, I was really in trouble. For the first time on the Camino, I felt a tremendous fatigue come over me; so bad I could have slept standing up. Making matters worse, the sky cleared up just in time for the afternoon sun to turn my face into a boiling drip-fest. Swarms of flies rushed my face, as I tried to brush them away. After a couple of steps, the swarm would return, entering my mouth, nose, and even my eyes. Then I started swatting at them with my hat. After a few attempts, I was tired of that too. My body was sweating so profusely that I got red, bumpy welts on both sides of my butt. Every time my underwear moved, it was like getting shaved by a cheese grater. "I have to be bleeding," I thought. But only one town separated me from my final resting place for the night. It was a tiny village called Tosantos, with a population of less than 60 people. I slowed my walk, pulled out my phone, and called the only albergue in Villambistia.

"Do you have a bed available for tonight?" I asked, with a tone of desperation.

"Oh, I'm sorry. We're closed today," said the host, as her words pierced my stomach and tore out my insides. "We're always closed on Wednesdays."

"Fuck," I said out loud. My body could not move any further. I needed to stop. Still moving through Tosantos, I found a green wooden bench in the middle of the Camino. In too much pain and fatigue, I could not even find the strength to unclip my backpack before sitting down. I sat there slumped over with my chin down and my brimmed hat tilted forward. I closed my eyes and drifted in and out of consciousness, waiting for the vultures to take me out of my misery. This was the hardest day on the Camino so far. But that was the same thought I had the day before. It just kept getting worse. And it was only Day 7. My naïve impression that "the body will adjust" was under serious doubt now. I wondered if this was it, if it was my time to go; if after 250 kilometers on the Way, my body had finally failed. Part of me thought I might die there on the Camino—it was that bad.

When I snapped out of it, I was still sitting on the bench, in a sideways position, with my backpack hanging halfway off the bench. 10 minutes had gone by. There was one albergue in Tosantos, which, unfortunately, was also closed. Next, I tried the local parish. They offered me a slab of concrete, no bed. That would not work; I was better off on the bench in the middle of the road. The next town after Villambistia was Espinosa del Camino. So, I pulled out my phone and called one of their albergues. My luck finally changed. There was only one more bed available, and it was mine. It was four kilometers away, which meant I had to tack on an extra two kilometers to my day's walk, making it a grand total of 47 kilometers on the day. Forcing myself up from the bench in Tosantos, I hobbled my beat-up body up the road. If I was going to die on the Camino, I was going to die walking. A wave of anger came over me at that point. I was angry at the road, and the large and inconvenient rocks that obstructed my path. I was angry at the flies that flew into my mouth and stuck themselves to my eyelids. I was completely full of anger.

An hour later, and after many stops to lean on my trekking poles, I made it to the albergue, panting, hunched over at the front entrance. It was owned and operated by an older German couple with a thick German accent. The woman greeted me at the entrance as I stumbled inside. Before anything else, she had a rather bizarre question to ask me.

"Are you allergic to cats?" she asked.

"No, I don't think so. Why?"

"We have a lot of cats…"

"Umm… OK," I uttered. I was too tired to care about the randomness of it.

"Take off your shoes and come with me to the kitchen." So, I did, grimacingly.

"Where did you come from today?" she asked, seeing my discomfort.

"Azofra."

"Azofra!?" she asked, shocked. "But that's… that's a long ways away!"

"47 kilometers." I said. Then, I paid her 12 euros for the night.

"Now, we also offer breakfast for a separate charge."

"I'm OK, thank you. I usually stop at the bars when they open," I said politely. Her face morphed into a stern look, as if she would not accept that answer.

"Listen," she said, as her eyes got bigger, "tomorrow morning you might not find a bar for many hours. And then what?" she said, trying to twist my arm to buy the breakfast.

"I think the next town is only 3.5km away."

"I think you're making a mistake. But OK, suit yourself," she said dismissively. It was unusual. I knew the Camino generated commerce, but the occasional salesman-style pressure irritated me.

Afterwards, I followed her upstairs to the second-floor dorm room.

After a couple of steps, a pack of cats came down the stairs. It felt like I was in a zoo, but I tried to keep it together. Almost at the top of the stairs, the woman's German husband was having a serious conversation with an American girl.

"I found bed bugs," she said to the man, holding up her jacket.

"Wait what?" I said in shock. This was every pilgrim's worst nightmare, after blisters, of course.

"I don't know if I brought them in, or if they were already here," she said apologetically.

"Where was your jacket?" asked the German host as he examined it. Still on the stairs, I did not move an inch.

"It was in my bag, but then I pulled it out and placed it on the bed as I was looking for my clothes," she said.

"Yeah, I can't stay here," I said to the German woman. I turned around and started walking downstairs to put my shoes back on. My feet hurt worse than before, wincing as I bent over to tie my shoes. The American girl followed with the German man, throwing the jacket into the washing machine in the lobby.

"I'm sure there's no problem in refunding my money, right?" I asked the German woman. The husband interjected immediately.

"Well, you already paid to stay here. We don't know if the bed bugs were here or if she brought them in," he said. He did not want to give me my money back. His face had the look of a shrewd businessman, not a happy-go-lucky Camino spirit.

"I understand, but I can't sleep in a place where you knowingly have bed bugs. I think it's only fair to give me my money back. I've been here for less than 5 minutes," I said. The look on his face changed abruptly. He seemed furious inside, but I think something clicked in his mind. Perhaps the fact that I would not fold easily, or even worse, that I was going to spread the word to other pilgrims about the bed bugs. He turned to his German wife and nodded. She left the room, then returned with my 12 euros. Few things traveled faster on the Camino than news of bed bugs. As I mentioned earlier in the book, albergues require your pilgrim's passport in order to stay there. While examining your passport stamps, if they see you stayed at an albergue known to have bed bugs, they will not hesitate to deny you a bed, as you may have brought the bed bugs with you to their albergue.

After the delightful experience with the cat-obsessed German couple and their "bed bug special," I went across the street to La Taberna de Espinosa. Inside, I walked up to the bar, where a man in his 60s asked if I needed a room. After explaining what had just happened, he had only two words to say: "No comment." After getting a bed in the dorm, the man's wife, Conchi, offered to wash and dry my clothes. Conchi was like a mother—caring and affectionate. She served dinner in the dining room, where I took my seat alongside a group of French pilgrims and a Swede. Beef fillets, French fries, yogurt, and melon—the meal was amazing. As I chewed away with a king's hunger, I looked out of the window and saw a torrential downpour. I narrowly missed it by a matter of minutes. It was a cheeky reminder that as bad as things got, they could always get a little worse. Maybe that was the purpose of Navy SEAL Training.

As humans, I think it is natural for us to swim against the current. What I mean by that is that when most people get overwhelmed by bad situations, they focus on all the pain and suffering, then completely give up on the fight. I believe Navy SEAL Training tests that mental fortitude. Those who succumb to the pressure and stress find themselves overwhelmed and in the dirt; they will not make it through "Hell Week." If someone can wrap their mind around a bad situation, and move forward with the current, they will be better prepared to fight. But then the question remains: for how long?

After entering Castilla y León, pilgrims come face to face with The Meseta, or "The Plateau." The 180km stretch of desert-like conditions is formidable. So much so that many pilgrims begin their journey to Santiago after The Meseta, to avoid it all together. To those who enter, beware. The person who exits is not the same as when they entered.

CHAPTER NINE:

THE MESETA

Before beginning his ministries, Jesus was baptized in the Jordan River, after which the Holy Spirit was revealed to him. In Matthew 4:1-11, the Holy Spirit takes Jesus into the desert to be tempted. And after 40 days and 40 nights, Satan came to him.

"If you are the Son of God, command these stones to become loaves of bread," said Satan.

"It is written, 'One does not live by bread alone, but by every word that comes from the mouth of God,'" said Jesus. Satan then took him to Jerusalem, the holy city, where Jesus stood on top of the temple, at the very edge.

"If you are the Son of God, throw yourself down; for it is written, 'He will command his angels concerning you, to protect you,' and 'On their hands they will bear you up, so that you will not dash your foot against a stone,'" said Satan, twisting the scriptures.

"Again it is written, 'Do not put the Lord your God to the test,'" said Jesus. Then, Satan took Jesus and showed him all the kingdoms of the world.

"All these I will give you, if you will fall down and worship me," said Satan.

"Away with you, Satan! For it is written, 'Worship the Lord your God, and serve only him,'" said Jesus. After this third attempt, Satan left Jesus, and angels came to his side.

As I prepared to enter The Meseta, I thought about the mythical way people talked about it. They talked about it like we were entering the world of Narnia, except we did not use an old antique wardrobe. Instead, we were to enter the high plains of Spain on foot and experience the furnace-like atmosphere that was The Meseta. But before I could begin, I had to reach the starting point: Burgos.

On Day 8 of the Way, I set out to Burgos, 42km from Espinosa del Camino. It was a miserable night of sleep, as there were four of us manly pilgrims crammed into a small room. With the door shut and the windows closed, we had zero airflow, turning our room into a sweatbox. My "growing pains" returned with a vengeance that night as I twisted, turned, and fidgeted around to get more comfortable. In doing so, my bunk bed squeaked loudly, surely disturbing the other pilgrims. I had taken a few pills of ibuprofen to help ease the pain, but it only helped a little. By 05:30, unable to sleep, I was more than ready to start my day. Sometimes I felt like I was suffering more by not suffering, if that makes any sense at all.

Leaving the room, I saw one of the Frenchmen coming out of the bathroom. I had seen the man at dinner the night before, feasting away on the fillets. When he came out of the bathroom, he was wearing his classy, gold-framed eyeglasses, a pair of white, skintight underwear, and socks almost up to his knees.

"Bonjour…" he said to me as I passed. It was funny, but also a little awkward. I gave him a wave and made my way downstairs to the exit.

At 06:00, I tried opening the front door—it was locked. "Oh no," I thought. I had heard of this happening at other albergues on the Camino. Most albergues had strict curfews for when you could enter or leave. The general rule of thumb was that doors lock up at 22:00. If you went to dinner, or stayed out for drinks, you might not get back in. The same was true when pilgrims wanted to leave the albergue—the doors stayed locked until morning. I know, I know. What about the fire risk, right? That is what I thought about as well. But as luck would have it, another pilgrim came downstairs, and together, we successfully unlocked the door. "Let the mission to Burgos begin," I said to myself.

The first 4km of the day were relatively flat. In the countryside, it always seemed like the trails had two lanes to walk in—you picked your poison. Sometimes, one lane appeared more heavily traveled, and had fewer rocks and stones, which hurt your feet like Legos on the living room floor. I typically moved back and forth between lanes every 10 minutes. Maybe I had good reason, or maybe it was just a way to occupy my mind. I constantly scanned the ground a few feet in front of me to avoid the bigger rocks.

After an hour on the Camino, the country road took me to the highway, as I straddled the edge of the asphalt, hoping not to get hit by a car. A little ways down, I reached Villafranca de Montes de Oca, a town of about 100 people. The relatively flat sections I had enjoyed until that point were short-lived. The Camino markers led me off of the main road, past a church, and up a steep cobblestone road. Around the corner, the steepness just got worse. I was beginning the Alto de la Pedraja, a 12km hike with no fountains, bars, or any other conveniences. After making sure my shoelaces were tight and my backpack firmly secured, I began the ascent.

The pass was like being lost in a forest. It felt isolating to be up there. It was extremely quiet, as nobody had any earthly business to do in those hills. This was, however, the site of the mass grave during the Spanish Civil War. In 1936, General Francisco Franco ordered the burial of 104 bodies in the Alto de la Pedraja. Nearby, he ordered another 31 people to be buried. Authorities arrested these young men in the villages I had just passed, such as Santo Domingo de la Calzada, took them to the mountain pass, and executed them with gunshots to the neck—yes, the neck. However, this heart-wrenching site is only one of 2,200 mass grave sites across Spain. To date, Spain has only exhumed 300, leading to the recovery of the remains of 7,000 people. There are still 114,000 people missing. This was difficult to grasp as I continued marching through the hills.

Along the path, I passed a couple of tents where pilgrims had spent the night. Sure, the forest was quiet during the day, but given the seclusion, it had the look of a place that came to life at night. It took guts to camp out up there. The narrow mountain path widened near the top, as the surface changed from inconveniently placed rocks to a clay-like mud that suction-cupped your feet with each step—ask the girl who fell 20 meters ahead of me. As painful as it was to hike up the pass, the occasional encounter of purple lavender plants gave the air a fresh, flowery aroma. Although I was breathing through my mouth, I could still smell the beautiful flowers the Camino had provided. That was a popular saying among the pilgrims. They loved to remind you not to worry, because "the Camino will provide." Need some water? The Camino will provide. Worried you might not have a bed at an albergue tonight? The Camino will provide.

The Camino provided about three hours of torturous climbing up the Alto de la Pedraja that day, finally giving way to San Juan de Ortega, 12km later. It is best known for a chapel built in honor of Saint Nicholas during the twelfth century. It resulted from a journey that Saint John the Hermit had undertaken to the Holy Land. Following the shipwreck, Saint Nicholas (the basis for the modern Santa Claus, or Saint Nick) rescued him. In return for his help, Saint John the Hermit promised Saint Nicholas that he would build a chapel in his honor, if he reached land safely. When he did, he went to work on building the chapel, which became a hospice, and eventually a full-fledged monastery. Today, it is undergoing a massive restoration, after being abandoned for many centuries.

San Juan de Ortega was my first stop of the day, as I found some park benches next to a potable water fountain. The cafe across the street was closed. Luckily, I had asked the wonderful people at La Taberna de Espinosa to prepare me a chorizo sandwich after dinner, in case I needed it for the hike. It was not until I reached the next town of Agés where I could finally sit down for my customary coffee with milk and pastry. The only bar open was a place called El Alquimista, or "The Alchemist." Inside was a spectacularly remodeled interior of an old farmhouse. The owner had preserved the large wooden beams that went across the ceiling, supporting the floor above. Green ivy had wrapped around the beams, flowing down the side of the wall. The wooden panel flooring helped keep its antiquated character. It had all the finishing touches, even some modern ones. The place also had a heart-shaped sink in the bathroom—winning! The Alchemist was a charming location. When I approached the small bar inside, I asked for coffee, then nervously looked around for my favorite pastry—napolitanas. Unable to find any, I asked the owner in a last-ditch effort.

"Excuse me sir, I don't see any napolitanas here. Do you have any?" I asked politely.

"You fucking kids, all you want is your damn napolitanas! They're made of shit, sugar, and fat! All of my pastries are made fresh, right here in the bar!" he said.

"Well, do you have anything close to a napolitana?"

"No!" This time, he turned his back to me and prepared the coffee with milk on the espresso machine. He continued talking to himself, complaining about the youth, and me, apparently.

While the angry guy prepared my coffee, I left my backpack on a chair next to a table, then went to the restroom. When I came back, it was on the ground. He must have taken offense to that, I assumed. I chugged my coffee and left the charming Alchemist.

The next several kilometers went in and out of the forest, momentarily escaping the blistering sun. Then began the ascent to Sierra de Atapuerca. The path was steep and slanted at times. Sections of the trail were completely invisible, cluttered with large rocks the size of my shoe. I was certain that those rocks sprained a few ankles. It was so bad I was not sure how goats or sheep delt with it, or even the army. The trail went around some barbwire fencing that was set up by the Spanish military. They ran exercises in those hills, and the metal signage warned not to cross over into their space. In the 1960s, before immigrating to the US from Spain, my father served in Burgos for two years, as military service was required of all young men in those days. Summiting the 1,080-meter climb of Atapuerca, there was a large wooden cross at the top, supported at the base by a cluster of stones. In the background, the city of Burgos came into view.

The stoney trail gave way to pavement as I passed the villages of Cardeñuela-Ríopico and Orbaneja-Ríopico. In Castañares, I walked the road with cars flying back and forth. There was no side path or trail to distance myself from the road—it was very dangerous. It snaked around the Burgos Airport and its airfields, protected by 10-feet-high barbwire fencing. I looked back several times to make sure I was heading in the right direction, checking for other pilgrims on the highway. The swelling in my feet and the growing-pain-like aches had returned. The pavement was taking its toll. I just kept telling myself that I was going to stop at the first bar I came across. Luckily, it was not far away.

On the outskirts of Burgos, in a very industrial part of town, I made a quick stop at Cafeteria Buenos Aires. All I wanted was an ice-cold Coca-Cola—regular, not sugar-free. The bar was full of truckers and other blue-collar types. In the bathroom, at the urinal, a worker argued with his boss on speakerphone. His boss was upset that he was not at the job-site. Instead, the guy was slamming a few cold ones at the bar. After 10 minutes, having demolished my high-calorie soda, I went to get up from the stool. My body had stiffened up again, from my back to my calves. My feet hurt so badly I thought they were going to explode. Even worse, it felt like I was stepping on broken glass—I had not experienced that yet. A million nerve endings had fired off in my foot, similar to that tingly feeling you get when you try walking on a foot that is still asleep. I wanted to loosen my shoelaces, but I never did. I thought it was better to deal with the pain than to loosen my shoes and have my feet sliding around, causing friction and more blisters. Using my trekking poles almost like crutches, the sidewalk led me into downtown Burgos, a straight shot from the bar. Although there was no shortage of places to stay for the night in Burgos, the most popular option was the municipal albergue called Casa del Cubo.

The "House of the Cube," built in the seventeenth century, alludes to the cubes atop the façade. It stood on a stone body with a beautiful doorway, which was flanked by balusters and finished with the family coat of arms. The albergue had six floors with about 40 bunk beds on each—it was humongous. But perhaps more notable than the albergue was the church that sat just meters away. The Cathedral of Burgos is among the most important Gothic churches in all of Spain. It comprises three bodies and two towers or steeples, all on a square plan, taking up the size of a city block. In medieval times, the city of Burgos was the capital of the Kingdom of Castile, making it a popular stop along the Camino. As a result, in 1221, they began constructing the great cathedral, serving as a tribute to the Virgin Mary. Since then, the cathedral has grown in size, and today it includes 15 chapels. As a true gem of the historical city center of Burgos, it is a sight to behold. Tired and beat-up from the 42km walk, I checked into the albergue and started my recovery.

The man at the front desk of Casa del Cubo was handing out beds like candy. I knew the place was big, but inside there were people everywhere. My bed was on the third floor, and luckily there was an elevator to take me up. In the dorm room, I began searching for my bed, walking down the aisles of bunk bed pods that stretched from end to end. Finally, at the very back of the room, I found my bunk bed. It was a top bunk, requiring me to climb up a rickety metal ladder with super sharp edges. There was no way I could climb it barefoot with my fucked-up feet. There was a woman in her 50s in the bunk below me. She was from Turkey. A few years back, she had done the Camino from Burgos to Santiago. And this time, she started in France and ended in Burgos, completing the full trip. Before I climbed up into the top bunk for the night, I threw my stuff up there and headed to the shower. There were several shower stalls, but only one toilet for the entire floor—not cool. After the shower, I resisted the urge to examine my feet, and hobbled outside to grab some food and make a critical stop before The Meseta: the pharmacy.

After grabbing food, I took the long staircase down the street to get some medical supplies. Each step I took, I tried my best not to bend my feet, because if I did, it felt like I was stretching and pulling the blisters on the bottom—it was excruciatingly painful. It did not hurt that bad when I was walking, but after having stopped for a while, the pain factor had increased tenfold. The townspeople stared continuously, as I had the look of an injured pilgrim.

When I entered the pharmacy, they barked at me for not wearing a mask—my mistake. So, the pharmacist handed me a mask, and I waited in line. Behind me walked in a beautiful Spanish girl. Everything was perfect about her. Long black hair, dreamy eyes, and a gorgeous dress.

"Next! How can I help you?" asked the pharmacist.

"Yes, hi. Can I get some needles and a box of alcohol pads?" I asked. The Spanish girl behind me probably thought I was doing drugs. She quickly left the pharmacy. Oops. Oh well.

"I can give you a box of alcohol pads, but I only have five needles left."

"I'll take them all."

When I got back to the albergue, I carefully scaled the ladder to get up to my bunk bed. I nearly tore the metal ladder from the janky screws that kept it secured to the bunk. Safely on top, I busted out my "surgery" kit, which was now a plastic grocery bag full of needles, iodine, alcohol pads, bandages, scissors, and anything else I had picked up by that point. I had Compeed bandages glued to my feet, covering up the oncoming blisters I had a few days before (light purple rings on the bottom of both feet). I lightly tapped the Compeed bandages to see where I had the most pain. The entire area hurt. The blisters were growing, and I could not pop them because I could not even reach them. I tried removing part of the bandage but I starting pulling my skin along with it. It was not looking good. To make matters worse, the blisters had grown and expanded to where the outside area of the bandage was purple and bruised. And now, every time I walked, it was like stepping on shards of broken glass. The only "surgery" I could perform was popping the blisters on my toes, which included a new blister on my right foot. Then, it was lights out.

On Day 9, I was furious that the albergue did not allow pilgrims to leave until 06:30. It seemed like I was starting my day at a disadvantage, already behind schedule. I had to walk 41km to Castrojeriz in the hot desert-like heat, and I wanted to minimize the time I would spend in the afternoon sun, inevitable as it was. So, when the doors at the albergue finally opened, I shot out like a cannon—a hobbled cannon. Still reeling from the pain in my feet and the tingly feeling bothering me, I walked past the Cathedral of Burgos and made my way through the streets of the historic old town. The signage was terrible, at least for me. Maybe I was still too tired, but I did not find the Camino markers well-placed. Perhaps the pain was too much of a distraction for me. Regardless, I found my way out of Burgos, and was 7km from the next village of Tardajos. The weather was already warm, even though the sky was mostly cloudy.

The first 15-20 minutes of the walk were terrible, as it took my feet some time to shake the tingly feeling and firing nerves. Whereas before, I found it difficult to take smaller steps with the trekking poles, one arm at a time, I was now a professional. Passing through underpasses and next to dried out grass fields, the walk to Tardajos was uneventful. I stopped for coffee and a slice of tortilla at Bar Frutería, as did most other pilgrims coming from Burgos. After coffee, the village of Rabé de las Calzadas was only 30 minutes away. The asphalt would be my companion over the short walk.

When I arrived in Rabé de las Calzadas, I whisked in and out like a breeze on a hot summer day; I was there, and then I was not. But just before I left, I found a water fountain at the top of a hill. It was a historical landmark of sorts. They called it the "Fuente de los Cuatro Caños," or Fountain of the Four Spouts. Since I had very little water left, I thought it would be wise to replenish. There was only one problem. I did not see a sign showing that the water was potable. The horror stories of my study abroad experience came rushing back. So, I wandered over to a group of men hanging out nearby; they looked like retired locals just trying to pass the time.

"Excuse me, sir. Is the water drinkable?" I asked, pointing to the fountain.

"Oh, that fountain over there? Yes, you can drink it, but then you'll die," he said with a grin, as his buddies laughed.

"OK, so it's not potable?"

"Like I said, if you drink it, eventually, you will die," he said again, to the amusement of his buddies. I could sense that he was messing with me, making a play on words, since eventually, everybody indeed dies, but not necessarily because they filled their water bottles at a fountain in Spain. Already in pain, having walked 13km, I was not in the mood for jokes. I had a "fuck you" attitude at that point, so I thanked the man and continued the Camino without stopping for water. In my head I thought, "fuck you and your historical fountain." Ironically, what I did not know was that this was the last town I would see for another 8km, until I reached Hornillos del Camino. There was only one problem with that: I was officially entering The Meseta.

The Camino began a gradual ascent up 150 meters from the valley into the great plains. The suffering was in full effect. When you go without water for a long time, your throat becomes dry and feels like it is covered in sharp spikes that scrape and tear the tissue. Not filling my water bottle was a terrible choice, and I was paying the price. The temperature was increasing, and the skies were clearing. I was baking in the Spanish countryside. The only thoughts that went through my mind were about water. As soon as my mind gravitated to another thought, the word "water" returned center-stage. Even worse, the gradual ascent made it seem like the climb was never-ending. Then, when I got to the top, I had to descend back down into another valley. My knees took a beating on the descent, as I tried to keep pressure off my feet. My legs felt like gummy worms, fatigued from the constant tension on the way down the hill. The only motivation was to reach Hornillos del Camino as quickly as possible, so that I could replenish my fluids.

Eventually, deep in the valley of The Meseta, I reached Hornillos del Camino. The stone-filled trail gave way to pavement at an intersection. In the center of town, there were several pilgrims sitting in the shade on the side of the road, next to a convenience store. Some were eating their sandwiches wrapped in aluminum foil, some were eating cookies, and others were pounding cans of beer—it was wonderful. All I wanted was a can of Coca-Cola, so I stepped inside to grab it. The man behind the counter emphasized that a cold can of Coca-Cola was more expensive than a warm one, but I was happy to pay the 50-cent difference. The bench outside was full, so I just took a seat on the curb and enjoyed the cold, fresh can of Coca-Cola. Drinking regular Coke was like quenching your thirst and eating a snack at the same time—it, too, was wonderful. I tried to mingle with a few pilgrims outside the store, but they seemed to want to keep to themselves. The look on their faces told you everything you needed to know; they were suffering. Girls had let their hair down, doing little to keep it out of their face, or hide their soaked armpits from strangers. The guys had a defeated look as they propped themselves up against the wall, resting both arms on the ground. Perhaps they looked dead more than they did defeated. But the hike to Hornillos del Camino was only a taste of what was to come.

After I finished my Coke, my next mission was to find some water. In the main plaza, next to the church, there was a tall fountain called the "Fuente del Gallo," or Rooster's Fountain—I promise, I am not making this stuff up. The Rooster's Fountain, tall and made of rock, had two brass spouts requiring a firm push for the water to jet out. Despite how badly I suffered on the way there, I only filled one bottle. This way, I would walk with less weight, causing less stress on my legs, particularly my feet. This decision would cost me dearly. The Camino markers took me back to the gravel trail and onto the next town of Hontanas, 11km away. Above, skies were mostly clear now. The temperature was rapidly creeping up into the low 90s. There was no wind, no breeze, and literally no shade to hide myself from the red-hot sun.

Two hours into the hike, I was in trouble. My water supply was completely gone. The intense heat had me trapped like broasted chicken, waiting to be devoured by hungry people. It was like vultures were circling above me as I licked the last few drops of water from my bottle. My brimmed hat was shielding most of my face from the sun, but the heat and sweat it generated felt like I had stuck my head into a boiling pot of hot water, much like a lobster. My breathing intensified, my pace slowed, and dark thoughts entered my mind—they revolved around death. "If I quit right now, I will surely die," I thought. My body was on the brink of heat exhaustion, or even worse, heatstroke. And I was feeling delirious. My temperature was rising, and my heart was beating rapidly. The effort I was exerting was fatiguing the muscles and draining me of my fluids. I wanted desperately to stop and take a break, but there was no shade. I also knew that if I stopped, or even sat down for a few minutes, I would not get back up. And if I did not, who was going to save me? I was in the middle of nowhere. I cannot emphasize that enough: the middle of nowhere. My surroundings were wheat and grass fields, as far as the eyes could see. And when you are telling yourself to hold on just five more minutes, it becomes difficult to maintain that hope when you reach a hill-top, only to realize there are many more hill-tops to come.

Physically, I was a mess. Swelling caused numbness from my ankles down to my feet, except for the soles, where it still felt like I was stepping on glass. My calves were gone, completely zapped of strength. My groin was sore, and my right hip hurt with every lunge forward. And my lips were all dry and cracked, just like in the movies and on TV. It felt like that scene from *Better Call Saul*, the spin-off of *Breaking Bad*, when Saul Goodman is walking through the New Mexico desert, with a shirt wrapped around his head, and his lips nearly bleeding from the dryness. Hope was fading.

Forcing myself to keep walking, for no other reason than not to die in the sun, I came across a sign for a nearby albergue with a bar and restaurant. But I could not see it in the distance. Was the sign a heartless prank? Was this my version of a mirage in the desert? An oasis that did not exist? I was not completely sure. Then, I saw it. There was a road that turned off the Camino, and about 50 meters down was Albergue Fuente Sidres. "This better be open," I thought. And it was. The place was empty inside. As kindly and politely as anyone could after being baked alive in the sweltering sun for nearly three hours, I asked the woman behind the counter for some water. She pointed me to a large jug at the far end of the bar. My hands shook as I flipped the release valve for the water to pour out into my bottle. If she had not been looking, I would have stuck my head under the spout and bathed in it. My hands continued to shake as I filled the bottle, which took forever to fill for a few gulps. It was not the fault of the spout, but of my hands, as my trembling caused the bottle to move around, spilling water all over the floor beneath me. I was in awful shape. The first few gulps of water made me cough, as I inhaled it by accident. I sat at a table with a window and a view of the dry plains in the backdrop. Closing my eyes for a few seconds, I tried to collect my thoughts and reset my mind as much as possible. 10 minutes in, I knew I had to move on. Hontanas was only a few kilometers away.

By the time I reached Hontanas, it was about 13:30 in the afternoon. Pilgrims occupied the terrace of Albergue El Puntido, sitting in chairs under the white umbrellas. There was an American woman with her daughter. They were eating chocolate ice-cream cones. After seeing that, I had to have one. I went inside the bar and bought one bottle of water, one Powerade, and one chocolate ice-cream cone. It was the best ice-cream cone ever. Sadly, things did not look any better for the remaining 10km.

The next 5km took me through the valley that housed Hontanas. Much of the trail was uneven and overgrown with strips of grass throughout. In contrast to my suffering and seemingly near-death experience on the way to Hontanas, I felt better now that I had plenty of water and Powerade with me. If I was going to die out there in The Meseta, at least thirst would not be my first concern. My entire body ached, and my feet were so swollen they were numb. But the most worrisome thoughts were now about the blisters on the bottom of my feet. When I got up from eating ice-cream, there were strange and uncomfortable pressure points with each step. Unable to see underneath the Compeed pads, I was unaware of the true extent of my blisters. I just had to get to the albergue.

When the trail turned to pavement, there were tall trees that lined the road. A few cars passed me by, but it was quiet, heading into town. A few kilometers out, I walked by the ruins of the old monastery of San Antón, built in 1146, on the order of King Alfonso VII. The convent was used to care for sick pilgrims, especially those who suffered from a disease called "Fire of San Antón," that once spread during the Middle Ages. The sixteenth century saw the addition of an elevated arch, complementing the stunning Gothic style of the ogival windows and façade. Today, the old convent is a pilgrim's shelter.

Passing through the arch of the old convent, around the bend to the right, there was a castle perched at the top of a mountain—it was glorious. A large moat isolates the eighth-century castle, adding to its medieval nature. At an altitude of 900 meters, the castle benefited from its strategic location. It was famous for resisting many attacks over the centuries, including those from Africa and Northern Europe. Today, like the old convent, only ruins remain of this once impenetrable castle.

Lucky for me, the first turn off the main road and into Castrojeriz had an albergue sitting on the corner. It was called Albergue La Rinconada. There was a woman waiting at the front door—another pilgrim.

"Do you know if they have any room here?" I asked, hoping I did not have to walk to the next albergue.

"They better!" said the woman, probably in her 50s. "I booked a private room just for myself."

"Whoa! You can do that? I thought we all had to sleep in the dorms."

"They aren't always available, but I thought, what the heck, I'll treat myself to my own room. It'll be nice to have my own shower and bathroom."

"And the snoring… you won't have to hear the snoring," I said, smiling. The woman laughed. Her name was Kirsten, and she was from Utah.

Eventually, the host came over and unlocked the door for us. The owners of the albergue also owned a bar and restaurant next door. Kirsten said she was going to settle in, then head over to the bar for dinner. I agreed to meet her over there, as I had eaten nothing besides a sandwich and an ice-cream cone. But my first order of business was to sit down. I was in pain as I walked, but standing idly in one spot was almost worse. I slowly climbed the stairs up to the dorms, holding onto the railings for dear life, pulling my body up with each step. This time, I could select my bed from the six available; I made sure it was a lower bunk. Then it was time to shower.

When I removed my thick wool socks, I remember the wretched smell that suffocated the air as they came off. My big toe had a huge blister that started at the end of the toe and went halfway down the left side. The end of my long toe had one of the same size, and my pinky toe, too. I covered my face with my hands, just trying to grasp the situation. Then I turned my right foot over to examine the bottom. The puffy purple and yellow bruising had gotten worse. The puffiness was now bubbling up around the Compeed pad. I flexed the toes of my feet up and down just to gauge the movement. It was excruciatingly painful. It had been under constant pressure as I walked, expanding the bruised bubble into the intersection with my toes. I could barely bend them. And my left foot was not much better. Where there used to be a blister between my big toe and long toe, there was a puddle of sappy fluid. The blister had formed again and popped during the 41km hike through The Meseta. It was weird that I had not felt it pop, but then again, when you feel you are walking on glass, not much else matters. I spent the next hour performing "surgery" on my feet, unwrapping old medical tape, cleansing my toes with alcohol pads and stabbing them with my needles from the pharmacy. The shower helped to remove some of the gooey puss that had built up, but the thought of infection was creeping into my mind. There were two questions that haunted me that night: 1) how long would I have before an infection took me off the Camino, and 2) was I physically capable of pushing through the pain? I had no answers for either.

After popping and draining the blisters on my toes, then re-wrapping all of them with medical tape, I tried standing up to gauge my condition. I could barely put any pressure on either foot. It felt like I was standing on daggers. I took a deep breath, with my head hanging low, grasping at straws to figure out how I was going to make it out of the situation. It was clearly my lowest moment. I had almost forgotten what it was like to walk pain-free. My medical knowledge was minimal, and I was unsure of the damage I was causing to my feet and to my body. Part of me wondered if simply wanting something was enough. My thought process had always led me to believe that if my will was strong enough, that I could get through anything. Stranded in the desert, Jesus endured 40 days and 40 nights with no food. Satan tested him in his weakest moments. I now felt stranded on the Camino de Santiago. A wave of fear had come over me. Living in my darkest moments and in my deepest despair, I needed something greater than my will.

CHAPTER TEN:

MOTHER MARY

He sits in his oversized bathtub, in his larger-than-life mansion, in the paradise of Miami, Florida. A Cuban cigar occupies one hand, while a black TV remote occupies the other. The bath water is sprawling with soap suds. A bottle of champagne is resting on ice, inside a silver-plated bucket. A plate of fresh fruit is off to the side. There is a bronze statue of a boy wrestling a fish, and a bronze chair that is empty. A crystal chandelier hangs from the ceiling, just above the bathtub.

"Hey, FUCK YOU, man! Who put this thing together!? ME! That's who!" says Tony Montana, played by Al Pacino, in the 1983 hit movie *Scarface*. His wife and best friend were with him moments before. His wife leaves the room after tempers flare during an argument, during which Tony makes a point that he has worked very hard to become a multimillionaire cocaine kingpin; the riches they enjoy are because of his hard work, he argues. His wife strikes back with an inconvenient truth.

"It's too bad. Somebody should've given it to you. You would've been a nicer person," she says before storming out of the room. After that, Tony takes up business matters with his partner, who is his best friend. His partner had taken the lead on arranging a business deal, but Tony tells him to stay out of it; he will take over for him. After diminishing his partner's contributions to their fortune, his partner takes offense. He, too, leaves the room. Tony continues his diatribe, claiming all the credit for his lifestyle turnaround, where he goes from a Cuban refugee to one of Miami's biggest drug lords.

"Who do I trust? ME!" says Tony. Just before the end of the scene, as the camera pans out above the bathtub, you can hear Tony quietly mumble a few last words.

"I don't need him… I don't need her. Fuck it… I don't need nobody," he says, smoking the cigar and watching TV.

That was my mentality when I paved the way for my father to become a permanent resident, also known as a Green Card holder, and then eventually a US citizen. Perched in my condo in Miami Beach, Florida, I saw the acceptance notice arrive in the mail, notifying us that my father was being invited to the citizenship ceremony. It had been a long journey. My parents had gotten divorced, and it separated me from my father for five years, while my mother raised me and my two sisters with little to no money back in the US. I remember thinking, "When I grow up, I'm going to put the pieces back together." The rupture of my parents' divorce was so ugly that I rarely imagined them getting back together. But that was not what I wanted. I just wanted us all to be close to each other; to be near each other. From early on, I took that responsibility upon my shoulders. I had to put the pieces back together. And, so, I took a great deal of pride because I eventually did. I carried that burden on my back for over 20 years, since the age of 12. But that was not the only time I felt the need to do something on my own. Not because I wanted to, but because I had to. I went to high school and aced my classes, got accepted to a private university in Washington, DC, graduated and landed a job with a Wall Street bank, generated a six-figure salary in my twenties, bought a condo by the beach in Miami, and have run with the bulls in Spain for six years. Over the course of my life, I have learned to rely on myself, and go bravely into the abyss alone. That is the way I felt on Day 10 of the Camino: a 45km trek to Carrión de los Condes.

The morning hours came early in Castrojeriz. I still felt alone, but technically, I was not. Kirsten had asked if she could join me at 05:30 to continue the walk through The Meseta—I obliged. She, too, wanted to get a head start that day, but she did not have a headlamp, and I did. Before we left, the host of the albergue had set out breakfast on the kitchen table. There was orange juice, pastries, sliced bread, and strawberry jelly packets. I knew then that I had a problem. The feeling of walking on glass was still there, but another feeling worsened it. It now felt like I was walking on bubbles. That is the best way to explain it. When a blister forms, a bubble appears. These bubbles fill with fluid and provide protection against friction. During the night, while my feet were off the ground, my blisters underneath the Compeed pads had formed large bubbles. I could feel these bubbles with every step I took in the kitchen.

The first few kilometers from the albergue took us up a gradual ascent through town. Kirsten was out in front to my right as my headlamp illuminated the path ahead—it was powerfully bright. I limped my way up the cobblestone hills, dragging out each step on my left foot, while trying to avoid putting pressure on my right.

"Don't worry about me," said Kirsten. "If you want to go faster, you can go ahead." I think she thought I was holding back, but I was not. I was trying desperately to keep up with her. Kirsten was a high school counselor back in Utah and was very sweet and considerate.

I was so focused on the pain of walking on my blisters and limping up the hill that I accidentally missed the Camino marker to turn down a street. When we realized it, the only way back was down a long, steep staircase, where a young teenage couple was smoking marijuana. There was a festival in town, and they were still out partying. We asked if we were going the right way. The girl was unsure, and the boy did not know what the Camino was. So, we began down the stairs. I could feel their eyes glued to us, as Kirsten flew down the steps, and I went down slowly in a side-stepping fashion. Surely, I was not in the best condition.

The town of Castrojeriz was like a horseshoe formation, wrapped around the mountain with the castle perched on top. I looked back a few times, but it was too dark to see before dawn. Before we knew it, Kirsten and I were back on the gravel trail, surrounded by grass fields. After 20 minutes, we crossed a wooden bridge, taking us over the Odrilla River. The sun was rising in the east behind us, shedding light on the 145-meter climb in front of us. Over the next kilometer and a half, Kirsten faded, losing momentum on the steep ascent—I waited for her, so that we could summit together. After all, Kirsten had unknowingly waited for me back in Castrojeriz, and I wanted to return the favor. At the top, we came across two Asian pilgrims— one from Japan and the other from China. They were taking photos of the rising sun. It looked like a white blip with a reddish orange glow around it. The sun gave light to the valley below as we said goodbye to Castrojeriz. Kirsten took a break at the top of the climb and mingled with the other pilgrims while I pushed ahead. Part of me marveled at their lack of urgency. I still had over 40km to go, and I did not have time to marvel. Still, part of me envied their seemingly carefree nature.

The path continued on flat terrain after the steep ascent, across the Mostelares plateau. It looked flat as far as I could see. There was really nothing in the distance other than the slowly illuminating sky. After 10 minutes, the path came to a sudden drop, along with my jaw, as I marveled at the sight in front of me. A magnificent landscape appeared out of nowhere. The Spanish call it the "Tierra de Campos," or the Land of Fields. It was like I had a view of the world, but there was nothing in it. All I could see were flat and sun-torched fields, with the occasional flash of green. These lands straddle the provinces of León, Zamora, Valladolid, and Palencia. The vast nature of the plains rests at an elevation of 720 meters. The trail was a compact clay of sorts, surrounded by dry, but very fertile lands. Farmers use dryland farming techniques to harvest wheat. During the winter, the area sees cool and wet conditions. This packs the landscape with all the moisture it will need for the hot and dry season that awaits.

My first few steps were tricky as I started down the hill and into the Land of Fields. I barely had enough strength in my knees to cushion the landing of each step. And my arms were dead from pulling my body up the ascent on the other side. The bubbles on the bottom of my feet made me grimace with every move. Drenched in sweat, I realized the best way to make it down the steep hill would be to jog down it. That way, I could leverage my momentum to avoid putting pressure on my knees, as well as my feet. It worked until I was at the bottom. Then, I had to start all over. The bending of my feet was dreadfully painful as I placed one foot in front of the other.

After 5km kilometers through the Land of Fields, I arrived in Itero del Castillo, where I crossed a Romanesque bridge called Puente Fitero, constructed during the age of King Alfonso VI. The seven arches of the bridge gave way to Palencia, uniting it with the province of Burgos that I had just come from. After crossing the Pisuerga River, the Camino markers took me off-road, en route to Itero de la Vega. In a rarity for this region, the tall, lush green trees provided me with refuge from the sun. Itero de la Vega was virtually asleep when I arrived around 08:30. Everything was closed. Then, I saw an older man walking with a cane. I asked him if there was any place I could stop for breakfast. His reply seemed fitting, given the condition I was in, and where things were going.

"Well, there used to be a bar that was open around this time… but then the owner died," said the old gentleman, waving his cane around as he spoke. I continued walking.

At the edge of town was a water fountain with four benches, surrounded by a few trees covered in leaves, wrapped with a two-foot-high brick border. I loaded up on water, then unzipped my backpack to find some KT tape. My right ankle ached with pain every time I put pressure on it. I likely strained it when I swiftly descended into the Land of Fields. A handful of fellow pilgrims sat on the bench across from me. When I took off my sock, the Italian pilgrims took notice of my medical tape. Every single toe had tape wrapped around them, some more than others.

"What's wrong with your feet?" they asked.

"Blisters."

"How can you walk like this?"

"I have to," I said, putting my sock and shoe back on after applying a strip of KT tape. I saw them again shortly after, when I stopped at an albergue in a town called Boadilla del Camino. Outside on the terrace, I ate chocolate brownies I had purchased from the host, who was originally from Amsterdam—not *that* kind of brownie. The Italians showed up at the albergue minutes later. They were a friendly bunch, and we kept each other company over the next 6km to Frómista.

Most of the walk continued on open country trails, in desolate, skin-burning heat. There was no escape. I was wearing my Patagonia windbreaker, with the zipper down as far down as it would go, my chest drenched in sweat. The blister bubbles were more pronounced now, after having walked about 22km. If my pain was on a scale of 1 to 10, it was nearing 10. There is only so much pain a person can take until they cannot take it anymore. The Italians were suffering too, especially the ones who wore sleeveless shirts. Their skin was beat red, and there was nothing they could do about it. Still, we continued to walk.

The final three kilometers before Frómista ran parallel to a canal. It reminded me of the ones we have in the Florida swamps. The water was stagnant in that way. Along the canal, I met a young American girl from Colorado. She was walking alone. Surprised by this, I asked her why, and she told me that her mother was waiting for her in Frómista. She had left earlier that morning, looking to beat the heat. Apparently, she suffered heatstroke on the ascent up the Pyrenees from St. Jean Pied de Port. They had to call emergency services to provide medical help. The prolonged exposure to heat was no joke on the Camino.

At the end of the canal, we walked over the locks that historically raised and lowered boats into the water. We stopped at the first store we saw. While I went in for the electrolyte-packed drink called Aquarius, the Italians opted for something else—beer. And why not? They had finished walking for the day. But I still had another 20km to go. Everyone took a seat on the sidewalk, drinking beer and speaking Italian. I caught every other word, as it seemed similar to Spanish. They were heading to the municipal albergue for the night, and wanted me to join them. They assumed I had also finished for the day, probably because I had told them so. As I walked the Camino, I became increasingly guarded about my objective of walking the entire Camino in 20 days. I also guarded my physical condition, but anyone with a cataract could have seen that I was hurting. After crushing the beer cans, the Italians proceeded down the sidewalk toward the albergue. I told the guys I would see them after I got some food, but I knew I would never see them again.

The many miracles recorded in Frómista earned it the name "Villa del Milagro," or the Village of the Miracle. Such miracles include the recovery of the paralyzed French girl's body, the healing of the German cripple, and the restoration of vision for the blind man. Locals believe that the Virgin Mary performed these miracles. Among the many miracles, perhaps the most famous one occurred during the fifteenth century. In 1453, a Christian man named Pedro Fernández de Teresa had asked to borrow money from a Jew. When Pedro failed to repay the Jew, the church excommunicated him and refused him communion from that point forward. After this, Pedro finally paid the debt, and assumed the matter to be closed. When he aged, he fell ill, calling a priest to his bedside. When the priest tried to give him the Eucharist, the piece of bread would not separate from the stack. It was stuck, and there was no way to remove it. The priest then asked Pedro if he had any sins that had gone unrepented. Pedro explained what had happened with the debt, and how he had first refused to repay the Jew. After this confession, the priest was able to perform communion with another piece of the Eucharist. Today, they still preserve the priest's stole, a vestment worn over the shoulders that hangs down to the knee, and there is a stone marker placed in front of the house where the miracle occurred.

The dry and desolate walk continued for me as I returned to the Camino, leaving Frómista behind. It took me another two hours to reach Revenga de Campos, where I hoped to grab lunch. Off the main road, I diverted down a street, looking for any place that served food. The first place I came across was a small boutique hotel. Inside, the host told me they had booked the whole place for a little girl's first communion. They told me to come back in a few hours—that was not happening. Nearby, I found a bar that looked like a local's hangout. Inside, it was empty, except for one woman eating alone at a table, and an older man behind the bar, who was presumably the owner. Not wasting any time, I waddled over to the bar and asked if they served lunch, to which the man said, "Yes." A wave of relief washed over me and my hobbled and hungry body. He handed me a menu with a list of options, but I did not need time to look it over. I ordered some jamon and eggs—nice and simple.

"Where are you from?" asked the woman, eating at the table. She had a Latin American accent.

"I'm from Miami," I said, walking gingerly over to the empty table beside her.

"You know, lots of famous people come here."

"Like who?" I asked, maintaining the conversation as I waited impatiently for my food.

"Alejandro Sanz," she said, referring to the Spanish musician who owns a house in Miami.

"Really? He came here?"

"This guy doesn't believe me," she said to the owner in a deeply condescending tone. "This is a small town, but people come from all over to visit!" she said, this time raising her voice. I think she worked at the bar. It was turning into a sales pitch for Revenga de Campos, with an oddly aggressive twist to it. When my food arrived, I inhaled it. They loaded the plate with a stack of jamon, three sunny-side-up eggs, a mountain of salad, and a pile of French fries. I still had 12km to walk, but I did not have the slightest care at that moment. Then, the conversation took a dark turn. I opened my mouth about walking over 40km a day, trying to reach Santiago in 20 days.

"You better watch it. They found a guy dead in The Meseta last year," said the woman, getting visibly more animated.

"Really?"

"Hey, Jose! He doesn't believe me! You think I'm joking!?"

"No, I believe you. I was just surprised."

"Wait 'till Paco gets here… just wait 'till he gets here. He's going to set you straight!" The woman was becoming unhinged. And I did not have any interest in meeting "Paco," whoever the hell that was.

I quickly asked for the bill and paid in cash—I needed to get out of there. When I stood up from the chair, I immediately sat back down. It was like a reflex that I could not control. During the 20 minutes inside the bar, the blisters on the bottom of my feet had bubbled up to new proportions. While sitting down at the table, there was no more pressure to keep the bubbles from expanding. It was as if they had time to grow and build up with fluid. The pain was through the roof. It felt like someone had cut open my feet, dug out a handful of flesh, stuck inside a ball, then taped it back up. I felt that pain deep inside my feet.

As I finally hobbled away from the table and back onto the Camino, there was no way to walk without my trekking poles—they were now officially crutches. My shoes scraped the bottom of the pavement with each step. My feet had to remain flat, as I could not bend them. Looking back, my physical, mental, and emotional state had flipped completely from my first day on the Camino; they could not have been more different. I was in pure agony. The way I was walking resembled a 90-year-old man walking from his front door to his mailbox. I was having trouble making it across the street, much less 12km to Carrión de los Condes. To help put things in perspective, until then, I had walked 374km from St. Jean Pied de Port in France. There were still 108km to go to reach the end of The Meseta, and 426km to go to reach Santiago de Compostela. My frame of mind was one of defeat; it was one of complete and utter desperation. Making matters worse, the massive meal I "enjoyed" at the bar was inducing a food coma, on top of the fact that I felt like I was carrying an extra 20 pounds from all the food. The oil and salt from the jamon I had eaten left me feeling dehydrated and dying of thirst. The relentless sun was baking me in The Meseta.

The 2km walk to the next village felt like 10km. In Villarmentero de Campos, I pulled off the path at a pilgrim rest area. There was a little shade provided by the pine trees, under which I found some tables and a small fountain that looked like a fire hydrant. There was no sign to indicate that the water was potable, but I filled up my bottle anyway. And because I was trying my best to limit the weight I carried, I was now only filling up one water bottle at a time—not a good idea, but I was stubborn that way.

Most of the path ahead was straight and narrow, with very few turns in either direction. As I walked, it felt like I was not making any progress, and the grass fields went on forever. There was a ditch to my left that separated the trail from the highway. I thought maybe the breeze from the occasional car that passed would be enough to knock me over and bury me in the ditch. But I never felt a breeze. The pain consumed my focus. And as badly as I feared stopping to take a break, I held out for as long as I could. Every once in a while, I would come across a bus stop. The benches were always empty. I would sit on the bench for two minutes, and not a second more. After what happened at lunch, I knew I had to stay on my feet as much as possible, or else the blisters would balloon up again.

The pressure was not just a matter of my feet, but also a matter of my mind, heart, and soul. As soon as I would shake the doubts of whether I could finish the Camino, they would come back with the aggression of an avalanche. The Meseta had me questioning myself. Ever since I started the Camino, there was always a lingering question of whether my body could hold up. In the rugged depths of The Meseta, I thought a lot about my father. After he first immigrated to the US from Spain, he spent his first several years living in the Idaho mountains, tending to sheep on a full-time basis for a local rancher. Rain or shine, cold or warm, he had to be up on that mountain, living out of a trailer that resembled something from the Oregon Trail in the 1800s. My father would spend months at a time living up in the mountains. He had no company, zero social interaction, and lived off of jars of peanut butter. And as I thought about my father, I remember passing by a grass field with some 20 sheep in an enclosure. The sheepherder was inside the enclosure, observing the sheep as they moved around, chewing on the yellow grass. His clothes looked torn and worn out, his arms blackened from the sun, and his face gaunt, with dark bags under his eyes. We looked over at each other, both nodding our heads.

Shortly after, I saw a sign for Carrión de los Condes. I was 6km away. The Camino was pilgrim-free after Frómista. Walking the Camino alone in the afternoon heat had become routine, as if all the other pilgrims vanished. But when I saw the sign, I noticed two pilgrims up ahead. When I caught up to them, they were an older couple from Tennessee. The older guy, Craig, was in his mid-sixties. He worked for a telecommunications company back in the US, and was contemplating retirement. Craig looked exactly like Hulk Hogan. He had the beard, the mustache, the sunglasses, the iconic bandana wrapped around his head, and stood well over six feet tall. His wife, Jamye, was a very sweet woman who looked to be having a hard time with the Camino. She too had blisters on her feet. Craig and Jamye were behind schedule, since they had to stay an extra night back in Frómista to care for Jayme's blisters. Craig and I made small talk as we walked the final 6km together. Jamye stayed a few meters back, taking her mind off of the Camino by listening to an audiobook.

What jolted my spirit during the Camino was how difficult some of those kilometers ended up being. On the last stretch to Carrión de los

Condes, I had no more water, not one drop. My throat became parched and prickly. It was so dry that it actually hurt to talk. I tried to wind down the conversation with Craig and minimize my input so as not to dry out my mouth. Craig and Jamye had water, but asking for it was out of the question. To me, that felt like I was failing to complete the Camino on my accord. I could not fathom asking for someone else's water. To me, it was akin to giving up, as crazy as that sounds. But I was in very rough shape. And as Craig kelp talking, I kept thinking about if I had pushed myself too far this time. I kept wondering whether I had finally reached the moment I would crumble. The pain, the swelling, the blister bubbles—it was all unbearable. Yet, I kept pushing, pushing and pushing some more. And when I finished pushing, I pushed again. I thought my foot was going to explode. And then it kind of did. I took a step with my right foot, when suddenly I felt a bursting-like sensation. It felt like the bottom of my foot had exploded. The burst sent nerves array, from the bottom of my foot to my upper calve. I paused mid-stride, cringing and grimacing from the pain.

"Is it a Charlie-horse? Which leg is it?" asked Craig, concerned.

"No, it's my foot. I think it just burst."

"Oh, that's not good."

As we passed over the gently rolling hills, the town came into view. It looked as though we were almost there. The funny (or not so funny) thing about seeing towns in the distance was that you knew you had another two to three kilometers before you actually reached them. It was pure torture. Running on fumes, we crossed the street, exiting the trail along the highway, taking a sideroad into town. We stopped for a few moments so that Jamye could re-tie her shoes. As I was standing next to her, leaning over my trekking poles, I looked down at my shoe and saw a dark residue above the toe box area. The burst had ejected some kind of fluid—puss, blood, or both—through two layers of socks, including the thick wool socks I wore every day. Yet, all I could think about was getting something to drink. It took every fiber in me not to leave Craig and Jamye behind as we waited for her to tie her shoes.

Once Jamye was done, we continued down the street, agreeing to stop at the first bar we passed. When we did, I made a bee-line to the counter. As I stood there in pain, looking for someone to take my order, I heard a voice behind the counter, but I did not see anyone. I leaned over the bar and there was a kid, not a day older than 10 years old. He was asking me what I wanted to drink. I did not waste a moment thinking about it. I immediately asked for a Coca-Cola. While the kid took his time attempting to open the glass bottle, I stood in agony, hunched over at the bar. He was still having trouble with the cap. Then, an adult, presumably his father, came over to assist. That crisp, cool taste of Coca-Cola was like a taste of heaven. Before I left, I bought a 100oz bottle of water, just for the walk to the albergue. Craig

110

and Jamye had taken a seat out on the terrace of the bar. Unsure of what they wanted, I asked the bartending-kid's father to tend to us outside.

After beers were served, we began looking frantically for a place to stay the night. We took turns calling different albergues around town, but they were all booked. Even the hotels were at full capacity. Apparently, the festival that was taking place in Castrojeriz was part of a larger festival in the area. With our lodging in question, Craig and Jamye wanted to relax at the bar before figuring things out, but I knew I needed to find something quickly. The pain in my feet was coming back, and I started getting spasms in my hamstrings. We said our goodbyes, then I made my way up the street through the center of town. In sheer pain, I stumbled from block to block, checking all the hotels and albergues in person, on the off chance that maybe they were saving spots for people arriving at the last minute. It was 17:30. I had been out on the Camino for 12 hours. The exhaustion I was feeling was something I had never experienced. Yet, I somehow found the strength to keep checking for a place to stay. And when everything seemed hopeless, there was only one more place to call: Albergue de Peregrinos del Espíritu Santo, or in English, "Pilgrims' Hostel of the Holy Spirit"—the local sanctuary.

"Do you have room for me?" I asked a woman over the phone.

"Of course we have room," she said, as I wiped the sweat from my forehead.

The front entrance of the albergue was closed, but they had signs pointing to another entrance around the back. A 10-foot wall with a large metal gate surrounded the albergue. Inside, I entered a small, chapel-like room, where the woman I had spoken with over the phone greeted me with a smile. I took a seat at her desk. Surely, I looked like death.

"Are you going all the way to Santiago?" the lady asked me.

"We'll see," I said with a nervous chuckle. "Only if God gives me the strength to keep going."

"Of course he will," she said with a tone of absolute certainty. Then she reached into her drawer and asked me to open my hand. "Here, take this."

"What is it?"

"It's a necklace of the Virgin Mary." It was made with a piece of cheap twine, and had a silver-colored oval pendant with the Virgin Mary on it.

"When you find yourself in trouble, and you need help, all you have to do is say, 'Mother Mary, please help me. Please grant me the strength to keep going.'"

Something inexplicable happened to me in that moment. A flood of emotion hit me with the strength of a thousand waves. It was a startling sense of comfort, with an overwhelming sense of guilt. I was milliseconds away from bursting into tears in front of this woman. Over the prior 10 days on

111

the Camino, I had experienced so much pain and suffering, and I had been storing and internalizing all of it. This small yet powerful gesture of faith and kindness brought me to the breaking point. But before I started crying, the woman stood up to help me leave the room. She saw it in my watery eyes that I was on my last thread, ready to lose it. I put the necklace over my head and around my neck, as she walked around the desk to help show me to the dormitory. I apologized for my physical state, telling her I was moving gingerly. She told me not to worry.

To access the dormitory, we had to climb a set of stairs on the exterior of the building. As we turned to go up the stairs, there was a woman soaking her feet in a kid-sized pool that was filled with cold water—her face said it all. She was in some serious pain. In the building, I kicked off my shoes—my socks were all bloody. I was dreading the act of removing my socks; it kept getting worse every time. And when I did, it took me 20 minutes, since the gooey material from the Compeed pads had completely fused to the socks. For the first time, I could see where the burst had occurred on my right foot, while walking into Carrión de los Condes. It was at the base of my toes, where I found it difficult to bend. The pressure had become too great, and the fluid finally burst out between my toes. My skin outside the pad was a flimsy, light-yellow color, covered in goo. I needed a shower immediately.

The showers were down the hall of the sanctuary. Nobody was inside, as the other pilgrims had arrived hours before. After placing my towel on the wooden rack next to the stall, I turned the lever to release the water. As I stepped under the showerhead, the water hit me like I was being baptized all over again. The tears flowed as the water washed over me, leaving me unable to distinguish the water from the tears. The guilt from earlier continued, like I was in the presence of grace and of everlasting forgiveness. It felt like someone was putting their hand on my shoulder. I then made a desperate plea for help, as the tears fell from my eyes.

"Mother Mary, please grant me the strength to finish the Camino. Please grant me the strength…" I said, tears flowing. I wanted the shower to go on forever, but the pain of standing was too great. I turned off the shower and tried to collect myself before returning to the dormitory.

My feet were in the worst condition yet. Nobody in their right mind should have even considered continuing to walk—my feet were that bad. Anybody with an ounce of sense would have gone immediately to an emergency clinic. But I did not. Instead, I took a needle and used the edge to make an incision near the spot where my blister had popped. Starting at the bottom of my foot, I pressed my skin away from the heel, like emptying a bottle of toothpaste, but in this case, emptying any remaining fluid I could drain from the blister. Then I grabbed my bottle of brown iodine and began dumping as much as I could into the open incision. The cold liquid burned as it flowed into the open blister, from my toes, halfway down the bottom of my foot. I was hoping to avoid a massive infection (if I did not already have one). But honestly, I was not sure if it mattered. I was practically dead.

We have all seen the final scene in Scarface, when the Colombians scale the wall of Tony Montana's mansion, looking to kill him. He sits in his extravagant office, surrounded by opulence and a mountain of cocaine on his desk. By this point, Tony has chased away his wife, and killed his partner and best friend. He made a few pivotally poor business decisions, but more than anything, his lack of trust and inability to keep people close to him ended up costing him—he dies in a hail of gunfire, with a shotgun blast to the back. I had been on the Camino for 10 days, and I had 10 more to go. The situation was dire. I felt I had reached the end of my physical and mental capacity and needed help. But I needed to put my trust in someone else. I needed to put my faith in someone else. And perhaps more than anything, I needed a miracle.

CHAPTER ELEVEN:

WE'RE HALFWAY THERE

Off the coast of Mexico, in a place called Punta Norte, a pod of orcas was ready to make its move. The orcas waited until high tide to move in closer to the beach, where seals and sea lion puppies frolicked. To hide their dorsal fins from their prey, they swam in a sideways motion, quickly approaching the shore. When the seals and sea lion puppies finally noticed the orcas, they made a run for the beach. But it was too late. The orcas beached themselves on the shore by coasting in on the tide. They snatched an animal or two, then used their razor-sharp teeth and constant head motion to tear them into pieces. This was hardly what I needed to see before sitting down for a meal. All I saw was how ferocious nature could be—downright ferocious.

Before going to sleep in Carrión de los Condes, I limped over to a bar and restaurant one block away from the sanctuary. It was around 21:00. The walls of the sanctuary closed for good at 22:00 that evening, so I had to be quick, which proved difficult in my condition. A couple of guys from Morocco ran the restaurant, so they geared the menu toward their culture. Everything on the menu sounded tasty, but I ended up ordering chicken thighs with French fries. Waiting for my food, there was a documentary playing on the TV. They were showing how orcas, or killer whales, hunt their prey.

When I rolled out of bed the next morning, I felt like the killer whales of Punta Norte had torn me apart. I put my right foot on the ground for a split second and felt the shooting pains of the popped blister. It had come back. I had a growing bubble on the left foot, but not as bad as the right. Just putting my shoe on and tying the laces was excruciating. It was Day 11 on

114

the Camino, and there were 40km to Sahagún. The first village on the way was a town called Calzadilla de la Cueza. It was a 17km walk, with no place to stop for food or water. The night before, I had asked the Moroccan restaurant to make me a chorizo sandwich for the next day. Since they ran out of bread, they used what was leftover from my meal. Running out of bread is a rarity in Spain, especially when you are walking through a region known as The Meseta, or in other, more affectionate terms, "Spain's Breadbasket," given all the wheat that is produced there.

The first 30 minutes of Day 11 were not just physically draining, but psychologically draining as well. Every 10 seconds, I thought about how farfetched it was for me to complete the Camino. There were plenty of reasons not to believe, two of them being my feet. But I started that day with a fuller spirit, something I had not yet experienced. I often repeated the prayer to Mother Mary, especially when I was alone on the trail. During my prayers, I made a promise. "If you can help me, if you can bless me with the physical ability to walk, I will endure the pain and suffering required," I said. In other words, please help me walk, and I will deal with the pain. And there was plenty of it on the way to Sahagún.

The 17km stretch from Carrión de los Condes to Sahagún was a solemn one. Initially, I found myself among a group of pilgrims who had also departed the sanctuary when the gate opened at 06:30. Others had come from the other albergues and hotels that had rejected me based on availability. As the walk continued, the crowd had noticeably thinned out. People would take breaks along the Camino, especially when they were in groups. When I was hungry, I slowed my pace a little, opened my bag to get the chorizo sandwich, and continued up the rock-infested trail. By that point, I had to make my stops count. If I was going to let my blisters bubble up again, such breaks needed to be few and far between. But what really took up my headspace that morning, and what got me through the 17km, was the feeling that God and Mother Mary were nearby. It was such an intimate and loving feeling. It felt like I was a soldier of God. I may have needed a medic, but I was on the warpath. And my motivations seemed different now.

When the 17km stretch was nearing its end, I encountered a cat in the middle of the Camino. Still 200 meters from the first town, the cat came up to me and started circling around. I pulled out my water bottle, which only had an inch of water left. Thinking the cat was thirsty, I stopped and poured out the water for it to drink. Then, I kept walking into town. Nearly all the pilgrims stopped at Albergue Camino Real. Outside, they had plenty of tables and chairs for us to take a seat. After ordering some coffee and a napolitana, I struck up a conversation with a woman sitting next to me. Her name was Cruz, and she was originally from La Coruña in Spain, but had been living in Ohio for many years.

"I was going to do the Camino in 2020, but then Covid happened," said Cruz. "I've always wanted to walk the French Camino. Ever since I was a little girl."

"What do you think so far?"

"It's very beautiful. My feet hurt from walking in these boots, but this is special for me. I'm thinking a lot about my father. He passed away a few years ago."

"I'm sorry to hear about your father."

"Come on, we better get moving."

Cruz and I walked together for a couple of kilometers until I pushed ahead of her. She had made some stops to take photos and videos of the surrounding countryside. The massive fields of bright yellow sunflowers were a sight to behold. And if it was not for the heat, I would have enjoyed it more. Cruz had given me a bit of a slingshot up the road, some much needed momentum.

The second half of the day was a scorching hot one. And as bizarre as it seems, I have almost no memory of what happened between that sit-down with Cruz and my arrival in Sahagún. There was, however, one thing that really stuck with me. Somewhere along the Camino, I stopped inside a hole-in-the-wall bar, in the middle of nowhere. All I wanted to drink was a cold can of Aquarius—the blue kind. It was the best. As I chugged the can, standing at the counter, I looked back and saw someone familiar sitting in a lounge chair, with their feet on a foot-rest. It was the woman I had seen at the sanctuary in Carrión de los Condes, soaking her feet in the kid-sized pool. She was a woman in her late 50s.

"Hey, I remember you," I said to the woman. She smiled. Her name was Melissa, and she was from the United States.

"You're doing really good," said Melissa.

"I'm in bad shape. These blisters on the bottom of my feet just keep getting worse. How did you get here so fast?"

"I took a taxi this morning. My ankle hurts too much to walk. But now I don't know what I'm going to do. I'm doing the Camino with my husband. If he keeps going, maybe I can follow him around in a taxi, but I don't know. It's just really disappointing. I was having such a good time, and I really wanted to finish. But I think my Camino is over," said Melissa. She had made it halfway to Santiago from St. Jean Pied de Port, and I could see how much it pained her to end the pilgrimage.

"You can always come back another year and finish," I said, trying to comfort her. But I knew in my heart of hearts it would not be enough. This was a once in a lifetime experience, and there was no guarantee anyone would have the chance to come back. After a few minutes, I said goodbye to Melissa, wished her the best, and continued on the Way.

From then on, rocks and stones of different sizes covered the Camino. They sent shots of pain through my feet and the rest of my body, especially when I landed on them unevenly. It was the constant pressure points on my sensitive blister bubbles that made every step a torturous experience. 5km outside Sahagún, my heart was beating out of control, and I was feeling delirious. The trail had led me over some rolling hills in the middle of nowhere. There were some tall bushes along the path, creating just enough shade for a person to stand in. I stopped for a few minutes, just long enough to catch my breath. My body was overheating. I contemplated vomiting off to the side, as I stood there hunched over, my long-sleeve shirt unzipped down to my stomach, with my necklaces dangling around my neck. But it was only getting hotter at 16:00 in the afternoon. I had to keep pushing.

Approaching town, a lightly wooded area provided a bit more reprieve from the desert-like heat. A few kilometers out from Sahagún, I walked over a stone-built bridge and passed by the Ermita de la Virgen del Puente, a hermitage dedicated to the Virgin Mary back in the thirteenth century. Built with brick, in a Mudejar style, the hermitage had one nave and a small chancel with a semi-hexagonal apse. The blind arches and corner friezes added to its beauty, despite its old and frail state. For years, the hermitage provided care for pilgrims on the French Way. Off to the left of the hermitage, there was a girl taking a nap on a flat-bed sculpture.

"You made it!" said the girl.

"What do you mean?"

"This is the geographical 'half-way' point along the Camino! This! This here!" she said, drawing an imaginary line with her finger. The girl's name was María. She was from Mexico. We exchanged a few pleasantries before I continued. I had to continue. I was running on fumes and needed to get to Sahagún as quickly as possible.

The trail left the lightly wooded area and took me back into the sun, where there were two tall statues, one on each side of the trail. The statue on the right looked like a knight in armor, with a sword pointing at the ground, while the one on the left looked like a priest or holy man carrying a bible close to his chest. After the statues, I could see Sahagún, the first town in the province of León.

My legs took me as far as the municipal albergue called Cluny, which was the old Church of the Trinity. As soon as I entered the former convent, it looked like a bomb had destroyed the ceiling. The brick walls that gave it its Mudejar style rose to a make-shift roof above. The downstairs area felt more like a chapel, where laundry services and bike storage were located. A squeaky wooden staircase took me up to the second floor, even though it felt much higher. The dormitory had over 60 bunk beds, spread out among eight rows of beds. Not wasting any time, I took a lower bunk bed in the first row. My feet were so swollen and beat up that I immediately removed my backpack, laid on my bed, and raised my feet as high as I could in the space-constricted bunk bed. There was an immediate relief when I did that.

An hour later, María showed up and took the bed next to mine. There was another girl in our row, but she was sleeping. As I rummaged around in my bag, the girl rolled over and introduced herself. Her name was Jojo. She was originally from Venezuela, but lived in North Carolina. Her personality was funny and upbeat.

"Ander, what is that? Are you taking pills right now!?" asked Jojo, as María wrapped her bed with a fitted paper sheet given to us at check-in.

"Yeah, it's acid. Goodbye…" I said to Jojo with a deviant smile. She burst into laughter.

"Wait, seriously, what the hell is that!?"

"Oh, it's Men's One-A-Day multivitamin. I gotta stay strong," I said, chuckling. Jojo kept laughing hysterically.

While I showered and got myself together for the evening, Jojo and María left the old church to go get their "Halfway Compostela." More formally known as the "Pilgrim Letter," this is a certificate that is provided by the Church of the Pilgrim in Sahagún. For three euros, you can get a one-page letter written in calligraphy, a nice souvenir to celebrate the geographical halfway point on the Camino. Souvenirs aside, it baffled me that something like this would be available. In a way, I felt like the Camino was tempting me to quit. I could barely walk without limping or using my trekking poles as crutches. But the concept of getting a trophy for not fully completing something was a mindset I could not adopt. I had cried too many tears the night before, praying for miracles. And I had made a promise that I was going to keep going, regardless of the pain.

The pharmacy was a few blocks down the hill from the old church, and I needed to stock up on supplies. The bursting of the blister on my foot, as well as its resurgence, needed additional bandaging, and I was skeptical of using Compeed to remedy the problem. After all, the Compeed pads cushioned areas with oncoming blisters. They did not heal infected flesh that had disbursed puss and blood everywhere. Instead, I stocked up on some large bandages, making sure they were water resistant so that I could shower with them on. I bought a couple of extra boxes so that I could cut some into small, custom bandages to wrap around my toes.

When I started my nightly "surgery" at the church, I had virtually zero light to work with. There were no lights on the ceiling, and no lamps on the bunk beds. We had one light in the bathroom and another in the kitchen area. And I had too much respect for my fellow pilgrims to take care of my business in either of those spots. So, I sat down on the floor in front of my bunk and used my cell phone flashlight to illuminate my feet. I had grabbed a huge wad of toilet paper to absorb the puss and fluid that drained out of my blisters. With the flashlight in one hand and my needles in the other, I had to be extremely careful not to stab myself on accident. I did a few times. I do not recommend it. An hour later, fluid and puss-soaked toilet paper and crinkled up medical tape covered the floor. And bandage wrappers were stuck to my arms and legs. Then Jojo walked by.

"Oh my God, what are you doing!?" asked Jojo.

"Honestly, I don't know what the hell I'm doing."

"Do you have blisters?" asked Jojo. Then I showed her my feet. She covered her mouth with her hands. Judging by her reaction, I knew the situation was not normal. She thought I was crazy. Even so, I remained convinced that I had to do it. There would not be an early victory for me. No halftime celebrations or piles of confetti. My ability to survive until the next day was my celebration. And my pile of used needles, alcohol pads, and medical supplies were my confetti.

I thought back to when I watched the killer whale documentary at dinner. The scene was so incredibly violent; the whale capturing an innocent seal or sea lion puppy, then tearing it to shreds, as a wave carried it back into the ocean. What I realized later was the risk the whale took to hunt its prey. By intentionally beaching itself, the killer whale risked being stranded on the sand. The whale risked being crushed, since it could not support its own weight while out of water. And if the whale could not return to the water within a couple of hours, it would die. Whether it was a seal, a sea lion puppy, or any other prey it was after, it was stunningly admirable of the whale to risk death to capture it. The whale's action was a true testament to its will and desire to live, by risking its very own survival. As grim as it sounded, I was willing to die on that Camino. I mean that with the utmost respect for life, and for those who no longer enjoy it—God rest their souls. "I am the killer whale," I thought to myself. And with all my heart, mind, and spirit, I was putting my faith first, beaching myself on the sacred trails of the Camino, waiting for a wave to carry me to Santiago. For me, death was a motivating factor.

CHAPTER TWELVE:

BEAUTY IN MISERY

"Ah, dear Juliet,
Why art thou yet so fair? Shall I believe
That unsubstantial death is amorous,
And that the lean abhorrèd monster keeps
Thee here in dark to be his paramour?"

—Romeo, *Romeo and Juliet*.

In the medieval city of Verona, Italy, two families have been feuding for centuries: the Montague family and the Capulet family. Romeo, son of the Montagues, has fallen in love with Juliet, daughter of the Capulets. The two struggle to keep their flame alive amid family bloodshed. Things take a turn for the worse when they banish Romeo from Verona, after he kills Juliet's cousin. Juliet's father arranges for her to marry a man named Paris, not knowing that Juliet has already secretly married Romeo. To avoid this disaster, Juliet, with the help of Friar Lawrence, concocts a plan of escape. Juliet will take a potion that makes her appear dead, and unable to marry Paris. Then, when she awakens, she will run away with Romeo and leave the dreadful history of Verona behind. But things do not go as planned.

I was nine years old when I saw *Romeo and Juliet* in 1996. The film was an adaptation of the famous play by William Shakespeare. I remember how it captivated people's imagination. It made them smile, and it made them laugh. But it also made them sad, and it made them cry. The story was the intersection of love, hope, hate, fear, and, ultimately, death. As a kid, I could not grasp why people found it so appealing. How could a movie about death illicit feelings of such heart-wrenching pain and sorrow, and also such heartwarming love and joy?

Albeit a Hollywood movie, *Romeo and Juliet* was my introduction to the famous playwright. For hundreds of years, William Shakespeare's plays have captivated readers and audiences across the world. From movie adaptations to Broadway plays, Shakespeare tuned into something unique. He tapped into the spirit of the human condition. He achieved the same effect with *Hamlet*. In this play, Shakespeare exposes the elements of life that drive us all—two of them being love and revenge. Hamlet is told to avenge his father's death by killing his uncle, the new king. Few of us are royal, and few of us will ever become royal, yet these plots reach inside and touch us all profoundly. There is a reason Shakespeare struck a chord with us, much like there was a reason I continued the Camino.

The windowless church stifled us inside the albergue at night. I was sweating in my bunk bed, tossing and turning on my fitted paper sheet. The plastic casing around the bed prevented the heat from escaping my body, causing my shirt to be drenched in sweat. I woke up around 03:15 in the morning, as someone made noise leaving the church. Laying in a puddle of sweaty nastiness, I got up to leave too. It was always best to pack up as much of your gear as possible the night before, to avoid waking up other pilgrims. And there were some 60 of them sound asleep. I took my shirt off, rolled up my bed liner, packed away my charging cables, and tiptoed down the creaky wooden stairs. Leaving the church, I left the main door open by a crack, just in case I forgot something. If the door closed, there was no way to get back inside.

In the dead of night, the streetlamps illuminated enough of the road for me to start the Camino. Day 12 was a 43km hike to Puente Villarente. Every time I jabbed my trekking poles into the ground, the clacking sounds reverberated off the surrounding apartment buildings on the quiet streets. But I had other things on my mind. I was walking on one leg—correction: hopping on one leg. There was a bridge at the edge of town, where I stopped for a moment to breathe and re-tie my shoes. The streetlights were fading, and it was only a matter of time before I had to pull out my headlamp. Once I had it on my head, I turned on the light. It was like I was in the middle of a snow flurry. Moths, big and small, started flying at my face. It seemed like the lamp was attracting all the moths in The Meseta. I tried frantically to swat them away. Some even started landing on the light bulb itself, encircling the light until it faded. I had to smack my forehead a few times. But one thing was for sure: there was no way I could have seen the path ahead of me without the lamp. It was pitch-black out there. Even with the lamp, there were still holes in the ground and uneven gravel trails. It was hard enough.

Four hours and 18km later, the sun was up, and the lamp was no longer needed. It was 17:30 when I entered El Burgo Ranero. There was a big, elegant cross erected at the entrance to the village, which was dedicated to Rufino Baños Lozano. The story goes Rufino was a soccer star in León, around the time of the Spanish Civil War. At the tail end, he escaped to France, and then joined the French army at the onset of World War II. During the war, the Nazis captured Rufino and his battalion and took them to a concentration camp. Miraculously, he survived. He was liberated by the Allies in 1945. Rufino lived the rest of his years in France, dying as an old man in 1980. His son, Jose María Baños Lozano, erected the statue in his father's honor. It was a beautifully touching tribute to a man who had experienced hell on earth.

Camino Real was the street that took me through the center of the village of El Burgo Ranero. I stopped at the first bar I saw. It was called Pensión Restaurante La Costa del Adobe. Having been up since 03:15, I was hungrier than usual. Besides my usual coffee with milk, I ordered some sliced jamon on toasted bread, lightly drizzled with some olive oil—delicious! Even though I sat down at a table, I kept trying to move my feet underneath, applying whatever pressure I could, hoping to minimize further inflammation and the expansion of the blister bubbles. While my feet danced around underneath the table, I heard a man speaking in English at the counter. It was American English. He was older than me, probably in his late 50s or early 60s. After finishing up my meal, I collected my things and stepped outside onto the terrace. The American was finishing his coffee, next to a woman. I introduced myself.

"Hey, I heard you speaking English. You're American right?" I asked.

"Yeah, I'm from Florida. Well, I'm originally from Illinois, but I've lived in Florida for the past 20 years," he said. His name was Michael.

"Did you stay here overnight?" asked the woman next to him. Her name was Kathy, and she looked to be the same age as Michael. Although she too was originally from Illinois, she met Michael on the Camino.

"No, I started early this morning in Sahagún. Someone left at 3 o'clock in the morning, making a bunch of noise, and I couldn't go back to sleep."

"You don't have ear plugs?" asked Michael.

"I did, but I lost them," I said. Michael and Kathy started getting up from their chairs, clipping on their backpacks, and grabbing their trekking poles.

"Want to walk with us?" asked Michael.

"Yeah, let's do it." It was a 13km walk to the next town of Reliegos. Over the next hour, we made some small talk, just to get to know each other a little better.

"Did you both start in St. Jean Pied de Port?" I asked Michael and Kathy.

"Yeah, but we didn't meet until later on," said Michael.

"I was walking with my sister, but she hurt her leg. Today she's taking a taxi from El Burgo Ranero to Reliegos, so we'll meet her later today," said Kathy.

In my injured state, my limping pace was still enough to lead the three of us through The Meseta. After breakfast, we spent the entire time walking on a dirt trail covered in gravel. At one point, Michael hopped over the ditch to the highway that ran parallel to the trail. Every pilgrim had their own techniques or at least attempted to experiment with changing surfaces—anything that could help ease the pain. From time to time, we stumbled upon a peaceful rolling hill, while intense heat, wheat fields, and masses of yellow sunflowers encircled us. As we progressed down the path, it just kept going straight. There was nothing to look forward to. Sometimes, Michael would call out our pace per hour, just to let us know we were making progress. Other than that, it was quiet among the three of us. I think that was a sign of our comfort with one another. It was quiet, but comfortable. Silent, but not boring. I could think, and I could process. Part of that thinking was about the Cruz de Ferro.

The Cruz de Ferro, or "The Iron Cross," is a wooden post with a cross at the very top. The cross stands at the highest point on the Camino, between the towns of Manjarín and Foncebadón—I was about four days away from passing it. At the base of the post, there is a huge mound of rocks and pebbles of all shapes and sizes. There is a tradition where pilgrims collect a small rock, either from home or on the Camino, and then leave it at the base of the post. This action symbolizes pilgrims leaving all of their burdens behind. I asked Michael about the cross.

"We're not that far from the Cruz de Ferro," I said to Michael. "Did you bring a rock with you?"

"Yeah, I got one in my suitcase that I brought from Florida," he said. Michael had sent his luggage forward using the courier service. He strained his shoulder, so he made the rest of the Camino with a light daysack, and sent his other gear to the next albergue.

"I didn't bring a rock from Miami. I'll have to find one before I get to the cross."

"I actually brought a couple of rocks with me," said Michael.

"Really? Why not just the one?"

"I brought one for me, and one for my fiancé."

"Oh OK, that's really nice of you. She couldn't make it to the Camino?"

"Well, we were going to do it together, but then she was diagnosed with cancer. She passed away a few months ago," said Michael. My heart sank.

"Oh... I'm sorry to hear that."

"Nancy was the one who really wanted to do the Camino. She loved to travel and was always so adventurous. And after she died, I made a promise to complete the journey for us. That's why I brought an extra rock with me."

"I'm sure she's with you in spirit."

"In a way, it's like she's with me. I only carry two things in my daysack: a bottle of water and a box with her ashes."

Behind the smiles, the small talk and laughter, Michael had suffered greatly. I realized he was carrying the burden of his late-fiancé. These were the kinds of moments and conversations that helped tie the Camino to a tapestry of human emotion. The Camino was a place of spiritual openness, a place of comfort for the suffering, one that is difficult to articulate.

About 5km before Reliegos, like clockwork, I ran out of water. I had forgotten to refill my water bottles at breakfast. As we got closer to town, there was another massive field with sunflowers. There was also an irrigation system that was watering the plants. Along the trail, there were some black rubber pipes sticking out from the field. The pipes looked broken as they poured out water onto the trail. It took every ounce of strength and common sense not to drop to the ground and drink the water. Surely, it was not potable water. And there was a good chance they had infused the water with fertilizer or plant nutrients. But watching the clear, refreshing-looking water being wasted like that was torturous.

In Reliegos, I stopped at a bar with Michael and Kathy. We ordered up some ice-cold cans of Coca-Cola and relaxed on the terrace under an umbrella. After a few minutes, we had to drag a second umbrella over to our table, as even the slightest bit of sunlight burned our skin. Before I left, we talked about my pilgrimage and mission to complete the Camino in 20 days. As I mentioned previously, there were only a few times when I told people about the 20-day mission. There were some haters out there. But maybe it was nothing personal, just the reflection of their own insecurities that shined through. Michael and Kathy were supportive, and said they would think about me on July 4th, when I planned to arrive in Santiago. We said our goodbyes and wished each other a "Buen Camino."

The arduous afternoon brought heat and suffering, but the town of Mansilla de las Mulas helped break up the remaining kilometers to Puente Villarente. I stopped at a bar for some tortilla, a quick refreshment, then pushed on, crossing a 150-meter bridge over the Esla River. There were people bathing in the water down below, near a rope swing that was tied to a long branch that extended out over the river. After the bridge, the Camino continued next to the highway, where the Civil Guard had set up a roadblock. The Civil Guard is the oldest law enforcement agency in Spain. They patrol rural areas all over the country, including highways and ports. From there, the path descended into a wooded area well below the highway. As I walked, I looked up and saw an officer exiting the Nissan patrol car from the passenger side. He looked down at me as he slowly stepped around the car, adjusting his belt. The off-road path blessed me with some shade, which led to a bridge across the Porma River and into Puente Villarente. I became a little teary-eyed when crossing the river into town. The end of each stage felt increasingly more significant. Almost like the mission was bigger than me. The emotion also stemmed from the fact that only 13km separated me from the city of León, which the Spanish consider the official "end" of The Meseta.

That night, I stayed at Albergue San Pelayo. The place was different. It used to be a cow barn but was now an albergue. Following the remodel, it still preserved the "bones" of the original structure. Like a typical Spanish barn, the interior flooring still ramped down with a gradient. The backyard had a bar that wrapped around the back of the house, complete with a patio and a neatly landscaped yard in the middle. But the cows were gone, and the pilgrims were in. And there were only a handful of pilgrims staying the night. We were a mix of different nationalities: American, French, Israeli, Italian, and Spanish. The host of the albergue served us a three-course meal. We enjoyed it communally, all of us sitting together at the dinner table. It started off with a mixed salad made of lettuce, tomato, carrots, corn, and tuna, drizzled with olive oil and vinegar. Next came the chicken legs and thighs. After that, we settled our stomachs with some digestive-supportive yogurt. Before I went to bed, I tried refilling my water bottles using the bathroom sink, but the water was dark brown—it was scary. I left the faucet on for a couple of minutes, but the color did not change. I had no intention of drinking it. I had come too far on the Camino to be taken out by rust or fecal-polluted water, calling off my mission because of an explosive case of diarrhea. Luckily, I spotted a water fountain on the way into Puente Villarente, about 100 meters from the albergue.

In the dark, early morning hours, I left the albergue and walked toward the fountain. The skies were clear, as the moonlight illuminated the path in front of me. The fountain was just off the road, under a cluster of tall and leafy trees. Despite the darkness, the shiny release valve guided me to the fountain. Alone in the dark, I refilled my bottles. Then, a whispering voice startled me.

"Are you on the Camino?" said a woman from behind, sending chills down my spine. My head spun so quickly I thought it was about to fly off. It was an elderly woman standing just a foot away.

"Oh, hey, I didn't see you… yes, I'm on the Camino… just getting some water before I start."

"I'm too old to do the Camino. I'm 86, you see?" she asked rhetorically. Hunched over in her frail state, she wore a light sweater draped over her shoulders.

"Do you live here?"

"I don't live far. But I wake up each morning and do my chores.

Then, maybe I come down to the fountain."

"This early in the morning?" I asked. It was 04:30.

"I like to see the pilgrims… yes, I like to see the pilgrims. You see, my body is not what it used to be. I'm much older now. The end is near…"

"Oh, come on," I said, trying to talk her down.

"I used to be young like you. Can you believe it?" said the elderly woman, as we smiled for a few moments. I could tell her mind was elsewhere.

"I better get going."

"Buen Camino," said the woman.

"Buen Camino." I then stepped out of the darkness and back into the moonlight.

I thought about what the old woman had said about her age, and how she daydreamed about her youth. Her morning walks to the fountain seemed to be a bridge to the past, a bridge to happier times. But those happier times only seemed so in contrast to her life as an old woman. Like *Romeo and Juliet*, the beauty of the Camino was unveiling itself through a prism of suffering. "What is beauty without suffering?" I wondered. I also wondered why she walked to the fountain in the dark. Maybe she felt her whole life had passed her by. And maybe her strolls in the dark, while the entire world was asleep, gave her the feeling that she was still alive. Maybe it was her poetic desire to cherish her little time left on this earth. With thoughts like these, I was not sure whether to smile or cry.

My Camino to Santiago was curating a newfound purpose in me. The beauty was not in its traditional form of colorful flowers, flowing rivers, or Roman architecture. It was difficult to localize, but with every step, and every kilometer, I was beginning to see the true beauty. My body was breaking down, and another was being built up—not in flesh, but in spirit. And tragedy and sorrow were the backdrop of a profound love and beauty hidden deep within the soul. It was almost time to say goodbye to The Meseta.

CHAPTER THIRTEEN:

GOODBYE, MESETA

"Two workers have died as a result of the high temperatures of recent days. Today, a farmer died in Cinco Casas. On Saturday, another 47-year-old man died from heat stroke working in an agricultural farm in Aznalcoya," said the news anchor on RTVE, Spain's state-owned news company. I was watching the newscast at Bar Santa Fe, in the industrial outskirts of León. They were covering the heat wave that had been passing through Spain in the last week. The deadly heat had caused a couple of farmers to drop dead while working in the open fields. I reflected on the times I was at my limit in The Meseta, ready to tip over and die. After watching the newscast, it did not seem so farfetched. I had spent four long days in the Spanish plateau, and it seemed like it would never end. But on Day 13, I was preparing to put it all behind me. After some coffee and glazed doughnuts at the bar, I left the industrial zone and crossed a bridge over a major highway. For the first time, I could finally see the city of León down below in the distance. The end of The Meseta was upon me.

The entrance to León began on a slanted sidewalk. With the sun still rising in the east, I walked in the shade provided by apartment buildings. The city of León is the capital of the province of León, which is part of the autonomous community of Castilla y León—confused yet? Anyhow, the beautiful city has Roman roots, and at one point served as the home of the Seventh Legion—a legion of the Imperial Roman army. The legion deployed in the year 74, and remained for over 300 years. León also has ties to the Knights Templar, who built castles there and in the surrounding areas. The Knights Templar was a military order of the Catholic belief, whose mission was to protect European pilgrims visiting the Holy Land. Although the seventh legion and the Knights Templar have been gone for centuries, the city of León still basks in its historic beauty.

It was about 08:30 when I passed through the city center. The narrow roads, the cobblestone streets, this place had it all. It was no surprise that pilgrims often stayed an extra night or two. And although I did not stop in the city, I observed two places along the way: the León Cathedral and the Parador de León. Although constructed later than other Spanish churches, the León Cathedral stands on the site of second-century Roman baths. They converted the Roman baths into a palace for King Ordoño II, who later gave up his palace and pledged to build a cathedral. This cathedral was to be built as a showing of gratitude to God for helping him beat the Arabs during a battle in the tenth century. Today, the remains of King Ordoño II are buried in the León Cathedral. I stopped my limping for a momentary gaze up at the cathedral, taking in the sight of its illustrious façade, as well as the towers on the left and right sides. The second landmark for me was the Parador de León. Nestled beside the Bernesga River, the Parador is a luxury hotel, and is part of a larger network of state-run hotels, of which there are 96 in Spain. The one in León is one of the most famous, if not the most famous. The hotel began as a hospital in the sixteenth century, and later became a school, prison, office and more. Originally built with a donation from King Ferdinand II, the hospital served pilgrims along the Camino de Santiago. But what made it special to me was that the fancy hotel was actually in the movie *The Way*, when Tom (Martin Sheen) invites his friends to crash at the famous Parador for a night. Together, they wine and dine, receive spa-like treatment, and wear bathrobes around their swanky rooms. I limped a little slower as I passed by, in awe of the large square in front of the hotel, giving way to the elegant façade. As did Burgos in the days earlier, the city of León offered a distraction from my pain as the saga of the bubble blisters continued. After the Parador, I crossed the bridge over the Bernesga River and headed west. Day 13 was a 45km day, all the way to Hospital de Órbigo.

Outside of León, I stopped at a pharmacy, hoping to find something for inflammation. I walked out with a small box of ibuprofen, anti-inflammatory spray, and some more needles. Small needles were the most difficult to find. In León, I needed the help of two pharmacists to pillage the back of the pharmacy to find them. And when they did, they only had a few, like all the other pharmacies I visited. That day, I thought my Achilles tendons were going to detach from my heels. Adding to the difficulties, my calf muscles kept going into spasms. Along the way, I suspected that my elastic knee braces may have been the culprits, but then I rolled them up and even removed them at one point, which did not help at all. So, I whipped out the aerosol spray with anti-inflammatory chemicals and went to town on my lower extremities. However, it only took a couple of kilometers before the pain returned, even after popping a few pills of ibuprofen. Some pilgrims say it is a bad idea to take ibuprofen or aspirin when walking the Camino. The reason is that pills make you less sensitive to pain, which alerts you to the damage you are causing your body—disturbing the natural alarm system, if you will. But I was walking 10-12 hours a day, with sustained levels of pain, and I was willing to try anything to help take the edge off.

The pain was so bad that day that I deployed a new strategy: do not sit down. Earlier that morning, when I had grabbed breakfast and watched the newscast, I stood at the bar the entire time. Even after standing idly for a few minutes, it took me at least 30 minutes to regain a semi-normal walking pace. It was a bad sign. The blisters kept getting worse, the pain kept getting worse, and worst of all, I still had no idea what was happening underneath the Compeed pads that were literally glued to the bottom of my feet. Nonetheless, my thinking was that if I did not sit down, I would save myself the pain and misfortune of having to start all over again.

Still on my feet after the pharmacy visit, I found a bar along the Camino, where I grabbed another slice of tortilla, along with some French bread—I needed to pack in some calories. I paced back and forth while waiting for the bartender to warm up the food. There were a couple of Norwegian girls at the bar as well; they were ordering popsicles. We left the bar around the same time, where the next several kilometers led us up a gradual ascent along the roadway. I was out in front of them for the first couple of kilometers, until we hit a few steep patches of terrain, when my calves started spasming again. After stepping off to the side of the trail, I used a Camino marker to stretch out my calves, hoping I could relax the muscle. As the Norwegians approached, I took out my bottle of anti-inflammatory spray and covered my leg with it. Moments later, the two girls passed me up. Determined not to be left behind, I grinded it out to stay with them for as long as I could; I was in a deep suffer mode. As I huffed and puffed, I would look up from the ground every few seconds, just to keep the girls in view. But little by little, I was falling behind. The girls would sometimes disappear for moments at a time if there was a bend in the path. When I came out of the turn, they would be a little further along. This went on for a few hours until I completely lost sight of them. Eventually, I saw them again while they were taking a break on the side of the Camino. They were eating lunch underneath a tree, enjoying the much-needed shade it provided.

"I would be doing the same thing as you, but I wouldn't be able to get back up," I said to them as I limped by.

"Oh, come on, we would help you!" said the Norwegian girls with kindness. They looked like a good time. But it was already 14:00 in the afternoon, and my "no-sit" policy was still in effect.

I had plenty of water for the next 12km until I reached Hospital de Órbigo. That was not an issue. What became an issue was the sudden swelling I was feeling in my feet. The pain was worse than ever. I considered spraying my feet with the aerosol, but I knew that if I took off my socks, the melted Compeed pads would be stuck, and I might tear my skin. So, again, I kept walking.

I coasted into town on fumes, completely alone in the sweltering summer heat. I beat my chest like a silverback gorilla, celebrating my arrival, and probably leaving a bruise with the violent impact of my fist. There were over 10 albergues in Hospital de Órbigo. When the first one picked up the phone, there was availability, but the host was giving me grief. His Spanish was Latin American, and even though I had spent most of my life living in the United States, the guy's vocabulary was a little foreign to me.

"Where do you originate from?" asked the man.

"Sorry, I'm not sure I understand the question."

"Do you even speak Spanish!?"

"Yes, I speak Spanish. I'm just confused by the word you used."

"Where do you originate from? Where do you come from? What town did you leave from this morning? Where do you hail from? Where did you come from?" he said condescendingly. This went on for about half a minute. When he finally finished, I answered his question.

"Puente Villarente."

"Call back tomorrow. Maybe something happens and you don't make it here," he said, not knowing I was doing two stages in one day.

"Sir, I'm already here. I just made it to Hospital de Órbigo."

"Oh… well, we have a bed available."

"Great, thank you." I was fuming after that conversation. It was the end of the day. Tired, hungry, angry, I pushed on into town.

The entrance to Hospital de Órbigo is famous for its thirteenth century stone bridge that spans 200 meters. Crossing the bridge over the Órbigo River, I was passing over a legendary site. They purposely destroyed the original bridge in the nineteenth century to slow down Napoleon's army. But what really made this site a place of legendary tales was something entirely different: it was the jousting tournament of 1434.

The story goes that Don Suero de Quiñones, a knight from León, hosted a tournament in 1434. He had fallen in love with a woman who did not feel the same way. The knight, overcome with sorrow, wore a metal collar to show his pain and suffering. Going a step further, he organized a jousting tournament as an ultimate means of relieving himself from the burden. He gathered up some of his closest friends, as they all took turns breaking lances on their challengers—300 in total. Following his victory, Don Suero had his metal collar removed in a ceremony. This was all done at the site of the 200-meter stone bridge I was walking across.

Nearing the end of the bridge, I noticed that the first building on the left was a hostel. The one I planned to stay at was another five minutes further into town. Not thinking twice, I went up the steps to Hostal Don

Suero de Quiñones (the namesake of the legendary love-stricken knight) and stayed there instead. My feet hurt so badly from all the pressure and swelling that I laid down with my shoes up, panting in pain, and looking for relief, as the blood flowed away from my feet. I held that position until I could slow down my breathing. Over the course of 45km walked during an 11-hour day, I had not stopped to sit down once, and I paid for it. That was the last time I did that. But the pain was not over.

When I placed my feet back on the ground to untie my shoes, the pressure returned instantaneously. Racing to get the shoes off, I tore a layer of skin on the bottom of my feet at the peak of the arch. As I had feared, the wool socks had glued to my feet. Suddenly, there was another pain to worry about. The socks were crusty and covered in dried fluid, while my skin remained smothered in blistery goo. The area of the blister kept expanding. I could now see a purple bubble forming around the bottom of the Compeed pad toward my heel. I pressed it a few times to gauge the pain, and when I did, I saw little crust-like flakes moving around inside the bubble. It was not good. The first thing that came to mind was "infection." Against the advice of pharmacists who had told me never to pop a blood blister, I did it anyway. The thought of an infection was more of a problem to me than bleeding. So, I used the sharp edge of a small needle to make an incision, leaking out most of the fluid. There were wads of toilet paper on my bed, as I tried to keep the bed clear of the nasty blister juice. I held my foot at an angle and poured in as much iodine as I could. I felt every bit of that iodine coursing through. When I was done, I popped and bandaged the smaller blisters on my toes.

That evening, I was feeling extremely hungry, having not rested at all during the day. There was a tiny market next door to the hostel, where I ravaged the shelves and deli for an epic feast. My red shopping basket included jamon and sheep cheese (enough for three sandwiches), a large can of green Spanish olives with anchovies, a Kit-Kat bar, a Snickers bar, three juice-box-sized cartons of chocolate milk and three of orange juice, one package of dried corn seeds, one package of walnuts, and two 100ml bottles of Aquarius. I ate almost everything that night, saving a few boxes of chocolate milk and the packet of corn seeds for a future binge down the road.

Still full from my pig-out the night before, I hit the road early the next morning. If Day 13 was the end of The Meseta, Day 14 would be the encore—not because of the terrain, which was much steeper in some areas compared to The Meseta, but because of the tiny reward I would get in Foncebadón. At 05:30, I began the 43km trek. In the dark, I turned on my light, which had been my companion for the last few days, since I was leaving an hour or more before dawn. The first major checkpoint for the day was a town called Astorga, 17km away. Pavement typically destroyed my Achilles, but I welcomed it that morning, since I experienced fewer bumps on the bottom of my feet. The gradual ascent to 900 meters of elevation led to the

Santo Toribio stone cross. It stood there elegantly, encircled by a large concrete ring, making it the focal point of attention. Rocks and stones of all sizes cluttered the concrete blocks at the base of the cross. It was a glimpse of what was to come at the Cruz de Ferro. Fields, trees, and some red and pink roses surrounded the cross, but the best part was the view down into Astorga—I could see most of the town from above.

The descent into Astorga was very steep. At first, it was feeling more urban again, walking by apartment buildings on both sides of the road. From there, the Camino took a detour back into the fields. The bright-yellow sunflowers that lined the path reminded me of The Meseta. The sunflowers then gave way to a path behind an agricultural building, surrounded by nothing but cornfields. I remember the sides of the building being defaced with graffiti, something I often saw on the Camino. The graffiti was not always in poor taste. In fact, most of it was usually friendly—"Come on Samantha! You can do this!" or "Only 270 kilometers to go… you are getting closer!" are just a few examples. The writing was usually big enough for me to read as I walked by. After going up five flights of stairs of a pedestrian bridge, in order to cross a set of train tracks, I came face to face with a punishingly steep hill on Calle de la Puerta Sol. My Achillies tendons were on the verge of detaching and recoiling like a snake after getting its head cutoff. But, nonetheless, I made it to the top.

Walking through Astorga, I passed ancient Roman ruins at the Plaza Romana, beautiful statues, gardens, and a plethora of bars in the old town. There was a bakery that served coffee, along with homemade biscuit cookies, so I made a quick stop. There was a family from Colorado sitting a few tables away from me. We exchanged a few laughs about the joys (and pains) of Camino life, appreciating its many quirks. Things like washing clothes by hand, people with sleep apnea in the bed next to you, and searching for clean bathrooms. But we also chatted about how lucky we were to be out there on the Way, following in the footsteps of other pilgrims over a thousand years ago. After chugging my coffee, I left Astorga through the Puerta Obispo (Obispo Gate), which gave an exit from the walled city.

Although it started on a sidewalk, it was not long before the Camino turned back into a rocky, gravel trail. The terrain was steep, as I passed the villages of Valdeviejas, Murias de Rechivaldo, and Castrillo de los Polvazares, all of which were very close together. With another 17km still to go, I made a second stop in Santa Catalina de Somoza. The bar was called Albergue El Caminante. Although I love the Basque Country, and places like Pamplona and Puente la Reina, the rest of Spain will typically serve you a free tapa with every drink order. This was common practice in the broader Spanish territory, but not in the Basque region. My Coke Zero came with a plate of two chorizo sausages. Locally sourced, they had an incredibly juicy and delicious taste. While I stuffed my face, I met another American. His name was David, and he was from North Carolina. David had a long career in the food industry, most recently serving as a Vice President, in charge of Wolfgang Puck's frozen food distribution.

"It seems like everywhere I stop for food on the Camino, it's always the same food," said David. "Beans, lentils, chorizo, eggs, tortilla, and bread... lots of bread."

"They do eat lots of bread," I said, still digesting the fact that he had rattled off some of Spain's most treasured meals.

"What I'd really like to do is open my own restaurant along the Camino."

"What would you serve?"

"I haven't found one place that serves organic and gluten-free food. I think that would take off. Plus, I've already talked to some local farmers near Pamplona that said I could work out a supply deal with them," said David. He was an energetic guy. After the Coke Zero and chorizo, we got back on the Camino together.

"Just give me a second," I said.

"Whoa... you're limping," said David.

"I know. I have blisters on the bottom of my feet. Whenever I sit down and take the pressure off, the bubbles feel like they swell and fill with fluid. Then, it takes me at least 30-45 minutes to go from a one-legged limp to a half-normal motion again. It's like the blisters need time to flatten out or something."

"You should really let me take a look at your feet. I was a medic in the Navy."

"Really? I don't know, they're pretty bad." Each day, it took me longer to establish a normal pace. Sometimes it happened sooner, when I felt a release of fluid, probably from the constant pressure I was applying to the blister bubbles.

We walked together for the next hour, along with another pilgrim David had met on the Camino. He was from Italy. David and I joked he looked like Bradley Cooper. But he kept to himself and barely uttered any words. David said the guy liked to meditate while walking, so we let him do his thing. After 4km, we reached a village called El Ganso. David and his Italian friend stopped for food at a restaurant next to the trail. I contemplated it, especially since David had offered to look at my feet, but I knew I had a decision to make. There were 13km still to go to Foncebadón, and most of it was a grueling climb to the top. It was getting late in the afternoon, and the heat was taking shape. If I stopped again, it might have taken me an hour to regain my momentum. So, I stopped in for a few minutes to refill my water bottles and continued on the route. David was understanding and hoped to see me in Foncebadón.

The highway was my companion as I made the gradual ascent toward

Rabanal del Camino. I encountered a large pine forest, which was a change of pace from my surroundings in The Meseta. The mountains of León were waiting for me in the distance. The flat and desolate terrain was being replaced with steep mountain climbs. I spotted the remains of ancient Roman gold mines along the way, but I did not bother looking for gold. Further on, the trail deviated from the road and took a sharp turn up the mountain. I had seen a group of pilgrims loitering in the area just before it, which made a lot more sense after I started up the steep ascent—it was treacherous. Large rocks and stones cluttered the path in front, waiting for someone to lose their concentration just for a moment—it was a sprained ankle waiting to happen. But at least I was ascending and not descending. In the meantime, I picked up a small rock the size of a gumball. I wanted to save it for when I made it to the Cruz de Ferro. The climb was hard, but short, and soon the surface leveled out into a narrow bike-path-like trail. Overgrown grass shrank the walking path as I moved through the forest. The barbwire fence on the right was full of religious crosses. Pilgrims had used sticks from the forest to make the crosses, then used pieces of twine to secure them to the barbwire. The display of crosses continued until the Camino led back to the highway.

The path ramped up again as I entered Rabanal del Camino. In cycling terms, I was beginning to "bonk," or feel like my muscles were running out of fuel. Skipping lunch saved me time, but I had gone through my energy reserves. The corn seeds would not cut it; I needed the sugar and calories of a Coca-Cola, which luckily, I found at a bar in town. But the worst of the climbing had not even started yet. Before long, I was back amidst the pine and oak forests, which gave a fresh scent to the air. But the struggle was on, as the village road turned into a narrow, rocky mountain trail. The twists and turns of the trail served as a distraction, as did the constant focus of my eyes on the stones below me. Rabanal del Camino was at an elevation of 1,153 meters, while Foncebadón shot up to 1,430 meters. This, after I had already ascended from the lower elevation of 820 meters in Hospital de Órbigo. It took me two hours to bridge the 6km gap between Rabanal del Camino and Foncebadón. It was not the hardest climb of the Camino, but it was hammering me in my weak condition. I beat my chest again with my fist when I entered the town. There were albergues and farmhouses, as well as a large cross cemented into the middle of the street.

The most moving part of this walk, and perhaps of the last several days, happened when I turned around for a moment. From an elevation of 1,430 meters, the mountain provided a 180-degree unobstructed view—it was priceless. From Astorga to The Meseta, I could see it all. But it was time to say goodbye. It was jarring to think about how far I had come. Through all the blisters, muscle spasms, fatigue, and the constant grind, I was beginning to feel like a different person. Rather than fighting the Camino every day, I was learning to open myself up. I was beginning to feel more open to the unknown, even if I had yet to let go of some of the anger that manifested itself through the pain and suffering I was enduring. The man I was before felt more distant than the man I was now, even though I still had 242km to go.

CHAPTER FOURTEEN:

JUST LET GO

It was Christmas Eve, 1993. My mother grabbed the Basque cheesecake from the refrigerator and placed it on the table, next to the brandy, cognac, and anisette. My father bit off the tip of his fresh cigar and fired it up, puffing a few clouds of smoke up into the dining room light. Across from my father, my grandfather stirred his glass of chamomile tea, while he poured in sugar and anisette. I sat at the foot of the Christmas tree with my two sisters, anxiously waiting to open our presents, as we did every Christmas eve. When it was time, I tore open the biggest box I could find, shredding the bright red wrapping paper. My eyes lit up when I saw it—the Nintendo Entertainment System. And next to the console, one of the bestselling games in Nintendo history—Super Mario Bros. 3. I stayed up all night playing that game, while my mother fell asleep on the living room sofa watching me. I was on a mission to save Princess Toadstool from Bowser, fighting my way through the seven kingdoms of the game. The best part was being able to hit the reset button whenever I was having a bad game, or whenever my lives ran out. I was always one button away from a new start, a fresh beginning. It was simpler that way.

Back on the Camino, I had spent the night at an old convent in Foncebadón. Instead of playing Super Mario Bros. 3, I was feasting on beef fillets and plates full of French fries. David and the Italian guy were staying at the convent as well. When they rolled into town, a few hours after I did, the Italian guy came down to the dining room, where I was eating dinner. Although he was previously silent during the hike, as he went into meditation mode, he took a moment to come over and say hello.

"How are you doing, buddy?" said the Bradley Cooper look-alike, curling back his hair and patting me on the back.

"I'm alive," I said, bringing my feet out from under the table.

"Oh my God! How are you walking like this!?" he said, pointing to my open-toed flip flops. Torn, stained, and worn-out medical tape covered my toes completely.

"I know, right? It's the price I'm paying."

"You know how this is possible? It's because of this… your mind," he said, pointing to his temple with a focused stare, not blinking once. "If you have a strong mind, you are more likely to have success in life."

"Thanks man, I appreciate."

"Listen, David and I are going up the street to the tavern to eat dinner. When you are ready, come join us for beers."

"Alright, I'll see how I'm feeling in a little bit." It was 20:00 in the evening, and I needed to change my bandages and perform the rest of my "surgery." There was no chance I would go out for beers, and even less of a chance that David could help with my feet.

Day 15 was a special day. I would pass the Cruz de Ferro, which has become an icon of the French Camino. With my rock safely secured, I turned on my headlamp and 05:00 and limped out of Foncebadón, back into the mountainous terrain. It was pitch black up there. The dirt path was rocky from the start. With a couple of quick glances to my left and right, I saw nothing but short shrubs and bushes on both sides. Then, out of nowhere, I heard the ribbit sounds of frogs. They were loud, very loud. There must have been a thousand frogs out there. As I kept walking, I almost stepped on one crossing the path. I had enough issues dealing with the colonies of moths, and now I faced a battalion of wild frogs. Alas, I kept moving. While I typically left early in the morning, before any rays of sunlight graced the earth, there was always a risk of injury, even with the headlamp. It was something I became increasingly respectful of as the Camino continued. I noticed I was being smarter with my steps, particularly around larger rocks and stones, where I could easily slip or lose my balance.

As dawn was upon me, I knew I was getting closer, as the path wrapped around the mountain range, going up and down hills. The tree line at the top kept getting closer. Then, finally, I turned the corner, and it came into view. The sky above was a light blue, as the hint of dawn provided a backdrop for the Cruz de Ferro. Standing about five meters tall, the wooden post had an iron cross placed at the top. At 1,500 meters of elevation, it was the highest point across the entire French Way. The post basked in the misty air and light morning fog, enhancing its majestic nature. The base was home to the renowned pile of rocks and stones that were collected over many years. It was touching to know that the rocks had belonged to people with different backgrounds, different feelings, and ultimately different motivations. Some rocks were tiny and pebble-like, while others were large, brick-sized stones that would have been a burdensome weight to carry up to the cross. Maybe it was the dimly lit darkness that made it more special, or how I was alone, but that place had a holiness to it, one that I had never experienced before. I was completely alone, yet, as I slowly approached the mound, it was as if someone or something was about to greet me. Even more, it felt like I was being helped up to the mound at the base of the wooden post. I felt a presence so strongly that I even looked around, shining my headlamp in various directions, expecting to see someone or something. Standing face to face with the post, I gently reached out my hand to touch it. It was a holy feeling.

Some rocks and stones had messages written on them with a permanent marker, usually a message dedicated to a loved one who had passed away. One stone read: "My soul knows you're at peace. Love you, Mom and Dad." Another stone had words of encouragement to other pilgrims on the Camino: "It's time to let go of everything holding you back." Some people had even taped photos of their loved ones to the wooden post itself, or left bracelets, folded up letters, and other dedications and items of affection on top of the mound. This was a place of love, and a place of grief, all at the same time. Knowing I could not stay there forever, I pulled out my rock that I had collected on the ascent up to Foncebadón the day before. I gripped it firmly as I stood at the top of the mound. Then I closed my eyes and said a prayer.

The thoughts that weighed on me were not about the Camino, getting through the Camino, or having anything at all to do with the Camino. They were not about the muscle strains, the back issues, or blister bubbles bursting on the bottom of my feet. My thoughts were with my family. I asked God to bless them every single day, and my friends as well. But I also reflected on my sins, and the things I could have done differently. There was guilt in my heart. It was impossible to pinpoint all of it. Maybe part of it was because I left my dad in Spain when I ran away to the US with my mom and sisters at 10 years old. What hurt me even more was what happened next. Just before Christmas, my father flew in, announced. He rented a car and pulled up in the driveway of my aunt's house, where we were staying. In a desperate display of love, his plan was to take us kids back to the Basque Country. As I detailed in my memoir, it all ended with a police-chase, my father being deported, and the United States revoking his Green Card and future travel privileges. My father suffered profusely over the years, living alone without his children; not even able to see them. I think part of me sought forgiveness for all of it. When I finished my prayer, I gently tossed my rock at the base of the Cruz de Ferro, then walked down the other side of the mound.

Once I resumed my Camino, the path became engulfed in thick shrubs and vibrant foliage, soaked in mildew after the drop in temperature the night before. The front of my feet were wet, but I figured they would dry as the day warmed up. It was a 43km day to Cacabelos, and a long descent awaited me. The first place I passed was an odd-looking refuge in a village called Manjarín. Having grown up in the Basque Country, this place reminded me of the barns we built using scraps of boards, plastic, and other salvaged materials. And it was all built on a few feet of stones, or the ruins of a former site. There were flags from several countries affixed to the structure, and countless wooden signposts with arrows showing distances to far-off cities like Jerusalem, Rome, and Mexico City. The unpredictable weather in these mountains, combined with the proximity to the Cruz de Ferro, likely drove the need for such a refuge. But it was unlike anything I had ever seen along the Camino. Although it was dead silent when I walked by, it is said that a man named Tomás runs it year-round. As the host, he invites pilgrims to drink coffee and take refuge there. It is also said that he claims to be the last of the Knights Templar. If I got caught in a storm, it would have been an interesting place to stay the night.

Further along, the trail was nestled with hordes of lavender plants. The mountain ravine sloped down on my left, as the trail wrapped around the mountain. There was a thick layer of fog about 10 meters below me. It seemed as though I was floating above it. Soon after, I began the official descent, as I could see the town of Ponferrada in the distance, several smaller mountain tops away. El Acebo was a village 7km away from Manjarín, which seemed like a good place to stop for breakfast. There was a charming cafe with enchanting décor inside. It looked like something out of *Alice in Wonderland*. There were beautiful plants, antique radios, and vintage furniture. The new locale was being run by a Dutch woman who had visited the village on the Camino, and opened a cafe soon after. This time, I went with two slices of toast, some strawberry and peach jam, a glass of orange juice, and coffee. Since the woman was Dutch, I could not resist bringing up a joke from the movie *The Way*, where Joost, the pilgrim from Amsterdam, says, "If it ain't Dutch, it ain't much!" She responded with a little smile, but did not find it as funny and clever as I did—oh well.

The stop was brief in El Acebo as I walked through the center street, made of cobblestone. As pretty as it looked, I dreaded the pain it caused. Being on the Camino really gave me an appreciation for flat, rock-free dirt, or flat, lump-free grass—that is what I always longed for, and rarely encountered. At the edge of the village, there were a few older women standing outside on a patio. This was probably their daily routine, watching and greeting pilgrims roll through their town. It is something I thought about often, how the residents of these towns grew up with the Camino and seeing strangers waltz through their villages; they were very welcoming. The two women shouted to me, "It will not rain today! You will be OK!" It was such a sweet gesture. And it was a good thing too, since the Camino went off-road again.

The next town was called Riego de Ambrós, where the first few buildings looked like something out of an old western movie. Balconies made of decaying wood looked seconds away from collapsing. The staircases leading up to the second stories did not have railings, and were being supported by a pile of large pre-historic-looking stones. But, with all its faults, the buildings were pleasant to look at, and gave you a nostalgic feeling like you had gone back in time. It was after this village that the descent became dangerous and downright treacherous.

Until then, the descent had not been too steep or too complicated. There were maybe one or two rocky sections, similar to the jagged edged rocks I encountered entering Zubiri on Day 1. But this part was a beast. Overgrown with trees and bushes, the Camino was full of large rocks that I had to navigate through, like a bomb technician. I had to be meticulous. It was as if someone, in some cruel and sick prank, had thrown sticks of dynamite up and down the steep trail. At one point, a Japanese pilgrim was passing me by and said, "This sucks…" It was funny, especially the way he flung his arms around, bouncing down the trail without trekking poles. On the side of the path, there was an Israeli girl sitting down for a break. It was not a great place to rest, but I understood the need for it.

Entering Molinaseca, I was never happier to be out of the mountains and back on a flat, paved road. There was a sign that read, "Voted one of the most beautiful towns in Spain." "Yeah right," I thought. I was sure every town felt that way about where they lived. And this town only had a population of about 800 people. But Molinaseca was truly beautiful. As I inched closer, there was an ancient medieval bridge that allowed me to cross the Meruelo River, where pilgrims were swimming in the water. Its seven arches made the bridge one of the longest I had walked across. I cannot emphasize enough the significance of this bridge in the medieval era. It made all the difference to pilgrims trying to make it to Santiago, who without this bridge or others, would have had to travel many kilometers just to make it over or around the river. Over the bridge and a few blocks over was the Church of San Nicolás, with its magnificent bell tower at the top, overlooking Molinaseca in all its splendor. The narrow stone street gave me a welcoming feeling. Its neatly condensed buildings, cafes, bars, and restaurants gave off a fairy tale vibe. The slate roofs, exterior staircases, ashlar facades, and popular use of chestnut wood made it even more magical. As I strolled through, I remember thinking how perfect the town was. I had not seen a more perfect town since St. Jean Pied de Port. It was that stunning. The next town would be beautiful too, but in its own *King Arthur* style.

The town of Ponferrada was 8km away from Molinaseca and took me about two hours to hike to. Ponferrada was a much bigger town than Molinaseca, with a population of over 65,000 people. What made it such a popular place was the Templars Castle of Ponferrada. It looked like a fortress, with its polygonal shape, moat, and drawbridge. The order for its construction came from King Ferdinand II in 1178. They named the castle after the Knights Templar, who protected Ponferrada in the Middle Ages. Two flags waved from the watch towers: Spanish flag and Castilla y León, the autonomous community in which Ponferrada is located. The castle itself was massive, covering 8,000 square meters. Popular belief says that the castle has an underground tunnel system that was to be used by the knights if the castle was under siege. As I walked up the hill near the castle, the symbol of the Knights Templar was everywhere, comprising a red cross on a white banner. The streets buzzed with people, packed restaurant terraces, and a jovial atmosphere.

Leaving behind the gallant town of Ponferrada, I passed through the smaller neighboring villages of Columbrianos, Fuentes Nuevas, and Camponaraya, stopping for a chocolate almond ice-cream bar to cool down a bit. Before reaching my last stop, Cacabelos, the Camino trail cut through some rolling hills of vineyards, poplars, wheat, and grass fields—far from any bars or restaurants. It was a sultry afternoon, with high temperatures. About one kilometer before town, I saw an old man trying to make it up a short but steep hill. He was barely moving. Even with my limp-style walk, I was gaining on him. The closer I got, the more I realized he was panting, almost dry heaving. He looked to be in his mid-70s. He had white hair, a baseball cap, and a backpack that looked heavy. I came to a halt, leaning in to ask if he was OK. He was so out of breath, he could not respond verbally, but he gave me a wave, as if to say he was fine, but clearly he was not. I then offered him the little water I had left, but he refused—he seemed to be a prideful, stubborn man. However, I waited with him for another 10-15 seconds, taking my time to situate my trekking poles and start up again. Although I kept moving, I had slowed my pace considerably, allowing the old man to keep me in his eyesight, providing a little motivation to keep going. I felt bad for him. After the steep hill, there was another one that crossed a major highway without a crosswalk. I stalled there on the side of the road for a few minutes, fussing with my phone, pretending like I was doing something useful. I glanced behind me to make sure he was still moving; he was, slowly. After crossing the street and starting up the hill, I slowed again, making sure he crossed the highway. He then stepped to the side of the path, sat on a stone Camino marker, and took a break. At the top of the hill, I passed a group of 8-10 people, a mix of kids and adults. They were the old man's family. I heard them talking as I walked by. They seemed annoyed that the old man was taking so long. The man was back there suffering in the Spanish heat, and they seemed careless. But, knowing his family was near, I focused on the path in front and pushed on to Cacabelos.

The Camino was nearing the province of Galicia, which is why my albergue was called La Gallega. The host there was wonderful. She cooked me up some fettucine pasta with chicken, a personal pizza, and threw together some greens in a mixed salad. It was another evening of gorging my face. We talked about the Camino, and my aggressive plan to complete it in 20 days.

"Tomorrow, I'll be entering Galicia," I said.

"Don't you have to climb O Cebreiro?" she asked. I had heard rumblings about that place since the start of the Camino.

"Yeah, I think I arrive later in the day." I could see the worrisome look on her face.

"They say that O Cebreiro is a very steep and difficult climb… be careful."

Despite the warnings and heed of caution from the albergue host, I did not dwell on the ascent I had to make the next day—naively or not. I was learning to take the Camino one day at a time. Other than the constant worsening of my feet, which was a real problem, I began to foster a "Nintendo mentality." At the end of each day, I worked hard to clear my mental memory. It was too much to carry around, piling up one day after another. I tried to enjoy my evenings a little more, savored my food with a couple of extra bites, and took a couple of deep breaths. I did not stop playing the "game," but I pushed the "reset" button when I could, or at least when my hard head would let me. Sometimes it took the shape of daydreaming about my first stop for coffee and pastries. Other times it was focusing on a tree line in the distance, just to set a near-term goal, keeping my mind present. I knew that with a little more time, and a little more pain, at some point, the Camino had to end. At some point, I knew I would reach Galicia, the home of Santiago de Compostela. At some point, I knew the Way would have to descend toward the sea. And maybe, just maybe, I could glide in on the holy air of the Galician province, where Santiago de Compostela was waiting, in all its splendid wonder and glory.

CHAPTER FIFTEEN:

SEND ME YOUR ANGELS

"The Camino will provide." Few things annoyed me more on the Camino than this popular saying. As I mentioned in earlier pages, pilgrims loved to repeat it. Are you packing too many clothes in your backpack? The Camino will provide. Are you worried about finding the next place to eat, sleep, or where to fill your water bottle? The Camino will provide. Most people do not say it outright, but the pilgrimage to Santiago de Compostela, in large part, calls for a minimalist approach. The backpack is probably the most violated form of the experience. Most pilgrims on the Camino had never even been on a hike, let alone an 800km pilgrimage, through a foreign country. It takes you out of your comfort zone, forcing you to fit your life into one little bag that is poetically strapped to your back, which you must then carry around everywhere you go. Because of this, your backpack symbolizes the burdens you carry with you in life. The days on the Camino, traveling between villages, often in complete silence, force you to examine these burdens—either knowingly or unknowingly. The implicit, unwritten agreement between you and the Camino is that it will provide what you need. That is something I struggled with, even as I approached the final arduous climb of the Camino: the ascent to O Cebreiro.

On Day 16, I left at 04:30 in the morning. A sixteenth century stone bridge led me over the Cúa River. Every morning I began, there was always a voice in the back of my head saying, "Could this be the day your injuries catch up to you?" When that happened (and it happened often), I pretended like I did not have growing blister bubbles and skin tears on the bottom of my feet. I tried to trick my body into thinking it was OK to walk normally, without any limping. But in the end, there was a reason I limped. It was because the pain of walking normally was practically unbearable. So, I limped, and slowly gained momentum en route to Villafranca del Bierzo, 9km away.

I walked along a highway, limping on one trekking pole in order to be on my phone and book albergues. In contrast to other stages on the Camino, most pilgrims book their albergues in Galicia well in advance. This was because most pilgrims began their journey in Galicia, when there were between 100-150 kilometers left to arrive in Santiago. The Pilgrim's Office in Santiago will only issue an official Compostela to someone who walks at least 100km. Because of this heightened demand, Booking.com served as an excellent resource, making the reservation process relatively painless—if you could make it on-foot to the albergue, anyway.

When I arrived in Villafranca del Bierzo, I knew I was walking slower than I had the previous couple of days. It had taken me three hours to cover nine kilometers. That did not bode well for the rest of the day. The town of Villafranca del Bierzo was a popular departure point, as evidenced by the high school tour groups that flooded the path. However, it was a welcomed convenience for me, since I did not have to pay too much attention to the Camino markers and yellow painted arrows, since I just needed to follow the groups. At first, a large group of 40 kids walked well ahead of me, but I could see which direction they turned in, and then just followed them. At one point, they made a sharp left turn into a little park area. To my surprise, by the time I made the turn, the entire sprinkler system had ignited, and I took a 15-second impromptu shower.

Once we were out on the edge of the road, the pavement slanted to the left. It was an ankle breaker of sorts, as the slanted surface caused a burning friction on the bottom of my feet. On the road, I came across a middle-aged American couple from Chicago. It was their second day on the Camino, and their enthusiasm radiated from their lovely smiles—the face always showed how "green" a pilgrim was "behind the ears." Soon after, we met a couple of girls from New Jersey, a girl from Holland, and a woman from New York. It was mostly an American freight train, hiking up the Camino. Conversations on the pilgrimage were random. One minute we were talking about backpacks, and the next minute the conversation had flipped to how the Dutch government was restricting nitrogen emissions. The girl from Holland grew up on a farm, and the government had been pressuring her father, the owner, to shut it down. Apparently, livestock farms are one of the primary culprits of nitrogen pollution. As we debated the issue, the woman from Chicago was wheezing. She was working hard to stay with the group, which kept pushing forward. Her husband was doing well, and looked fit enough to keep pace. We stayed together as a group until we reached Trabadelo, where we ate breakfast outside on the terrace at Albergue Crispeta. It was a popular stop that morning, judging by the 15 other pilgrims taking up seats. On the Camino, stops for breaks were risky business—for everyone, not just me. Getting too relaxed, or having a taste of food, was enough to make anyone unravel at the seams, given the discomfort of hiking.

When we started down the road, the group broke apart. The blonde-haired girl from Holland, carrying a pep in each step, led the way ahead of everyone. I followed five meters behind, giving it everything I had to keep up with her. Given how slowly I had walked so far, I knew I needed to up the pace if I wanted to make it into Galicia as I had planned. The woman from Chicago, holding back her husband, was at the back of the pack. They held on until we reached La Portela de Valcarce, then dropped off at a bar on the side of the road. The girls from New Jersey stuck around until I noticed they were gone. It was just me, Kimberly from Holland, and Moe from New York. It was the Camino's version of *Survivor*.

Moe, a recent retiree, had also just started the Camino; it was her third day. She was making the pilgrimage with her son, but he had taken an alternate route that day, off the official Camino path. Apparently, it was more scenic. Back in New York, Moe had been a hospice nurse for most of her career. She was sharp and gave me some good advice about my feet.

"Ander, you really need to remove those Compeed pads you've slapped on your feet. You have no idea what's really happening under there. It could be bad," said Moe, drawing on her nursing experience.

"I want to, but they're glued to my feet."

"When you get into the albergue tonight, run it under hot water and see if it'll come off." Moe had a true mother's instinct. She was caring in that way.

Moe held strong until she needed to stop for water at a roadside fountain in Ambasmestas. As I stopped for a moment to talk with Moe, Kimberly darted ahead like she was on a mission.

"Don't worry, if you need to go ahead, don't feel bad," said Moe. I wanted to wait for her, but I knew the ascent would soon kick up. We were nearing O Cebreiro.

"If I stop now, or even slow down, I'm not sure I'll make it to the top," I said.

"I know," she said with a smile. The kind of smile pilgrims made when they realized we might not see each other again. Then, I was off to catch the Dutch girl.

Kimberly was a fast walker, but she finally settled into a steady pace, one that I could chip away at. I caught her off guard when I reached her.

"Hey! You made it!" said Kimberly. "I would have waited for Moe, but I'm trying to walk more kilometers today."

"Yeah, I wanted to wait, too. But I guess we all go at our own pace, right?"

"So, why are you doing the Camino?" asked Kimberly.

"I've probably given a different answer every time someone's asked me that."

"Is it because of the movie all you Americans watch?"

"Haha! That's part of the reason. Have you seen it? Have you seen *The Way* with Martin Sheen?"

"Yes, I've seen it. It's actually a good movie," said Kimberly.

"Have you ever felt like you started something with one intention, but then finished it for another?" I asked.

"Well, I was working at my job. I thought that's what I wanted to do, but then I quit. Does that count?"

"Yeah, that counts. Why'd you quit?"

"I was bored at my job. I was doing marketing projects for the government in Amsterdam, and I just got tired of it. I wanted something different. And then my life changed."

"What do you mean? New job?"

"No, I got pregnant. I'm still pregnant. This happened just a few weeks ago," she said. Kimberly was in great shape. She was slim, fit, and did not show a bump at all. I would not have guessed she was pregnant.

"Oh, congratulations! That's so cool!"

"Thank you. I was already planning the Camino, so I did it anyway. My boyfriend was going to come too, but he couldn't make it because of his job."

We had been walking for over an hour, and stopped for a light meal. The town was called Las Herrerías, and the outside terrace faced a big open field. Kimberly ordered a couple of boiled eggs, while I went with jamon on toast, drizzled with olive oil. And of course, coffee with milk. I wanted to pack on some calories for the brutal ascent to O Cebreiro. Although it was not as long and drawn out as the Pyrenees, it was unforgivingly steep. As we enjoyed our food, a familiar face surprised us. It was Moe from New York.

"Moe! You made it!" I said in disbelief.

"Ugh, it was tough, but I'm here!" she said, before going inside to order some coffee. When she came back out, she took a seat at our table.

"OK, Ander, let's see those feet," said Moe.

"Really?"

"Yes! Go ahead and take off your socks." I looked over at Kimberly, who had already finished her food.

"OK... let's do it." I could not remove them completely, since the melting goo of the Compeed pads had fused to my socks.

"Oh, wow... well, that's not good!" said Moe, as Kimberly and I laughed, while I sat slouched in my chair with my feet on the table. The big toe on my right foot had a huge blister; from the tip, all the way down near the intersection of my long toe. Moe rifled through her medical supplies.

"We need some cotton, some disinfectant, and something to wrap it with," said Moe.

"I have some medical tape!" said Kimberly, offering her own supplies for my sake.

"Oh, perfect! That's what you need right there. The self-adhesive kind is the best," said Moe. Kimberly cut a few pieces of tape, while Moe applied the disinfectant. The blister was a deep purple—not good. In case it burst, Moe wanted to clean up the surrounding area. She placed the cotton in between the big toe and long toe, then bound it with Kimberly's medical tape.

"This will keep your toes from rubbing together. That's what's causing the blister," said Moe.

"What do you think?" I asked, looking up at Moe. "Have you seen worse?"

"You might have an infection under the Compeed pads. If your blisters keep getting worse, it means there's friction. The Compeed pads might be doing more harm than good," said Moe.

She then turned her attention to the other blisters on my toes. I had used water-resistant bandages to fully wrap each of them, which effectively glued them to my toes. Moe gave me a few extra pieces of cotton to take with me, and Kimberly gave me some of her self-adhesive medical tape. I put my socks back on and thanked them both profusely. I was a complete stranger to them, and yet, they took care of me like I was family, in the middle of a small village on the Camino. I had little time to process, as Kimberly stood up from the table, preparing her gear to move on. So, I did the same. I gave Moe a big hug before I left.

"God Bless you, Moe. Thank you, thank you, thank you," I said as we embraced each other. Moe was staying behind to have lunch, and wished us a "Buen Camino."

Kimberly took it slowly for the first hundred meters. I was limping badly, and as usual, I had to regain momentum.

"Are you sure you're OK?" she asked.

"Yeah, this happens every time I stop. It's OK," I said. I think she could see the way I gripped and handled my trekking poles was not normal. I was suffering, greatly.

When we got to the end of the village, the mountain kicked up. We began our ascent to O Cebreiro, from an elevation of 675 meters up to 1,300 meters—an ascent of 625 meters across 8km. There would be two villages along the way: La Faba and Laguna de Castilla. At first, the road was flat and paved. I kept up with Kimberly's quick pace as the path twisted and turned around the mountain. Soon after, the Camino took us off-road, under the cover of tall trees. And then the rocky ascent began for real. It seemed like a merciless video game, with large rocks and stones dropped inconveniently throughout the trail. My Achilles tendons had maxed out, as they remained under constant pressure, with my body leaned forward at an angle on the steep mountain slopes. The sweat dripped from my hairline down to my face and off my nose. My mouth was open, sucking in as much air as I could, working feverishly to keep up with Kimberly. Staying within a few feet of Kimberly meant I was "still in the fight."

Once Kimberly established the rhythm, I switched my focus to the large stones that obstructed the path. The most frustrating part about climbing slopes with scattered stones was the fact that you had to avoid them, which forced your steps to the left and to the right, almost making you zigzag your way up the mountain—it was not a straight-line path to the top. I continued to find the next best landing spot for each foot and rarely lifted my head to look up. In total suffer mode, I felt like my lungs were going to explode out of my chest. I thought for sure that Kimberly would have to take a break, but she just kept moving—and she was pregnant! As we climbed further up the mountain, I was totally on the limit. We had been climbing for about an hour. Finally, after a sharp turn, we spotted a house. It was the village of La Faba.

There were a few women resting just a few meters before the house. As we passed the women, waving "Hello" and "Buen Camino," Kimberly looked over at me.

"Oh, my God! You are sweating!" she said. It was the understatement of the year. I looked like I had stepped out of a shower.

"How are you not!?" I asked. Kimberly had not even broken a sweat, not even a droplet.

We thought the hard part was over, but we were wrong. A steep cement path took us from the wooded trails into the village of La Faba. It was so steep that three or four of the locals, likely in their 70s, were clapping and cheering for us to reach them, where there was a popular cafe on the right. We stopped for a break, allowing just enough time to order a couple of cans of Aquarius to help replenish our electrolytes. Everyone stared at me as I limped into the bar and came out with the drinks. It startled people to see someone hobbling around the Camino. After all, the Camino was supposed to be a "fun" journey, they said.

"Want to split this doughnut with me?" I asked Kimberly. I had been saving it since Cacabelos.

"Umm…" she said at first, eyes glued to the doughnut.

"Come on, we'll split it."

"OK, maybe just a little piece," she said, as I gave her a solid chunk of the doughnut. It was the best glazed doughnut I ever had.

The break at the cafe was short-lived, as Kimberly and I decided it was time to move. Against our most inner wishes, we threw our heavy backpacks on and proceeded toward Laguna de Castilla.

The mountain trails were just as bad as before, if not worse in some areas. Now, we were subject to the hot summer heat, as the cover of trees we previously enjoyed was no more. The path narrowed significantly in sections, allowing for little room to tip-toe around the stones and jagged rocks we encountered. Other than the pain, the most miserable part about climbing this section was that we could not see where we were going. At every zigzagging turn, we might have been able to see about 20 meters ahead of us, and that was it. But it was a 3km push from La Faba, so we knew it could not take much longer than 35-45 minutes. And just as La Faba had suddenly appeared, so did Laguna de Castilla. We sat down to have a real lunch— meaning, sat down on a bench with an old wooden wine barrel as a table, and demolished two plentiful plates of spaghetti. We knew we still had another 3km to go, but we could not resist. As did many pilgrims, Kimberly took her shoes off for a little while, letting her feet air out. This was common on the Camino, and heavily advised. The only reason I did not take my shoes off was because the swelling would get worse and then it would be a challenge getting my shoes back on. We took our time savoring the spaghetti, leaving little behind. But O Cebreiro awaited us.

Knowing we were almost to O Cebreiro took some of the bite out of the last stretch of hiking. The view down the ravine was becoming more beautiful with every step, as we neared 1,300 meters of elevation. It was the beginning of the end for pilgrims. It was sinking in that we were almost in the province of Galicia, the final province of the Camino de Santiago. And then we passed the large stone marker that read, "Galicia." The stone had a large red cross, accompanied by the coat of arms. Soon after, the right side of the trail had a six-foot-high stone barrier, probably to keep the mountainous terrain from sliding down and destroying the trail. We were almost at the top. Then, moments later, we reached a cobblestone road with a perfect, wide-open view of the valleys below. It was breathtaking. We had made it.

There were several "Zen-like" moments along the Camino, and reaching the top of O Cebreiro was one of them. It was Zen-like in that the panoramic view of the peaks and valleys was more than just that. The view was a nodding of the Camino, a handshake of sorts, almost a pat on the back. But also, it was a sign of proof, a gift receipt, a way of telling me that the Camino had not forgotten about me, that it was holding firm to its commitment, our agreement, to provide what I needed. On Day 16, I needed angels, and the Camino had delivered. My angels had plucked me up off the trail and taken me high above the clouds of the Galician mountains. However, from atop O Cebreiro, the descent was now imminent.

CHAPTER SIXTEEN:

A HAPPY THOUGHT

"What's wrong, Peter?" asks one of the Lost Boys.

"I can't stay and play. I've done what I came to do, and now I have to go back."

"No, Peter, please," say the Lost Boys, pleading for him to stay.

"Tink, make my kids glow," says Peter. After Tinker Bell sprinkles some pixie dust on his two children, Peter tells them how to fly.

"Jack... Maggie... all you have to do is think one happy thought, and you'll fly like me."

"Mommy!" shouts Maggie with glee.

"My dad," says Jack. Soon after, Tinker Bell takes them up into the sky, as Peter bids farewell to the Lost Boys.

I must have watched *Hook* a thousand times as a kid. I found myself captivated by Robin Williams as "Peter Pan" and his sword duels with Dustin Hoffman, who played "Captain James Hook." When Peter first arrives in Neverland, he is a middle-aged lawyer motivated by greed, and prioritizes his job over his family. In Neverland, he earns the trust and respect of the Lost Boys, and ultimately joins them in their quest to defeat Captain Hook, who reigns terror over Neverland. But when the battle is over, and an enormous crocodile devours Captain Hook (you have to watch the movie), Peter finds himself torn. In Neverland, away from his family, he realized how much he loves and misses them, and vows to live differently. But also, he knows he must leave the Lost Boys and his sword-fighting adventures behind forever. He must leave Neverland for London and return to reality. Although my journey to Santiago was slowly coming to an end, I could not help but think about the journey and my affection for it. I wanted desperately to finish, yet it had been my teacher for the better part of three weeks. I wondered how I was going to explain it all when I landed back in "reality"—if I landed back in reality.

Kimberly and I had parted ways shortly after finishing the climb to O Cebreiro—she stayed behind at the municipal albergue. O Cebreiro was a charming village, popular among pilgrims for its rich history and "pallozas," which are round stone huts with straw roofs. People inhabited these huts at 1,330 meters of elevation until the 1960s. Aside from the ancient architecture, the lodging house of San Giraldo de Aurillac has been operating since the ninth century, and is a real gem of the Camino. However, it is the Royal St. Mary's Church that takes the cake in that town. It is the oldest remaining fully intact church on the entire Camino de Santiago. Built in 836, the church has sunken floors, serving as protection from the harsh winter storms. For centuries, locals say, the church bells rang to help guide pilgrims through the mountain mist, en route to O Cebreiro.

After O Cebreiro, I continued on for another 6km to Hospital da Condesa. The evening was relatively uneventful, aside from some leftover empanadas I scored at a nearby bar—the only place with food. It was the first thing I did after checking into the albergue. The bartender told me that the kitchen was closed until dinner, which would not start for another two hours. After telling her I would be physically incapable of returning later, she took mercy on me and gave me some empanadas her mother had baked— chorizo and tuna. Besides the empanadas, I bought two ice-cream cones and a can of Aquarius. Then, it was shower, "surgery," face-gorging, and lights out.

When I woke up on Day 17, after the grueling ascent to O Cebreiro, everything hurt. I was still standing, but barely. And worse yet, I had a 45km day ahead, which started out with a 5-hour mountain descent. The target was a town called Barbadelo, which is about 4km past a major Camino hotspot: Sarria. I was alone that morning, navigating the darkness of the Camino, something that had become routine. To my delightful surprise, I still had climbing to do to reach Alto do Poio. The mountain trail turned into a brutally steep, back-breaking ascent—hardly the first thing I would have wanted to encounter at 05:30 in the morning. But, at the top, it rewarded me with the bronze statue of a pilgrim fighting against the wind, with one hand on his hiking stick and the other on his head, trying to keep his hat from flying off. At 1,337 meters of elevation, this was the highest point of the Camino within the Galician province. From there began the descent.

It did not take long for the rugged mountain terrain to begin its decimation of my feet. Despite my best efforts to tie my shoes tightly, my feet kept sliding around inside my shoes, all the way down the mountain. At one point, it literally felt like someone had taken a cheese grater to my toes, then bashed them on top with a sledgehammer. Bar none, it was the most painful descent I had experienced. I stopped only once in a failed attempt to remedy the situation. With nowhere to sit, I performed a balancing act on one foot, partially removing my right sock. I moved the cotton bandages and taped up most of the skin exposed on my toes, hoping that would work—it did not. Still, I kept moving down the mountain in pure agony.

Triacastela was the first notable village on the way down. Most pilgrims ended their stage there. Lucky for them, the short stage from O Cebreiro offered a chance to recover from the physical exertion made on the previous day's ascent. Among the few attractions in Triacastela, there is a windmill, and a handful of churches to visit if one has the time. From there, it was onto Sarria. At the edge of Triacastela, there was a junction in the road. The left-hand path was flatter and had easier terrain, while the right-hand path was 6km shorter, but included an extra 238 meters of climbing. As you might have guessed, I chose the shorter, more difficult route. The path led to asphalt, and then to a dirt trail, leading the way to A Balsa. The steep hills were full of inconveniently placed rocks, forcing me to sidestep them all the way up. I was not alone that morning, as I noticed a pilgrim about 50 meters behind me. As we climbed through the proverbial landmines, the man was gaining on me. Meter by meter, every time I looked back, he was that much closer. At that rate, I thought he would surely catch me. But after a little ways, I looked back again, and he was gone.

The road smoothed out, but remained difficult. After some ankle-breaking climbing, the Camino led me to meadows full of oak trees and lush, isolated nature. Although I was in pain, it was impossible not to recognize its beauty. I just remember how quiet it was. There were no other pilgrims around, just me, which made it easier to stop momentarily in the middle of the trail when my groin started acting up. Every 100 meters, I stopped and stretched, using a lunge-like motion. A few years back, I had torn my groin running with the bulls, and it still gave me issues from time to time. Nonetheless, the meadows were something to behold.

After the peaceful descent through the shade-filled forest, I stopped at a restaurant on the Camino called Casa Cines Restaurante. I think their specialty was pizza, judging by the large sign out front. However, I went with something lighter. I had already walked about 34km, but I still had another 7km to reach the town of Sarria, then almost another 5km to reach Barbadelo. So, I skipped the pizza, and instead, I ordered scrambled eggs with pieces of jamon. When it arrived, I was less than impressed by the tiny two-cup portion served, especially after paying around 10 euros. But, in moments like that, when I was hungry, I "charged it to the game," as the youngsters say nowadays.

The path to Sarria took me past a roadside farm of sorts, where twenty goats sat in the shade of a tree next to the sidewalk. I stopped for water at a nearby fountain, then made my way into town. Sarria was one of my favorite places on the Camino. The people were pleasant and radiated happiness. Even at the pharmacy, where I stopped for a resupply of needles, bandages, and iodine, the pharmacist was lovely. The Galician people spoke with an accent, with high and low-pitched affectations, similar to the way Italians speak; more emotion. Their primary language, of course, is called "Gallego." This ancient language goes back to the third century BC, where its roots trace back to the Celtic tribes that settled in Galicia. However, scholars formalized the language during the ninth century. Besides the people, the town and its architecture were gorgeous. The medieval castle, the Convent of A Madalena, the thirteenth century Church of O Salvador and its early-Gothic style, the steep staircases and cobblestone streets, it was all exquisite. Its random scattering of bright yellow, orange, and teal-colored buildings made Sarria even more vibrant and unique. Apart from being on the route, Sarria is the place where King Alfonso IX of León died, while making the pilgrimage to Santiago in 1230. And after I passed through the city center of Sarria, I too felt like I might not make it.

Nearing the highest point of Sarria, I passed by a cemetery and a tall, stone cross along a narrowly-paved street. The descent from Sarria toward Barbadelo was a short, but super steep one. If a pilgrim was not careful, they probably could have fallen and rolled down to the bottom. Using the Aspera bridge, I crossed over the Sarria River. The bridge was old and narrow, made of layered stones and constructed in the Middle Ages. At the other end of the river, the path had changed from a bustling, urban metropolis to tree-filled meadows. And 4km later, I arrived in Barbadelo.

At the albergue that night, I had given my bag of dirty clothes to the host to wash. For six euros, I thought it was well worth the expense. The biggest convenience of this was not having to walk. The washing area was outside the albergue, and would have required multiple trips to hang and dry everything on the clothesline, hoping they would dry in time. But what started as a convenience quickly became an inconvenience. When I had given them my clothes, they said to come back in two hours. And I did. I hobbled my swollen and blistered feet from my room to a nearby restaurant area where they were holding my clothes. When I got there, they were not ready. They said to come back in another 30 minutes. When I did, they gave me damp clothing stuffed inside a laundry basket. They were still not ready. I returned yet again after another 30 minutes, where this time, a woman came out with the basket, dropped it at my feet and said, "Here you go," then walked away. Most of the clothes were dry, except for a white sock they did not remove from my laundry bag—they washed the laundry bag too.

When I started Day 18, I had to chuckle to myself. I tied my wet white sock to the outside of my backpack. I did this with my t-shirts almost daily, as I would completely sweat through the shirt I wore in the morning, as well as the one in the afternoon. But the sock was sort of funny. Who dangles just one white sock from their backpack? Nobody, just me. A few hours into my morning hike out of Barbadelo, a family of Spanish hikers were walking behind me.

"Excuse me, I think you lost a sock," said one kid.

"Oh, no, it's just the one, thank you," I said. The kid's face was priceless. Then their father chimed in.

"I feel like I've seen you before. Do you run with the bulls?" he asked.

"Yeah, I go to Pamplona every year."

"I thought you looked familiar. I think they interviewed you, right? You're the guy from Miami?"

"That's me," I said. "They were looking for runners to interview before the bull run, and they just asked if I would do it."

"That's great that you love the bull run. Our family loves the tradition—it's a big part of our lives."

"Maybe you'll see me on TV this year. Hopefully, I'll be running well," I said in jest. During the brief conversation, their little girl was hungry, so they veered off the Camino and went looking for a cafe. I trudged ahead, alone.

There were exactly 18 villages on Day 18, making it a busy day. It was a 44km trek to a town called Palas de Rei. I had already passed little towns such as Rente, A Serra, and also a town called Morgade, where just ahead of it was the famous "100km" marker, where I officially began the last stretch of the Camino. I silently celebrated the marker, despite my obvious discomfort. That day, the blisters on the bottom of my left foot hurt worse than those on the right. Unfortunately, it was not because my right foot hurt any less; the left foot just hurt more. Each day, I began setting new thresholds for my pain tolerance. I felt like I was one or two blisters away from being unable to walk. But walk, I did.

On the outskirts of Portomarín, I walked down a makeshift staircase made of large uneven stones—I was asking to break my leg. The staircase led down a steep hillside, surrounded by walls made of layered stone on both sides. The walls continued until I arrived at a highway, where I crossed the street and made my way toward the bridge over the Miño River. It took a few minutes to cross the 300-meter-long bridge. Watermarks in the river were visible from above. The water level was very low, and because of that, I could see the remnants of a village that once stood there. In the 1960s, the Spanish government ordered the formation of a water reservoir, which caused the uprooting of an entire village—literally. Brick by brick, the Spanish government ordered churches and other historical buildings to be moved, piece by piece, to the new site of the town. They moved many average homes and residences as well, but not all of them. So, even today, when the river's water level is low enough, people can still get a glimpse of the houses and buildings that remained. In some ways, it was a sad sight, knowing that many families were likely displaced forever. Still, the town was lovely—the new town, anyway.

I entered the town of Portomarín around 10:30 in the morning. After crossing the river, I scaled a staircase up the slopes of the city center. I stopped at a bar for glazed doughnuts and coffee. The whole time I was there, a Galician couple was arguing at the far end of the bar. Their voices echoed off the walls of the empty locale—I did not understand a word. As I was eating, a small group of foreigners approached the bartender at the counter, asking for directions. Without hesitation, she kindly obliged the foreigners and showed them the Way. The couple arguing took notice of it. When the group left, the couple switched from Galician to Spanish, but only for a moment. It was just long enough to tell the bartender she should have left the pilgrims to fend for themselves. It was a foul thing to say, but I did not let it bug me. If a pilgrim asked me a question or needed help, I would offer it, no questions asked. We were in it together, and so were the locals. A few minutes later, it was my turn to walk.

Carefully and gingerly, I strapped my backpack on, re-tied my shoes, and set out down the hill toward the river. My pace was half that of my normal speed, as the pain in my left foot was excruciating. Adding to the situation, I was so used to putting most of my weight on my left foot that I had to train myself to do the opposite. The long, downhill road did not help, as I felt the slope putting more pressure on the front of my feet, where most of the blisters were located. I was already taking ibuprofen and using anti-inflammatory spray, but they did little to lessen the pain. As I walked down toward the river, there was a parked charter bus; it was full of tourists, and they were all watching me out of the window. Surely, they would think twice about walking the Camino after seeing the look of sheer pain and suffering on my face.

Shortly after reaching the river, there was a fork in the road. The Camino offered two routes to continue, which would meet up later on. I pulled out my phone to understand the difference between the two. The path to the left was the principal route, while the one on the right was a shorter, alternate option. As I grimaced while putting my phone away, collecting the energy to push forward, a couple of Asian girls approached the fork—they too were confused, lost. They kept looking up from their phones to see what I was going to do.

"I didn't come this far to take a shortcut," I said with a smile. They laughed.

"OK, we will follow you," said one of the girls. Her name was Dove.

"OK, let's go."

"Wait, what happened to you?" asked Dove.

"Blisters, muscles, back… everything is old. I am old."

"We will call you 'Old Man,' then."

"Yes, you will return home with tales of the 'Old Man.'"

We followed the markers over the paved road, quickly veering up a steep gravel trail.

Dove and her friend, MJ, were studying abroad in Spain for one semester. They were making the pilgrimage to Santiago before returning home. In Korea, they belonged to a Catholic university, and were serious about their faith.

"In Korea, they taught us about the Camino de Santiago. It's very important. Many students travel to Spain to do it," said Dove. "I want to see Saint James, but I'm also doing it for God."

"Where did you start from?" I asked.

"We started in Sarria. We don't have much time, so we started there," said Dove. As Dove spoke, I noticed MJ falling behind. Dove and I were pushing hard up the hill. As banged up as I was, I was extra motivated to stay upfront.

"Is MJ OK?" I asked. MJ was a few meters behind. It was her second day on the Camino, and the Spanish hills appeared to be taking their toll on her.

"Yeah, she's OK, she just walks slow uphill," said Dove. And the hills, as few of them as there were that day, they were about to get harder.

During a 10km stretch of hiking, we passed the villages of Gonzar and Castromaior. Much of the Camino had been pleasant, offering a mix of gravel trails through shady pine-tree forests, wide-open fields, and roadside shoulders. But after Castromaior, we came face-to-face with a 700-meter climb. It was steep, very steep. It was so steep that we saw pilgrims scattered about the slopes of the mountain range, taking brief breaks before continuing the punishing ascent. Sometimes, the rocks and loose gravel made it tough for me to keep traction with my worn-out New Balance shoes and obliterated soles. The only saving grace of the vicious ascent was that the climb took some pressure off of the front of my feet, placing more on the heel, Achilles, and calves. I preferred that pain to the one on the bottom of my feet. My body was simply falling apart.

The heat was so bad, each time we passed through a shaded, wooded area, I wasted no time in removing my brimmed hat. On one such occasion, I was so irritated by the sweating furnace that was wrapped around my head that I violently threw the hat up and over my head. It had a string attached from side to side, which kept it secured to my neck, preventing it from falling off—or so I thought. When we exited the shade, I went to put the hat back on, but it was not there. I ended up having to retrace my steps for about 50 meters before I found it on the ground. It took me 30 minutes to catch back up to the girls, who I had ushered ahead and told not to wait.

"The 'Old Man' made it!" said Dove.

"Barely…" I said.

The girls were staying at Ventas de Narón, a small village along the Camino, popular among pilgrims who stop at a nearby chapel, serviced daily by a blind volunteer. When we arrived, the girls went to check-in to the albergue, while I darted straight for the bar counter, where I ordered a Coca-Cola and a chocolate almond ice-cream bar—I needed to cool down. I was a little bummed that me and the girls did not say our "goodbyes," especially after spending the better part of the day together. Thinking they would not return, I got up from the chair and left the bar.

"Ander! You weren't leaving, were you?" asked Dove outside the bar. "We wanted to say bye!"

"I thought you left! Thanks for coming back," I said.

"Where are you going now?" asked MJ, the quiet one.

"I still have another 12km to Palas de Rei. That's where my albergue is."

"Wait, before you go, let's take a selfie together!" said Dove. The three of us then squished together for a photo, waved goodbye, and I continued on my journey.

Before setting out to Palas de Rei, I found a water fountain next to the famous chapel. I filled up both bottles and started the 12km hike. The 12km should have only taken a couple of hours, but it took me closer to three. The terrain was not particularly difficult, since it was a roadside trail for most of the way, with some sections of pavement. But what made it difficult was the time it was taking to regain my momentum after leaving Ventas de Narón. I kept getting passed up, which was frustrating. The road went up and down the hills a few times, passing a handful of villages in proximity—Ligonde, Airexe, and Portos. The frustration was mounting, but it was mixed in with a wave of emotion that was hitting me. I think it was the fact that I had one more full day to walk before arriving in Santiago. I was less than 48 hours away. It was difficult to fathom; all that time, almost 18 days on the Camino until that point. I think I was beginning to believe that I could really make it, that I could actually finish. I was getting teary-eyed just thinking about it. But I also knew I was worn out, fatigued, broken-down, and all the above. So, after a few minutes of sentimental self-indulgence, I forced myself to stop thinking about the finish, and stayed focused on the Way.

When I arrived in Palas de Rei, I loaded up on groceries at a convenience store. Similar to my recipe in Hospital de Órbigo, I went with jamon, cheese, and chocolate milk. This time, I added some chorizo, and for good measure, a tasty pre-packaged Caesar salad. After feasting and performing some "surgery," I threw an extra pillow under my feet to keep them as elevated as possible. Sleeping had been a problem throughout the whole Camino. It was mostly the throbbing pain from my back down to my toes. The worst of it would resurface at 01:00 or 02:00 in the morning, just as the ibuprofen was wearing off. Trying to be a tough guy, I did not take more at that point. Instead, I just got used to tossing and turning for the final few hours of sleep before starting my day. But alas, my time in "Camino-Neverland" was nearing its end. Most nights the pain would be so bad that I would dream I was still on the Camino—climbing up a mountain, descending a ravine, crossing a river into a seemingly forgotten town, and meeting strangers along the Way. The pain felt real, and so did the dreams. But when all of it was over, and the pain was finally gone, I wondered if I would keep the Camino with me. "If I am enough," I thought.

CHAPTER SEVENTEEN:

BEING ENOUGH

It is the night before the final race. A driver sits alone in his hotel room, studying photographs of the track. He memorizes each turn, every bend, and every slope with the intensity of a determined champion. The silence is nerve-wracking. The pressure to win and the intensity of the competition have driven him to his limits. But deep down, there is something bothering him. His coach then enters the room, asking if he wants to join the rest of the team for dinner. The driver declines. Instead, he works up the courage to ask his coach a burning question. It is an uncomfortable question, and with it comes a heavy truth. Before he can even ask, his coach interjects.

"You want to know why I cheated, don't you?" asks the coach, referring to being caught cheating at the same Olympic event years before.

"Yes, I do," says the driver. His coach had already won two Olympic gold medals. He was a legend. Then, he cheated to win another.

"That's a fair question. It's quite simple, really. I had to win. You see, I'd made 'winning' my whole life. And when you make 'winning' your whole life, you have to keep winning... no matter what," says the coach. "You understand that?"

"No, I don't understand, Coach," says the driver. "You had two gold medals... you had it all."

"A gold medal is a wonderful thing. But if you're not enough without it, you'll never be enough with it," says the Coach.

"How will I know if I am enough?" asks the driver.

This exchange was from the 1993 Disney movie, *Cool Runnings*. The driver is Derice Bannock, played by Leon. The coach is Irv Blitzer, played by John Candy. Loosely based on the 1988 Jamaican bobsled team, the movie tells the story of four Jamaicans representing their country at the Winter Olympics in Calgary. The doubts that lie within Derice Bannock are all too familiar. Similar to Derice, I put a lot of pressure on myself to win. With that said, I am nowhere close to being an Olympic athlete. However, the same burning questions lingered in my mind: "How will I know if I am enough? Even if I make it to Santiago, what meaning will it all have?" I only had a little more time to figure it out.

Day 19 was a rough day. But every day was a rough day. I guess the only thing that made it unique was the bad start. That, and trying to put the Camino into perspective. Most of the time, I felt like I was in too much pain to reflect in the moment. I just simply focused on the next step in front of me—that was hard enough. But Day 19 was the first day that my bubbling blister did not seem to soften or ease up as I tried to walk off the pain. Sometimes, after enough pressure, I would feel the fluid and puss squirting out from the bottom of my foot. It was the greatest feeling in the world, because I knew it would get a little easier to walk. Like I have mentioned before, the fluid and puss would miraculously reappear when I took a seat or stopped for a few brief moments. But that morning, it was more difficult than usual.

I turned on my headlamp at 05:30 in the morning. It was dead silent out on the streets. It was a 41km hike to Salceda. Leaving Palas de Rei, I knew there would be at least 350 meters of climbing on the day, but I was not expecting such difficulties in the early going. Slabs of large and uneven stones led the way out of town. They would have been aesthetically pleasing if it were not for my feet. No matter how I positioned them, each step gave me the familiar stabbing and tearing feeling on my blisters—it was too early for that. Within minutes, I found myself completely soaked, sweat pouring down from my nose. It was nearly impossible to garner any momentum in the first 20 minutes. Adding to that, the surface made it impossible to use my trekking poles, as they constantly slid around all over the place; I almost fell a few times. Then, the stone slabs took me to sidewalks made of slippery, cobble-like concrete. And again, I could not get any traction with the trekking poles, which I desperately needed to support my weight and pull myself forward. Things got a little easier once I began the small ascent to San Xulián do Camiño, even though my forearms felt like they were on fire as they propelled my body up the mountain. Oak trees and eucalyptus filled my view each time I glanced to the side of the trail, along with old stone-built farmhouses. The slopes continued for some time. By dawn, I began a descent toward Casanova, filled with wooded surroundings and lush green nature.

Eventually, I crossed over a river and into the village of Furelos. My pace came to a crawl as I tiptoed around the stones and out of the village. Shortly after, I arrived in Melide, which was a bustling urban town with apartment buildings, cars, traffic lights, and roundabouts—and churros, lots of churros.

I had not eaten since the start of the day, and I thought churros would surely give me a sugary boost. I found a seat outside Alborada, a churro and ice-cream establishment on the main drag in town.

"Please tell me you speak Spanish, yes?" asked the waiter.

"Of course," I said.

"Oh, thank God... I'm so tired of all these entitled Americans wandering through our town with such rude and impolite attitudes."

I ordered coffee, jamon on toasted bread, a side of orange and tangy jam, along with a dozen churros—it was a lot of food! I was so happy, though. As I ate, there was a cute, rough collie dog laying down a few meters away—his owner was at the table next to mine. The dog looked so happy, watching people walk by to give him friendly pats on the head. The dog looked exactly like "Lassie," from the 1950s TV show. I chuckled inside, thinking about how that dog lived only in the present. The dog did not know what tomorrow was going to bring, whether he would have food, or if someone would take care of him. The dog felt safe, and he felt loved, too.

With 15km in the bag, and after adding some fuel to the tank, I left the urban setting and returned to the forest. I passed smaller villages, such as Boente and Ribadiso. I faced a hard climb on asphalt, where I had to stop to take off my shirt, taking advantage of the stop to reapply some sunscreen lotion. However, I cannot forget to mention the bar I visited just a few kilometers outside of Arzúa. There was a happening, upbeat terrace where pilgrims were drinking beer. Perhaps we were so close to Santiago that everyone let their hair down. I stopped inside for a Coca-Cola, and more importantly, a stamp for my pilgrim's passport. To not be rude, I asked for the drink first, then paid, and then asked for the stamp, which I did not see on the counter. After stamping my book, the old lady at the bar put away the ink-filled tin can and stamp, just as a woman was walking in. The pilgrim asked for the stamp, but the old lady denied her, saying she did not have one. However, the pilgrim had already seen me get it as she walked through the door; it was awkward. The pilgrim, looking puzzled, went to the restroom at the back of the bar. As she did so, the old lady spoke to me in Spanish, telling me how rude it was of pilgrims to walk into a business and expect a stamp.

"I'm trying to run a business," said the old lady. "I can't just be giving out hundreds of free stamps every day."

As a finance professional back in the US, I understood her point. She too needed to make a living—on the Camino or not. But I thought it was cold to deny the pilgrim, especially when they asked so politely. After leaving the restroom, I gave the pilgrim a subtle wink, beckoning her to join me. I explained to her in English what happened with the stamp.

"Oh, really? I was going to buy something anyway," she said, laughing. Afterwards, the pilgrim approached the counter again, but this time ordered a beer. After getting her beer, she asked again for the stamp, and this time she got it.

As I prepared to leave the bar, I heard a Spanish-speaking pilgrim make a joke at the counter. The name of the bar, which I will not mention here, was an obvious reference to the owner ("Jose's" bar, for example).

"You're not Jose, are you!?" asked the pilgrim, snickering with his buddies.

"No…" said the old lady.

Part of me wondered if maybe the owner, "Jose," had passed away, leaving the old lady responsible for the bar. What if it was up to the woman to manage the bar, only to make sure its namesake, her husband's memory, lived on? Not everything was as it seemed on the Camino. And our quick and casual encounters, as were most on the Camino, sometimes resulted in quick, unforgiving judgements of people. I left the bar in a bit of a funk after that.

I had no more encounters that afternoon. But the heat was brutal. I entered Arzúa with one sweaty shirt on, and another dripping sweat, as it hung from my backpack. Despite the heat, all of my "feelers" were spiking. There was something unexplainable about it. Despite being a beautiful, vibrant town, Arzúa is famous among pilgrims for being a place of legends. There is the story about a healing fountain, which was said to dry up if people restricted its use to paying customers only. Then, there is my favorite: the legend of the bread miracle.

During the early, ancient days of the Camino de Santiago, it is said that a young pilgrim arrived in Arzúa. Needing a little food to recover and continue his Camino, he stopped at a house where a woman with an oven was baking bread. The pilgrim asked the woman if he could have some, and in return, he promised he would pray for the household in front of the tomb of Saint James the Apostle upon reaching Santiago. The woman refused, saying she would only accept money for the bread, and if the young pilgrim had none, there was no bread to be had. With nothing to eat, the pilgrim tried the home of another woman. This time, the woman of the house gladly welcomed the pilgrim inside. She offered him a place to rest and recover while she baked the bread. While grateful, the pilgrim said it was unnecessary, and that he only needed a little food to continue down the road; he had no time to stop. The woman told the pilgrim that the fresh bread was not yet ready, but if he insisted on continuing without rest, she said to him, "All I can give you is some bread from yesterday." The young pilgrim gladly accepted the offer, and the woman went back to her kitchen to fetch the bread. When she returned to hand him the old bread, the young pilgrim was gone. The woman then left the house in search of the pilgrim, thinking he could not have traveled far. But when she looked into the distance of the long and straight road, he was nowhere to be found. However, when the woman returned to her home and opened her oven, she found a shocking surprise: the fresh bread had turned into gold. Meanwhile, the woman who refused bread to the young pilgrim had her own bread turned into stones. Yet, there was one last twist to this story. People believe that Saint James himself was the young pilgrim who had visited Arzúa. It was clear: the Camino expected selflessness and empathy from both pilgrims and locals.

The road out of Arzúa was like that of the story; it was long, straight, and of course, covered in cobbles. As I neared the end of town, there was something mystical about the path. It started by passing through fields and private farmhouses. From there, it allowed me to bask in the shade provided by the trees that arched their way toward the Camino. The trail then passed by the French fountain, across the River Vello, and descended to the River Brandeso. There was a little climbing left to do, as I gripped my trekking poles with everything I had left, heading up to Preguntoño. I was about a kilometer away from Salceda, as I started feeling my calves giving out. My thighs felt fried, and my knees were toast, as I had no strength left in them. My groin hurt with every move, and my feet felt like they were going to explode from the pressure of the swelling. When I arrived at the albergue, I thought to myself, "If I had to go one kilometer further, it would be an interesting 1 kilometer."

Inside the albergue, the host was tending to two other pilgrims. They were taking forever as he helped them check-in.

"What's the Wi-Fi password? I can't connect," said the English pilgrim, as I was standing, hunched over, with my palms on the edge of a table. I could barely stand. The pain was worse than when I was walking. The blisters, the swelling, and the muscle cramping, it was horrendous. If I had not been so embarrassed, I would have collapsed to the ground in agony, but I could not. Instead, I started pacing back and forth with my hands on my hips, desperately waiting for the English pilgrims to be done. Finally, the host showed the pilgrims to their room, then returned to help me check-in. He immediately showed concern for my condition.

"You don't look so good," said the young man. He had a hip way about his look, complete with a trendy man bun.

"I'm exhausted. And my body hurts everywhere," I said.

"Are you going to Santiago tomorrow?"

"Yes, it's my last day on the Camino, but it's going to hurt badly. I've been dealing with blisters, especially since The Meseta. They're very, very painful."

"Where are the blisters?"

"On the bottom of my feet. Both of them. They're also on almost every toe."

"You know, if you are in these conditions, it's best not to make yourself suffer. I mean, why should you suffer?" he asked.

"I have such a short way to go, I can't quit now," I said.

"Why not just take a taxi to Santiago? Then you can spend the day there and relax. You know, I did the Camino de Santiago a few years ago, before I got this job at the albergue. I was in The Meseta, when I felt a sharp pain in my ankle. It was very difficult to walk. So, I got a taxi to the next town."

"Did you continue after that?"

"No, I ended up taking the train home. I was in no shape to walk. I mean, why suffer?"

What nobody knew, including the young host, was that I had made a promise to God, and I had made a promise to Mother Mary. I prayed for them to give me the strength, health, and ability to finish the Camino. In return, I promised to deal with the pain, and to put in the effort. I was not about to go back on my promise. They had brought me within 28km of Santiago. Despite the allure of the taxi and the appeal of a day of relaxation, I refused to give in.

That final night felt surreal. It was going to be my final night staying in an albergue on the Camino. Before I left Miami, I had booked my stay at a hotel in Santiago, given that vacancy is slim to none as you get closer. All of those nights of communal sleeping, dealing with the snores, the constant noises, loud telephone calls, having to climb up to the top bunk of a rickety metal bunk bed, having to perform "surgery" on my bed in front of other pilgrims; it was all coming to an end.

I spent the evening laying down on my bed, eating some microwaveable noodles I bought from the front desk. It was something I would never have eaten in the US, and yet, the chicken flavored noodles were incredibly delicious. It was a microwavable miracle. I thought back to that scene in *Cool Runnings*, when bobsled coach Irv Blitzer is having an honest and intimate discussion about "being enough." Derice Bannock, the driver, remained perplexed at why his coach had cheated years before, even after winning two gold medals. The quote that rang in my head was from Irv, when he said, "A gold medal is a wonderful thing. But if you're not enough without it, you'll never be enough with it." What Irv meant is that if you do something for the wrong reasons, you never quench that thirst; it will never be enough, as long as you, yourself, are not enough. You could pile Olympic gold medals to the sky, and yet, you would still feel incomplete and unsatisfied.

"I had made winning my whole life," says Coach Irv. Ever since I was a kid, I guess I had done the same. After my tumultuous childhood, filled with my parents' divorce, the separation of my family, and all the uncontrollable situations I endured, I had developed an ultra-competitive mindset. This competitive mindset had served me very well in college and in my career. Taking this competitive mindset to the Camino was different; it was holy ground. I had started the Camino to achieve a physical feat, but the objective seemed so alien now. Thinking back to the scene of "being enough" in *Cool Runnings*, I'll never forget the follow-up question asked by Derice Bannock when Irv explains the perils of being obsessed with winning.

"Hey Coach... how will I know if I'm enough?" he asks.

"When you cross that finish line... you'll know."

CHAPTER EIGHTEEN:

SANTIAGO DE COMPOSTELA

When I was 9 years old, living in the United States, I remember my father traveled to Spain for a week to be with his mother, who had fallen ill with cancer. The disease had progressed devastatingly quickly. When he left, my mother dropped me off at my grandmother's house in Portland, so that she could watch me while my father was gone. Running the hamburger business and watching all three kids was going to be too much for my mother. However, I butted heads with my grandmother. For example, when it was time for bed, she prepared the pull-out sofa bed for me in the living room. As soon as she left the room, I turned on the TV and started watching movies. She would scold me every time she had to get up to turn it off. Other times, I used profane language, or refused to eat the food she prepared—it was always super healthy. Adding to the friction, my grandmother was a devout Catholic. And I was not a saint.

While I stayed at her house, she always made me pray. Before going to sleep, she would take me into her bedroom and make me kneel with her next to the bed. She would make me recite the words of the Lord's Prayer, and those of Hail Mary—both popular Catholic prayers. I had been through my First Communion, but my parents rarely took us to church—they were too busy performing miracles just to make payroll at the hamburger restaurant; my parents rarely, if ever, took a day off. And my father's trip to Spain to see his dying mother was certainly not a vacation. In short, although I completed my First Communion, I did not have a firm grasp of the bible, or much less, the daily rituals of a practicing Catholic.

One Sunday, during my one-week stay at my grandmother's house, she took me to church. I sat with her near the front, as she always preferred to be near the front. I felt a little nervous as Mass went on, knowing my grandmother would send me up to receive Holy Communion. And sure enough, she did. I stood in line, dreading that the person in front of me would take a step forward. When I came face to face with the priest, it was like I was having an out-of-body experience—not because of anything holy, but because I was so nervous. It was like being center stage, with all the eyes in the room fixed on me. The priest said a few words, of which I registered none, zero, nada. Then, he asked me to put out my hands, with the palms up. After the priest gently placed the Eucharist in my hand, I closed my fist and walked off—this was a big "no-no." As a Catholic, they taught me to consume the Eucharist in the priest's presence before walking back to the bench. Noticing this, my grandmother scolded me when I got back to my seat.

"What are you doing!? You are not a Catholic! You made a fool of yourself up there! What is wrong with you!? That is the last time you will be going up there!" she said, reprimanding me in front of the others—they all watched the fireworks.

When I woke up in Salceda, on Day 20, my plan was to arrive in Santiago in the morning. This was because the Cathedral of Santiago held a daily "pilgrims' Mass" at 12:00. They also held one in the evening, but typically, they would be at full capacity within minutes. So, to make sure I had two chances to attend it, I was shooting for the one at 12:00. Because of this, I had set my alarm for 03:00—the earliest I had set my alarm while on the Camino. As I mentioned previously, my left foot and right foot took turns being the most painful; each day, they would flip. Although far from comfortable, I always had one foot to put most of my weight on. On Day 20, my "luck" ran out—both feet were absolutely, positively cooked. The blister on the bottom of my left foot had spread well outside of the Compeed pad, and I had even torn a thick layer of fresh skin underneath the blister—ouch! It had exposed the skin, which was dark and red. I tried slapping a bandage on it, but it was on the middle of my foot, where the skin stretches with each step or bend of the foot. The feeling of putting hardly any pressure on it sent sharp pains up my back, causing a recoiling of my leg off the ground. Then, there was my right foot. The blister had also expanded well outside the area of the Compeed pad. Part of it naturally drained out from the incision I made after the blister had burst open in The Meseta. And toward the heel, there was still a pocket of light purple fluid with little yellow, crusty flakes floating around—it was nasty. I had drained it once before by making an incision, then poured iodine into the blister, hoping that would help tackle any infection that was brewing. For this final stretch of the Camino, I slapped on some bandages over the entirety of both soles, just to add as much padding as I could. Then, I set out to Santiago.

I left the albergue through the back door. Outside, I tiptoed around the building to get back on the highway. The pain was worse than ever. I could barely withstand the momentary pressure I was putting on each foot. It was as if I was supporting my entire bodyweight with my trekking poles. Immediately, the thought crossed my mind that I might not make it to Santiago. At that pace, and at that pain threshold, there was just no way. But again, I prayed. I prayed to Mother Mary, asking for strength, and I just kept going. Every second seemed like a minute, and every minute felt like an hour. It was the epitome of "going nowhere fast." I had just left the albergue, and I was already in a full sweat. I knew it was not normal to be suffering so much, but it was my cross to bear, so to speak. Whether it was my lower back, groin, thighs, hamstrings, calves, Achilles, or my feet, it did not matter to me. I needed to throw everything I had left in the tank, which was nothing but fumes, hope, and a heart full of spirit. Although I felt every ounce of that pain, I set aside my worries of injuries and infections and set out to leave it all on the Camino—even if it meant putting at risk my physical ability to run with the bulls.

From the highway, the gravel trail took a brief detour into the wooded countryside. Dogs barked as I passed a couple of farmhouses in the early morning hours. I stomped my feet on the ground, trying desperately to shake off the pain, and settle into a groove, a decent pace. Each time I did, it felt like my feet were being prodded with electric cattle rods. After a bit, the Camino found its way back to the highway, then back again into the eucalyptus-filled forest. The villages of A Brea and Santa Irene were the first I encountered. I limped from village to village, jamming my trekking poles into the ground—the noise kept waking up the dogs.

The moonlight gently reflected off of the black road next to the trail. I had reached O Pedrouzo, about 7km into my hike. O Pedrouzo was a popular starting point for pilgrims' final stage of the Camino. As I passed the albergues, I noticed a couple of older pilgrims quietly exiting the buildings to resume their journeys across the Galician landscape. The clacking sounds of my trekking poles were more pronounced there as I walked along the concrete sidewalks and paved roads. Each clack reminded me of the effort, and the need to earn every step along the Way. A large oak forest awaited me after the quick visit to O Pedrouzo. A demanding climb followed next.

It was dark in the forest, as I did my best to illuminate the path in front with my headlamp. The moths were all over the place, flying into my eyes, mouth, and even into my ears. I kept swatting every few seconds just to clear the ones that had landed on my light. I was completely alone out there, except for wild animal noises that made me glance behind me from time to time. Halfway up the climb, to my surprise, I approached a group of girls from the United States. It was 06:00, which is considered an early start on the Camino. The mountain trail narrowed significantly in some parts, making it difficult for me to pass them. I had finally found my groove, a solid pace, and there was no stopping me. Just before I asked for space to move up, one girl alerted the rest to move over, and they did. I left them in the dust after that. The forest had tree branches extending over the trail. Some branches were so close overhead, I could have reached out and grabbed them. Following the 2km ascent through the forest, the trail reached a paved road, where I walked the fenced perimeter of the Santiago Airport—I was getting closer.

The light of dawn was seeping through the sky, as the pale moonlight was fading. I passed a couple of villages where ancient pilgrims stopped to bathe and freshen up before arriving in Santiago. As the legend goes, "among the rivers of fresh and wholesome water to drink is Lavacolla, because in a leafy spot through which it passes, 10km from Santiago, the French pilgrims on their way to Santiago took off their clothes and for love of the Apostle used to wash not only their parts but the dirt from all over their bodies." This comes from the *Codex Calixtinus*, a famous manuscript compiled between 1138 and 1145. It served as the witness for the "Liber Sancti Jacobi," or in English, "The Book of Saint James." The purpose was to provide background and advice to prospective pilgrims on the Camino de Santiago. The manuscript is a compilation of sermons, miracles, works of art, among other notable aspects of the Camino.

After crossing the Sionlla River, I faced an uphill climb on asphalt— it was steep. I spotted a few more pilgrims in the distance. I fixed my eyes on them and tried feverishly to cut the distance between us, looking for any form of motivation to keep my pace. It had been close to five hours of walking without a stop, break, or moment of rest—nothing. I was throwing everything but the kitchen sink at this final sprint to Santiago. I could feel the damage I was inflicting on my body; it was pure punishment. But my tunnel-vision was intense and narrowly focused on reaching the great cathedral.

The birds chirped as they flew by up above, amidst the glorious light of the morning sun. The sky was blue, the weather was mildly warm, and I had made it to the Monte do Gozo. Atop the hill, I began descending a long and straight road. I could see it. I could see the towers of the Cathedral of Santiago. Even though it was far in the distance, it was there, it was tangible, and it was very real. It sent a tingling shiver up and down my spine, as well as a shot of adrenaline through my veins. I teared up a little, displaying a big grin on my face. The moment was so intense, so wonderful, and so unimaginable. Santiago himself was waiting for me, just 4km away.

I powered down the descent through a handful of twists and turns and crossed over a few highway overpasses. I had tears in my eyes as I walked by a big sign that read, "Santiago de Compostela." It was a tall metal gate, almost like a grid with little squares, with large letters attached to it. Behind the metal gate was a condensed patch of beautiful ivy and lush green leafy trees. The letters had stickers of all kinds, which were left by pilgrims who had arrived in Santiago. Although I was still about 3km away from the church,

I was making good time. It was 09:00 in the morning, and the pilgrims' Mass was starting at 12:00. Full of adrenaline, excitement, and all the above, I felt confident enough to stop for coffee and a napolitana, one last time on the Camino. After I placed my order at the bar, I felt a tap on my shoulder. It was Moe from New York! She had bandaged me up before the ascent to O Cebreiro.

"Oh my God! No way! I can't believe it!" I said, giving her a great big hug. "What are you doing here!?"

"I hurt my foot after climbing O Cebreiro, so I took the train here to Santiago with my son, Ryan," said Moe. I still could not believe she was standing there.

"Oh, I'm sorry about your foot. I hope it's nothing too serious."

"I think it'll be OK. I just needed a few days to recover. After we do some sight-seeing here in Santiago, we'll hit the Camino again and continue on to Fisterra, on the coast of Spain."

"That sounds like fun!" I said. I continued to marvel at the fact that I was standing next to Moe. I thought I was dreaming. "What are the odds that we'd be here, over 100km later, ordering coffee in a bar in Santiago? I really didn't think I'd see you again."

"It's so good to see you. I guess that's the Camino, always full of surprises," said Moe with a smile. Before I left, I used my Spanish to help Moe order coffee. The bartender was super busy attending a full bar, and my Spanish helped speed things up.

"What do you want to drink?" I asked.

"Just a coffee with some milk," said Moe, to my delight. That was my favorite drink on the Camino.

"No problem." After the order, I gave Moe one final hug. We embraced each other for a few seconds longer than before. This would be the last time I saw Moe.

Back on the street, it was 09:15. Next stop: the Cathedral of Santiago. The cobblestone sidewalks led me through the busy city streets, traffic lights, and crosswalks; cars were everywhere. Then, I encountered a couple of older pilgrims from France. They both looked over at me.

"Only two kilometers left. Be sure to enjoy it," said one of the Frenchmen. But I could not help myself. I wanted to get there. I wanted to see Santiago.

After a few more crosswalks, for which I stopped for none, I passed by a small park called the Plaza Porta Camiño—I was 500 meters away. Next, the narrow streets kicked up as the Camino maneuvered around the buildings of the old town. The path opened up at the top of the hill, where a fountain stood in dedication to Miguel de Cervantes, the legendary Spanish author of *Don Quixote*. Down the hill and to my right was the Mosteiro of San Martiño Pinario, the second largest monastery in all of Spain—200 meters away. I could hear the sounds of bagpipes up ahead, as they reverberated off the stones of the plaza, where the cathedral awaited. The street narrowed as I approached the glorious archway entrance. I took my beaten body under the archway and down the stone steps, passing a musician on my left—20 meters away. The sun was shining down on me from the east, creating an enormous shadow in front of me. There were two people in the shadow, but nobody was next to me—5 meters away. My heart was pounding, my adrenal levels spiked, my spirit was full, and I felt no pain at all. And then I exited the darkened archway and stepped into the light-filled Plaza del Obradoiro. When I looked up to my left, my eyes could not believe what I was looking at. It was the Cathedral of Santiago—I had made it. It was "mission accomplished," or perhaps more appropriate, "journey accomplished." I stood in awe of the sheer majesty and beauty of it all. The granite masonry was stunning. The imposing but magnificent façade was breathtaking. At the top, there was a statue of Saint James, dressed as a pilgrim. The bell tower on the left, and carraca tower to the right complemented the picturesque, Romanesque cathedral. I was simply speechless.

Through all the pain and suffering I had been through on the Camino, all the doubt, the constant setbacks, the physical and mental grind, and the spiritual fortitude, I was there, at the footsteps of Saint James, on Day 20, as I had planned. I am not sure if I will ever be able to truly describe what I was feeling, but I will try. The feeling of joy, fear, elation, sadness, and triumph all converged at once inside of me. It was as though I had accomplished something miraculous, but also as if I had finally repaid a long overdue debt. Arriving in Santiago ended the journey, not just the hiking, but also the experience of something truly holy. If I could have summed up my Camino in one sentence, it would be this: it was like I was walking with God. After all, I spent 20 days with Him, and it was difficult to let go.

After gazing up at the cathedral, I walked to the end of the plaza, where the downhill slope led to a staircase. The Pilgrim's Office was just down the street on Rúa das Carretas—it was time to collect my Compostela. Inside the office, the building was buzzing with energy. Pilgrims, like myself, still carried their backpacks and the rest of their gear. Their faces were brimming with smiles from ear to ear. Sighs of relief and bottled-up emotion were all over the place. I stepped up to the kiosk, where I inputted the details of my trip: my nationality, when and where I started from, and my reason for walking the Camino. Those who marked "culture" or "sport" as reasons for their Camino received a non-religious version of the Compostela, called a "Certificate of Welcome." I marked "spiritual" as my reason.

With my ticket number in-hand, I lined up with the other pilgrims until my number was called. At the counter, the volunteers asked for my pilgrim's passport, verified the countless stamps, and even gave me one final stamp to mark the end of the journey. They printed and signed my

Compostela, then gently handed it to me. Although written in Latin, below is a translation of its text:

"The Chapter of this Holy Apostolic and Metropolitan Church of Compostela, custodian of the seal of the altar of the Blessed Apostle Saint James, offers authenticating letters of accomplishment to all the faithful and pilgrims from all the lands of the Earth who, for devotion or by taking a vow, have come to the Church of the Apostle Santiago, Patron and Tutelary Saint of our Country Spain, and makes known to each and all who may inspect this letter that Ander Etxanobe has devoutly visited this most holy temple for reasons of piety."

After collecting my Compostela, I dropped off my gear at the hotel and returned to the cathedral. Outside the church, a long line of pilgrims had already wrapped around the perimeter, waiting to attend Mass. I picked up a can of Coca-Cola at a convenience store next door, then took my spot in line. Once the door opened up, which was called Puerta de las Platerías, church officials checked for backpacks and other large items. Those with such things could not enter the church as a matter of safety. Inside, it was dimly lit across the Latin cross-like floor plan and three naves. There was a display of candles next to a wooden donation box. I dropped in a couple of euros, then grabbed a candle and lit the wick, using another pilgrim's candle. Once lit, I gently set the candle in a holder on the rack. I gazed upon the wooden and stone-made chancels that took up the space around the altar, the two organs in the central nave, and the dome up above where some light was seeping through. The ambulatory and its five side-chapels wrapped around the main altar. In one of these chapels, called the Chapel of the Reliquary, it is said that the gold crucifix is from 874, and it contains a piece of the True Cross—the real cross Jesus was crucified on. And then there was the altar—the gloriously spectacular main altar. The barrel-vaulted nave gave way to this altar, which contained groin-vaulted aisles of eleven bays, while the transept comprised six bays. Semi-columns looked to be painted in a mesmerizing gold. The baldachin included a thirteenth century statue of Saint James. Above him were angels carrying a canopy, where at the top was a statue of Saint James the Apostle on horseback. I could have stared at the altar for hours. Before I stepped away, I closed my eyes and said a prayer.

The cathedral benches were mostly empty as pilgrims explored the cathedral. I noticed a man sitting in the first row, seated nearest to the aisle. I sat next to the man. He was a Dutchman and had completed his Camino the day before. It was already his second Mass. The man, whose name I did not learn, had told me that our bench provided the best view. And he was right. When Mass began, the benches had filled up, and we had a front row view of it all. The priest started by welcoming us to the church, even noting the national origins of pilgrims who had arrived in the last 24 hours, such as myself. After that, part of me sort of blacked out. My emotions unraveled as

I sat on the bench. My eyes welled up with tears as the priest repeated a few prayers. The Dutchman looked over at me a few times—surely he noticed. I looked up at the "Botafumeiro," the largest censer in the world. Weighing 53 kilograms, and one meter and a half tall, a system of ropes and pulleys kept it sustained in the air above the altar. On special occasions, the censer swings from a height of 20 meters, dispersing sage throughout the church as it reaches speeds of 68km/h. Though I did not observe this, it was even more poetic as it remained suspended in the air. The whole thing was very emotional.

Before Mass was over, it was time for Catholics to rise and accept the Eucharist. Two priests prepared the Eucharist and established two lines for pilgrims on each side of the main aisle. They asked only baptized Catholics to step forward for Holy Communion. The Dutchman stood up first, and I slowly followed. When it was my turn, I stepped up to the priest, who uttered a few words:

"This is the Lamb of God who takes away the sins of the world. Happy are those who are called to His supper," said the priest. I opened my hands as he placed the bread in the middle of my palm. Looking into the eyes of the priest, it was another holy moment for me. It was an out-of-body experience. I calmy but promptly took the round bread piece from my hand, placed it on my tongue, and consumed it in front of the priest. Then, I returned to the bench.

When Mass was over, there was a rush for pilgrims to go to the crypt of Saint James, which lies beneath the main altar. Moving as quickly as my blistered feet would take me, I lined up with the others as the line slowly moved toward the entrance. A small staircase led down into the crypt, with a plaque above that read, "Sepulcrum Sancti Iacobi Gloriosum," or in English, "Tomb of the Glorious Saint James." I ducked my head under the narrow passageway and down the staircase. Behind bars and to my left was the silver reliquary. Inside the chest was a cedar box, which contained compartments with the remains of Saint James, along with his two disciples, Saint Theodorus and Saint Athanasius. I said a small prayer as I stared into the crypt, then moved along to make way for the pilgrims behind me. Up the opposite staircase, the line led to the bust of Saint James, situated atop the main altar. As is the tradition, I carefully approached the bust of the Apostle, and gave him a gentle, but affectionate hug, placing my left hand upon his left shoulder, and wrapping my right arm around his right shoulder. Then, I left the church.

Outside, I noticed the priest who had given me Holy Communion. Dressed in his black liturgical vestment, he was walking away, up the staircase and through the archway that I had used to arrive at the cathedral. I immediately chased him down.

"Excuse me, father!" I said, doing my best to slow him down.

173

"Oh hey, I remember you," he said, taking off his black sunglasses as he stopped to speak to me.

"I just wanted to say, 'thank you.'" As fate would have it, he was American. Father Michael was a guest priest from Cincinnati, Ohio, having finished his own Camino the day before.

"Can I give you a blessing?" asked Father Michael.

"Of course! I would be honored!" I said, closing my eyes as he did the Sign of the Cross on my foreword, softly uttering a few words. Other pilgrims continued walking by as we stood on the steps in the middle of the staircase. When he was done, he put his sunglasses back on, then continued up the staircase. The experience left me speechless; it felt biblical.

In the Bible, one of the most profound passages is in the Book of Job. In it, we come to know Job as a wealthy man who has it all. He has a large family and plentiful livestock. Then one day, Satan appears before God in Heaven. After God boasts of the righteous life that Job is living, Satan responds that he only does so because God has blessed him with an abundance of good fortune. After Satan challenges God, He accepts. God allows Satan to torment Job and disrupt his perfect life. In the span of one day, Satan kills Job's livestock, his servants, and all 10 of his children, believing this will cause Job to turn away from God. And while Job mourns and is distraught with grief, he still prays to God and shows his faith in Him. Satan tries one last time to make Job turn away from God by giving him a terrible illness.

"So Satan went out from the presence of the LORD, and inflicted loathsome sores on Job from the sole of his foot to the crown of his head."—Job 2:7.

Now, at his lowest point, Job curses his own existence, and even asks for God to kill him. Eventually, God intervenes and speaks with Job. He asks him a series of rhetorical questions about His power and the wonders of creation. After a humbling encounter, Job acknowledges God's limitless power and glory, and he once again finds favor with Him. God forgives Job, cures his disease, and blesses him with twice as much livestock, new children, and a long life ahead.

The story of Job is a touching one. No matter how strong or indestructible I think I am, no matter how tough and enduring I believe my mind to be, I always need God in my life; I need God to lead me.

"But he knows the way that I take; when he has tested me, I shall come out like gold."—Job 23:10.

God had a plan for me when I began the Camino. He knew why I was going, even before I did. In June and July of 2023, I was called to the Camino to be broken down, to be humbled. I believe God allowed this to happen, so that through Him, and through my faith, I could become a better man. He knew the path I was on, across the entire 800km journey. He and

His angels, along with Mother Mary, observed and watched me over countless steps—from the Napoleon Pass to the Hill of Forgiveness, from The Meseta to the ascent to O Cebreiro, they never lost sight of me. I am blessed.

Miracles are not always for the naked eye to see. Sometimes, miracles are for us to feel, they are for us to question, and they are for us to seek understanding. Sometimes, miracles are not instantaneous, either. Sometimes, miracles take 20 days on bad, blistery feet. And with a little time, and a little faith, such miracles can take shape. Is not pain such a beautiful part of life?

CHAPTER NINETEEN:

I NEED A DOCTOR

"If a man has not found something worth dying for, he is not fit to live."—Martin Luther King Jr. It is one of my favorite quotes of his. And although he said it regarding the Civil Rights Movement of the 1960s, the words still echo their importance across all aspects of life. Ever since I could remember, I always wanted to be a bull runner. My grandfather would sit me down on his couch and play old, recorded VHS tapes of the running of the bulls. The screen would light up with the traditional red and white clothing worn by the runners. People flooded balconies above the cobblestone streets, just to get a glimpse of the brave men (and women) running in front of the charging bulls. These animals can weigh up to about 600 kilos—they are massive, made of solid muscle. Thinking back to those days with my grandfather, what attracted me most to the event was the brazen act of it all. I watched as runners rounded "La Curva" (The Curve), the most dangerous turn on the run route. They ran with rolled-up newspapers, extending them out behind them, getting the bulls to lock on. The bulls, unable to decelerate in time, would slam into the wooden barrier of the turn, then continue charging up the street toward the bull ring—it was absolutely thrilling. And it filled my grandfather with great pride; I could see it in his eyes, and I could feel it when he spoke. But while watching the footage, I also saw when someone got trampled, tossed, or even gored. That was when I realized that death was an actual possibility. Despite that, all I wanted was a chance to take part, a chance to join the fraternity, and ultimately, a chance to wager my life for the age-ole tradition.

By the time I had walked the Camino de Santiago, I had been running with the bulls for six years. Along the way, I had seen injuries, but nothing major like a goring or even a bone fracture. There was the time in 2019 when I tore my quadriceps in Pamplona, requiring the help of my dear friend Aaron Marshall, who wrapped me up each morning before the run. We would meet up at a friend's apartment at 06:30, with a roll of ACE wrap and other medical supplies. Aaron would bandage me up from my knee to my waist. Then, there was the time in 2020, when I tore my groin in Ciudad Rodrigo, luring lone bulls into the bull ring all day long. Then, there was the time in 2022, when I sprained my ankle in Pamplona after colliding with a guy who had climbed up a drainpipe on the side of a building—yes, he climbed a drainpipe during the run, and did not even make sure he was out of the way of the runners. But never had I taken part in the running of the bulls in such poor form—both physically and mentally.

After Mass at the Cathedral of Santiago, I went back to my hotel and spent the next few hours removing all of my bandages from the Camino—even the Compeed pads. I had not done that previously because I thought I might tear the skin attached to the Compeed pads, which fall off on their own. Fearing an infection, or something worse, I took the chance and tore them off. When I did, I had never smelled a more rancid smell in my entire life—it was bad. It was bad enough to make me gag, just being in proximity to it. The bandages had a moist, but crusty, yellow gunk on them. So, I crumpled up the bandages and tossed them in the wastebasket near the bed. Chunks of dried-up puss and blister fluid had also formed around the blisters on the bottom of my feet. I took a warm paper towel and gently cleaned the area as best I could. Unfortunately, when I removed all the bandages, I had torn the dark red skin that was underneath the blister skin. And for the second time, it was at the spot on my foot where it bends. It is nearly impossible to take a step where your foot does not bend. Still in shambles, I had one more errand to run before I left Santiago.

When I go places, like on vacation, or to sightsee, I rarely buy souvenirs. Mostly because I find them overpriced, cliché, and easily forgotten once I bring them home. But my pilgrimage to Santiago was different. Although I already had the Compostela, and the spiritual experience that I will carry forever, I needed one last thing—a rosary from the Cathedral of Santiago. I stopped by and grabbed one, throwing it over my head along with my necklace of the Virgin Mary. I felt like a man of God. The Camino was a deeply spiritual experience for me, and the rosary served as a reminder to cherish it and live righteously.

On Day 21, with the rosary around my neck, I was ready to catch the train to Pamplona. After boarding, I placed my backpack in the overhead bin, then took my seat next to the window. It was an eight-hour ride from Santiago to Pamplona, with 13 stops along the way. Luckily, the train had a bar at the back, where I could order drinks and snacks. As the train moved along, it was surreal to be passing some of the same towns and villages I had passed through on the Camino: Ponferrada, Astorga, León, and Burgos. It felt like I was doing the Camino de Santiago in reverse, but lightning fast, and without 40 kilometers of painful daily walking. It was amusing to witness the section from León to Burgos from the comfort of an air-conditioned train—it was a hot mess outside, and I knew it all too well. The swelling of my feet and the aches persisted, even on the train. I was still wearing my thick, wool hiking socks, since the pressure, though it caused swelling, helped to numb some of the pain.

My friends Bill and Paula came to pick me up in Pamplona. The train station was absolute chaos, as police were conducting searches for narcotics. It was July 5, and it was less than 24 hours before the official start of the Fiesta of San Fermín. Festivalgoers packed the train I rode in on, eager to settle into town before the festivities kicked off. Bill and Paula were excited to see me, and I was too. We had not seen each other since the last fiesta in 2022. Bill has been going to the running of the bulls for almost 20 years. He is originally from Chicago, where he grew up a Golden Gloves Boxing Champion. Years later, he discovered a passion for literature, earned his PhD, and now teaches back home in Chicago. Bill spends so much time in Pamplona that he even met his wife there. Paula was born and raised in Pamplona, and has a strong affinity for the city, the bulls, and the Basque and Spanish cultures at large. It was love at first sight for Bill and Paula. A few years after they met, I was Bill's "Best Man" at the wedding.

When they picked me up, Bill and Paula were quick to notice my limp, which was even worse now, considering the skin I tore at the bottom of my foot.

"Oh my God, Ander, how are you going to run like this?" asked Paula. I had texted with her and Bill a few times during the Camino, but did not let on how bad things had gotten.

"Today's July 5th, so I have two days before the first run. I'll be ready," I said, trying to keep us both calm. I knew I had to call someone. And there was no better person to call than Aaron Marshall.

Aaron was always there for me whenever I got hurt in Pamplona. He is an Emory University graduate, with a Master's degree in Public Health. In the past, Aaron has served as an Incident Commander for Team Rubicon, an Emergency Medical Technician and Helicopter Crewmember fighting wildfires, an Emergency Management Specialist at the Capitol Police in Washington, and he is currently a Director at the Federal Emergency Management Administration (FEMA) in Mass Care and Emergency Services—in short, Aaron is the guy you call in dire situations, and this was one of them. After phoning Aaron, who himself had just arrived in Pamplona, we agreed to meet at Hotel Yoldi, where I stay every year for the festival. Hotel Yoldi is a boutique hotel that has earned legendary status in Pamplona. It is the place where bullfighters stay when they are in town.

Ernest Hemingway was also a frequent visitor during the early twentieth century.

"Alright, let's see what you have going on here," said Aaron, as he examined my feet, sitting in a chair next to my bed. I was eager to hear his response. Aaron did not overreact to situations, much less during the running of the bulls, but he also gave it to you straight.

"What do you think? Is it bad?" I asked.

"Well, at least it's not as bad as I thought it would be."

"Think I can run?"

"Oh yeah, you can run… it really just depends on your pain tolerance."

"I've been taking some ibuprofen to help with the pain," I said, showing him the 200mg pills I had purchased on the Camino.

"Umm, yeah, I see what's going on here. We gotta go to the pharmacy," said Aaron. "First, we need to get you something stronger. Then, we need to get some disinfectant cream… that thing looks nasty. I'll wrap it for you, but you have to be sure to air it out. It doesn't look infected, but it wouldn't take much."

I went with Aaron to the nearest pharmacy to pick up some supplies: acetaminophen (1,000mg), tube of disinfectant cream, more Compeed pads, bandages, moleskin, and iodine. His lovely fiancé, Caroline, joined us on the mission. Caroline is a medically trained flight attendant—I was in excellent hands all the way around. When we returned to the hotel, Aaron cleaned out my blister bubbles using a bidet, pumped them full of iodine and disinfectant, then bandaged me up.

The next morning, on Day 22, I was going to miss the opening ceremony of the running of the bulls—I had to work. In 2021, I joined a "peña" (social club) in Pamplona called, "La Unica," which means, The Only One. It is the oldest of the 16 social clubs in Pamplona, with roots going back to 1903. These clubs are the heart and soul of the fiesta. They parade through the streets from dusk 'till dawn, accompanied by "txarangas" (bands) with an assortment of musical instruments. Members of La Unica are easy to spot at the fiesta, since they wear green "pañuelos" (handkerchiefs) and "fajas" (sashes). As a member of La Unica, I was required to work two different shifts during the fiesta. And, unfortunately, one of those shifts was on July 6 at 08:00, just before the opening ceremonies.

Nestled in the old town of Pamplona, the clubhouse is on the infamous Calle Jarauta, where most of the other social clubs are located. La Unica had recently purchased a new building for its headquarters—a big, beautiful building with four floors, three bars, a commercial-sized kitchen, and a bodega on the basement level. On July 6, my job was to be a waiter and busboy. Each year, the club hosted a late morning breakfast for members. Before I walked over, I popped a few tablets of acetaminophen, then met up with my buddy, Iker. What made that morning shift fun was being able to wheel around the food carts with Iker for five hours. There were over 300 guests packed into the building, so there was a lot of work for us. We started by lining the long tables on each floor with tablecloths, plates, glasses, napkins, spoons, forks, and knives. Afterwards, we went back to the kitchen to collect the trays full of food. We had jamon serrano, chorizo, fried eggs, garlic-fish soup (traditional of Navarra), and bread, lots of loaves of bread. With over 300 plates on the tables, it was easier to drop off the large trays with the guests and let them share or distribute the breakfast. And of course, what is a meal in Spain if you do not have wine? Iker and I loaded up on bottles of red wine, txakolin (Basque sparkling white wine), and plenty of Coca-Cola.

Still reeling from the Camino de Santiago, I took every chance I had to lean on the food cart or against the inside of the elevator shaft—standing up was a problem. My legs felt like they had just completed the New York Marathon. But actually, the New York Marathon is only 42km, and technically, that was an average day for me on the Camino. Still, I had to work. So, Iker and I did a little something to take the edge off—we "snuck" a couple of beers into the kitchen. What also helped to take my mind off of the pain were the special guests we were going to have at breakfast. Cash Lawless, my friend from high school and real estate entrepreneur, was in Pamplona for the entire Fiesta of San Fermín—he brought his whole family with him too. Courtney, Cash's wife, had already been to Pamplona twice before, and this time, she brought her 14-year-old son, Jude. Along for the ride were Cash's brother, TJ, a motorcycle parts manufacturer and custom bike builder, and their sister, Chevy, who works as a technician in the medical field—this was the first fiesta for both TJ and Chevy. We assigned them a table toward the front of the main floor, just to keep an eye on them—they spoke limited Spanish, and absolutely zero Basque. Overall, I think they did OK for themselves, as they made great friends with the table next to them. However, it may have been the wine, seeing as though they all walked away from breakfast as drunk as a skunk—the magic of San Fermín.

After the Lawless family and the other 300 guests left La Unica, Iker and I spent the next couple of hours bussing the messy tables, collecting food scraps, removing plates, and tossing out countless empty wine bottles. But once we clocked out, we took to the streets to get sloshed. The difference in atmosphere before and after the opening ceremonies is night and day. Before the 12:00 launching of the rocket at the town hall, signifying the start of the fiesta, there is certainly an undeniable buzz of energy throughout the ancient city. But once the rocket goes off and the confetti falls, it is nearly impossible to walk down a street without squeezing through the masses. Despite that, we all gathered for food and drinks. Joining us also were Ane, Iker's girlfriend, as well as Aaron and Caroline. The meetup point was La

Mejillonera, a place we refer to as "Mussel Bar." People know the standing-room-only bar for their small plates of food—mussels, calamari, patatas bravas, and fried green peppers. To drink, half of us ordered "kalimotxo", which is a mix of Coca-Cola and red wine, and the other half got "tinto de verano," a combination of red wine and lemonade. Although both are great, tinto de verano was my drink of choice—refreshing, yet it got you drunk. And the more I drank, the less pain I felt, which was nice too.

After some time at Mussel Bar, I retreated to Hotel Yoldi to get some much-needed rest. The crew came along for a quick celebratory drink—we found many reasons to celebrate. The sky was blue? Let us drink. We are in Pamplona? Let us have another. We are at a bar? Why, let us have one more. And at Hotel Yoldi, there was only one drink to be had—"champú." This white, Cava-infused lemon sorbet concoction helped put Hotel Yoldi on the map. They only serve it during the Fiesta of San Fermín, which was all the more reason to enjoy it. Served in chilled glasses, the icy and refreshingly awesome drink was one of the few things that quieted the group. You always had to savor that first sip—it might as well be the law.

Back in my hotel room, the first thing I did was lay down and elevate my feet. The bonus of being back in a proper hotel room was the assortment of pillows I had at my disposal—I was living my best life. I did not want to remove any bandages, for fear that I might tear more skin—my feet were bad enough as they were. But the bandages also made showering difficult. I had to contort my body just to get in the tub and keep my feet dry. While on the Camino, I had seen what water could do to wet bandages and sensitive skin—it wreaks havoc upon them. The Compeed pads were especially keen to keep dry, since I noticed they absorbed water and ballooned up. It also made them gooey and stick to everything, including my socks.

After cleaning up, I laid out my gear for the running of the bulls. My red Nike Lunar Epic shoes had been with me since 2017, my first year running. The traction had held up well, despite the six years and over 50 bull runs they had been through. The shoes are spectacular. They are comfortable, lightweight, sleek, and have a grip that even Spiderman would envy. They also feature a high collar or bootie style wrap at the top, which keeps my feet tightly secured to the shoe—a luxury considering how easy it is to get stepped on while running with thousands of other runners. The only downside of the terrific grip was the very nature of the pressure-mapped soles. The circular cracks and crevices allowed every small rock or pebble in its path to get stuck inside. My only remedy was to sit on the ground with a fork and carefully dig them out. But it was worth it. Aside from the shoes, the rest of my Nike ensemble included long black compression pants (yes, tights), black running shorts, and a sleeveless Nike Dri-Fit shirt. Some of you might ask, "But what about the red and white attire? Isn't that the uniform?" Well, yes, and no. While most runners and festivalgoers-alike do indeed wear the traditional red and white clothing, they have not always done so. Old photos from the early twentieth century show men dressed in dark suits and caps, while running with the bulls in Pamplona. As the years went on, the red and white clothing took over the run. It helped unify runners under the banner of the fiesta and its homage to San Fermín, maintaining a level of purity in the bull run. By purity, I mean taking the attention away from any one individual runner, and focusing more on the "toro bravo," or "Spanish fighting bull." However, not everyone feels that way. Typically, the runners who are local to Pamplona will run in red and white attire. However, those who visit from other towns across Spain will frequently wear a sports jersey, perhaps that of their favorite soccer team. In recent years, this has become more controversial, and even made its way to the newspaper opinion pieces. Nevertheless, I wear the black Nike gear for two reasons: it promises optimal athletic movement, and it looks rad.

Before I jumped into bed, we had organized a dinner with the group at La Cuchara de Martin, my cousin's restaurant. It has become an annual tradition. Each year, we reserve a banquet and isolate ourselves from the rest of the restaurant and partygoers. It provides a much-needed break from the madness outside. By this point in the day, we still drink, just not as recklessly as we did earlier on. My go-to food choice at the restaurant is the "solomillo," an utterly delicious beef tenderloin that has incredible flavor, especially when cooked rare or medium-rare. One of my favorite parts of this dinner is hearing Iker's "tour stories." July 6 is always busy for Iker, as he takes hundreds of people on "bull running tours" through the run route. And on this day, Iker had been at it since we finished bussing tables at La Unica—he looked exhausted.

"Hey man, glad you could join us," I said to Iker. "How'd it go?"

"Hey, yeah, thanks. The tour went well. There was this guy toward the end... it was just him, nobody else in the group. Whenever I said something, he'd be like, 'Whoa!' or 'Wow, that's crazy!' and it was like that for an hour. I mean, I'd be showing him a wooden barrier, and he'd be like, 'That's crazy! This is crazy! We're crazy, right!?' and I just wanted it to stop." The entire table laughed. As Iker told the story, it sounded like a scene from *Bill and Ted's Excellent Adventure*. In Pamplona, we found laughter in most everything, except the bull run itself.

On Day 23, my alarm went off at 05:45 in the morning. When most people wake up, their first thought is, "Hot or cold," or "What time is it?" When I wake the morning of a bull run, my mind is already thinking about the bulls and how I am going to run. I am thinking about my strategy: my starting point, when to take off sprinting, and where I plan to exit. Over the last few years, my place has been at The Curve. My objective is to "run on the horns" of the bull, just in front of it. That is the goal of most runners. But more than that, my objective is to round the corner of The Curve, looking back into the eyes of the bull coming up behind me. I do so while holding out a newspaper toward its snout, bringing the bull around the dangerous curve, just a few feet or sometimes inches away from me. In general, everyone ends up running away from the bull, no matter where they start their run. But I feel like very few people actually enjoy their moments with the bulls. When you look back and stare into a bull's eyes, you have an instant relationship with that bull—its might, its power, and even its grace. It is an unbelievable feeling. The Curve is also one of the most technical and chaotic points of the "encierro" (the Spanish term for the bull run). Many people panic there, as the bulls often collide with the barricades, after stampeding down Mercaderes, the street that leads to The Curve. But I love it there.

Before leaving the room, I popped a 1,000mg acetaminophen tablet, stretched for 10 minutes, then limped out of the hotel. Anybody with an ounce of common sense would have stayed in bed. They would not have left at 06:30 to go run with the bulls. There are only eight bull runs in Pamplona each year, and missing even one of them was a non-starter for me. I can honestly say that it is the only reason I continue to stay in shape: running every week, lifting weights almost every day, and eating the right foods. The irony was that I had never been in such bad shape before a bull run. It hurt badly to walk on my blisters and the open, bloody flesh wounds on the bottom of my feet. But this would be the first time I actually ran on them, if it was even possible. Throughout my life and my career, I have been able to accept failure—not passing an exam, not getting the girl I wanted, being passed over for a job, or even having "bad" runs at the running of the bulls. Although I despise failure, I can learn to accept it. But I cannot lay down without trying. That got me out of bed that morning.

Down in the lobby, the hotel desk clerks wished me well during the run. The hotel is family-owned, and the siblings run the place together. After several years of staying there, they became like a little family to me.

"Good luck, Ander! Maybe we will see you on TV," they said. "But be careful. There are always too many people on the first day, and it can be very dangerous."

When I left the hotel, dawn was breaking. It was still dark, and the air was cool. As I approached the run route, I did not want people to observe my condition. So, I tried to walk as normal as possible, gritting my teeth with each step. Still, anyone with a half-sober eye could have seen that something was up, something was off. Young partiers were walking away from the route. They had been out drinking all night long and were finally making their way home. It was the ultimate contrast. Most of them were so drunk they did not even notice me. Even though I stuck out like a sore thumb, wearing my all-black Nike gear, it was as though I was invisible. It was as though I was dead.

I picked up a newspaper on a street called Santo Domingo, near the corrals where the bulls were being held. I drank coffee with milk at a bar just off the run route, at a place called El Redín. As I sipped my coffee, someone tapped me on the shoulder. It was Aaron Marshall and his fiancé Caroline.

"Aaron, what are you doing here? I thought you weren't going to run this year?" I asked. Aaron suffered a serious injury the year before while running with the bulls. He was running through the town hall section when other runners tripped him up and trampled him. He broke his arm in three places, requiring extensive surgery.

"No, I'm not running this year," said Aaron.

"Then what are you doing up this early?"

"We're here for you," he said. Aaron was the guy who gave you the shirt off his back. His friendship and care for others is second to none. And Caroline is the same way. They are two peas in a pod.

"Thanks, you guys… I wouldn't be here without you." I said. I was so blessed to have them.

"Who's running today?" asked Aaron, referring to the ranch where the bulls came from. Each of the eight bull runs featured a fresh set of bulls from a different ranch across Spain.

"La Palmosilla," I said.

At 07:45, it was time for me to head up the street, near the doorsteps of the town hall. There, I would start my run at the top of the hill, with the street of Santo Domingo in my sight. I rolled up and flattened my newspaper repeatedly, making it tighter each time. The police inspections had just taken place, weeding out the "bad apples," such as people who were drunk, on drugs, or carrying GoPro cameras. But the town hall was still overflowing with people, since it is a popular spot for new runners, making it even more dangerous. Bulls are dangerous, but so are new runners, given their unpredictability when panic sets in. The cool morning air was full of tension and anxiety, as runners fidgeted their hands and began breathing heavily with their mouths open. The façade's analog clock made the excruciating wait for the bulls even worse. Runners looked up at it with a nervous twitch every five seconds, just to see if the big hand had moved. The spectators amplified the anxious energy. They watched from their apartment balconies, and lined the wooden barricades along the route, which kept the bulls, and the ensuing chaos, in the street. I remembered how I had passed the town hall while on the Camino. Compared to July 7 at 07:59, the streets were relatively empty. The atmosphere was calm and carefree. Now, I was standing on those same cobbles, surrounded by hundreds of other runners, all waiting for the big bang.

Moments later, the clock bells rang from atop the façade of the town hall, signaling it was 08:00. People clapped and cheered the sound as the bulls were about to be released from the corrals down the hill on Santo Domingo. After a few seconds, the loud sound of a rocket exploding reverberated around the old town of Pamplona. They opened the gate, unleashing a thundering stampede of 600-kilo fighting bulls onto the cobblestones. People jumped in place, loosening themselves up for the run of their lives. My rosary dangled around my neck as I bounced from side to side, left foot to right foot, trying to shake up my legs and stay loose. When I did that, I felt the shooting pains of a thousand nerves being disturbed on the soles of my feet. It was then that I realized I had no "lift" in my legs—they felt like Jello-O. I could not even jump.

The people in front of me continued jumping up and down, this time trying to get a glimpse of the bulls charging up the street. When they did, they began running at me frantically, causing a stampede of their own. They flung their arms, shoving and knocking over anyone in their path. Still, I held my ground for a few seconds longer. When the herd was about 30 meters away, I turned up the street and began my slow jog around the town hall and onto Mercaderes. As I trotted down the street, I looked back every few seconds to gauge the distance to the bulls, which I could not yet see. I knew they were close, as the escalation in panic was more and more intense. When the grown men full of freight began yelling, I knew they were just 5 to 10 meters away. At that point, just as I was arriving at The Curve, I clutched the newspaper with my right hand, looked back, and extended the paper out behind me, pointing the tip at the herd—they were on my tail, just a few feet away. They were coming for me.

Once I had the herd locked onto my newspaper, I began sprinting up the cobbled incline of Estafeta—the longest stretch of the course. I made it about 25 meters up until I noticed I was losing my footing. It was like it was happening in slow motion. My form went out, my velocity slowed, and I felt an eerie silence for what felt like an eternity. And then, I hit the ground. My face slammed into the cobbles, with the entire herd of bulls and the black cloud of death behind me.

CHAPTER TWENTY:

PAIN AND GAIN

They tied him up in an obscure warehouse. Badly beaten, and deprived of sleep, they prod his testicles with electricity. And yet, Victor Kershaw is still alive. Ex-con and bodybuilder, Daniel Lugo, and his pals from the Sun Gym have kidnapped and extorted Kershaw for his mansion, fancy cars, and untold South Florida wealth. They keep him blindfolded and tied up to a chair in a warehouse while they move into his waterfront home, drive his exotic cars, spend all of his money, and live the lavish lifestyle they have always dreamed of. Through crooked notaries and forged signatures, they think they are getting away with the perfect crime. And there is only one thing left to do: kill Victor Kershaw.

The "Sun Gym Gang" devises a whacky plan. They force Victor Kershaw to drink hordes of liquor to alter his mental state, put him inside his own vehicle, jimmy-rig the gas pedal, then send him flying into an excavator parked underneath a freeway overpass. Shockingly, Kershaw survives the wreck. Their next idea is to douse the car with gasoline and set it on fire. The vehicle goes up in flames. Surely, he is dead—nope. Kershaw steps out of the car, swatting at his shirt as he tries to extinguish the flames. The gang, in disbelief, remains intent on killing him. So, they try ramming him with their van as he stumbles away from the fire. Kershaw goes down, but he is not dead. While he is laying on the ground, they put the van in reverse, then slowly back up, as the weight of the van appears to crush Kershaw's face. Their job is done, so they think.

These are the events portrayed in the 2013 film, *Pain and Gain*. The movie was based on a shockingly true story, and played by Hollywood elites Mark Wahlberg, Dwayne Johnson, and Anthony Mackie. When I hit the ground on July 7, I felt like Victor Kershaw. I had spent 20 excruciatingly painful days on the Camino de Santiago. It felt like the Camino had tortured my feet, hit me with a truck, and left me for dead. Then, a day or two goes by, and I am lying face down on cobblestones, with the most ferocious and feared animals chasing from behind.

After I rounded The Curve, I clearly remember seeing the entire herd on my coattails. I had stuck out my rolled-up newspaper to attract the bulls and bring them around, following me in a straight line. Instead of hitting the wooden barrier of the curve, the lead bulls maintained their speed and momentum, causing me to lower my paper and sprint straight up the street—or risk getting trampled, gored, or worse. I felt my right foot give out, which sent me directly to the ground. My forehead slammed into the unforgiving cobbles that lined the narrow street of Estafeta. As I was laying there, facedown, there was absolutely nothing I could do, and that was downright terrifying.

With my body stretched out from head to toe, I did not move an inch. I laid there like a dead man in the street, at the mercy of the bulls, the runners, and San Fermín. My eyes were closed as I clutched the newspaper. I felt the world move around me, like a tornado tearing through a town. The noise of bells rang as the entire herd began leaping over me. A hoof rocked my temple, then the back of my head, then the temple again, then stepped on and scraped up my back. The noises continued as the ground shook, but I remained still. I grunted in pain and anguish as the hooves made contact. A throbbing headache came on immediately—it was pounding. Once the entire herd had jumped over me, I felt a few taps on my shoulder and a few hands helping me up. They were two well-respected runners, and they were my friends, too.

"Ander, come on, get up!" said Isaac Ferrera.

"Ugh..." I said in agony. It felt like my headache was flopping around in my head as I stood up with their help.

"Are you OK!?" asked Jose Manuel Gomez.

"Yeah, I'm good, I'm good..." I said, as they helped me over to the wall. Their eyes were gigantic as they looked at me with terror.

"You don't look so good. We need to get you help," said Gomez. Ferrera was waving his arms in the air, yelling to get the medics' attention. The nearest medics had a station 25 meters away.

"No, really, I'm fine..." I said.

"You hit your face, there's a huge red lump on your forehead," said Gomez. The medics rushed over with a gurney, though I did not need it.

With the medics' help, we walked slowly over to The Curve, where the station was located. Standing against the wall with a horrified look was Ryant Bennett, my buddy from Texas. He had both hands on his head as he looked at me in disbelief.

"I can't believe you survived that... I thought you were gone," said Ryan. I gave him a hug as he waited to make sure I was OK. Then I ducked through the wooden barricades to receive medical attention.

A team of five medics rushed to spot-check me for any gorings. Bill, my friend, has been gored three times while running with the bulls. He says that you have so much adrenaline pumping through your body that sometimes it can feel like a small prick of a needle, even though a giant horn has impaled your skin. Thankfully, I had no gorings. The medics examined the welt on my forehead, telling me to put ice on it right away. They dabbed the scrapes and cuts on my skin with alcohol and iodine—the palms of my hands had it the worst, as I extended them out to break my fall on the cobbles. After removing my shirt, the medics discovered bruises and cuts on my upper back. I had another welt on the back of my head, as well as on my right temple—even the slightest touch was extremely painful.

"Does your head hurt? Are you experiencing any headaches?" asked one medic.

"No..." I said. Meanwhile, the migraine-like pain was getting worse.

"If you begin to experience headaches or pains, you need to go to the hospital," they said. Then, they released me.

After I left the medics at The Curve, I started walking over to Bar Txoko, a bar made famous by Ernest Hemingway. He frequented the place over the many years he attended the Fiesta of San Fermín. Bar Txoko was in the Plaza del Castillo, which was only a few hundred meters from The Curve. Almost immediately, I ran into Aaron and Caroline, who had watched the run from a barrier down on Santo Domingo. Unaware of what happened, I gave them my version of the events.

"I went down," I said.

"No way..." said Aaron.

"What happened?" asked Caroline.

"I timed my run from the town hall so that the herd would reach me at The Curve. When the pocket opened up and the herd was behind me, I realized they were flying. So, I sprinted up the street. Four or five seconds later, I was on the ground. It felt like my shoe slipped or something."

"Did you hit your head?" asked Caroline.

"Yeah, I guess it stopped my fall. How bad is it?"

"It's a good size bump... you need to get ice on that right away," said Aaron.

"Let's go to Bar Txoko," I said.

"Here, take this..." said Aaron, handing me a 1,000mg tablet of acetaminophen.

"Dude, you're the best! My head hurts like a bitch," I said, popping the tablet immediately. Aaron looked concerned, but not worried. He performed a quick check to see if I had a concussion. Then, he told me to get rest, keep ice on it, and to let him know if the pains became worse. In the end, he knew I would run with or without the concussion.

The drinks flowed that morning on July 7. It was 08:15, and I was already tipsy from slugging a few "lugumbas," which is a traditional drink among foreign runners. It is a combination of chocolate milk, cognac, and a couple of ice cubes. After the run each morning, we gathered together at Bar Txoko and ordered drinks from the outside counter. People took turns going in and out of the bar, where that morning's bull run was on slow-motion replay. It was the first time I had seen the footage since my fall.

"You got taken out!" said Cash, standing below the television screen mounted to the ceiling of the bar.

"Wow..." I said, "I have no memory of that." The steer, which is a castrated bull that leads the herd up the street, had practically run me over.

"You didn't see it coming at all?" asked Cash.

"No man, nothing. I saw the herd behind me at The Curve, then I darted up the street and lost my footing... that's what I thought, but I guess not."

"Oh, shit! The bulls ran right over you!" said Courtney.

In the video footage, I left The Curve with the herd directly behind me. But there was a group of people to my right that blocked the view of a steer. When I made it up the street, runners had cleared out to the sides, and the steer appeared out of nowhere. I was running in the center of the street, while the animal was gravitating toward me, then it used its left horn to level me to the ground. I watched in slow motion how each bull passed right over my outstretched body. It was a miracle that nothing worse happened. Still, I was pretty banged up. Before I went back to the hotel, I saw Ryan Bennett again. He ran right up to me and gave me another big hug.

"Dude, don't ever do that to me again," he said.

"Thanks for being there, man. You were one of the first people I saw when I got up," I said.

When I got back to the hotel, I took off my shirt and found my chest stained with dark purple dye from my rosary. That thing saved my life, as did my necklace of the Virgin Mary. The rosary had a soothing lavender scent to it. It helped put me at peace. And the acetaminophen helped too. Getting trampled on the first day of the running of the bulls seemed fitting, considering I had just walked 800km across Spain. I had become accustomed to things getting harder. So, to start off the running of the bulls with a thundering bang, I welcomed it, even if I had added to my growing list of injuries.

The crew gathered again for a late breakfast around 09:30. In years past, we loved going to a place called La Raspa, only a few blocks away from Estafeta, where I hit the ground. La Raspa has become the most popular place for the contingent of foreigners who return to Pamplona each year. It is largely the same group of people who get together at Bar Txoko for morning lugumbas. Unfortunately, the restaurant did not have any space, as all the tables were swarming with eager eaters. Eating is a tricky issue at the fiesta, as you almost always have to book in advance. That is why so many first-timers walk around eating sandwiches all day—it is often the only food you have access to, unless you go well outside the party area, or down to the carnival, which is a 20-minute walk. However, sometimes you can get lucky. After being turned away from La Raspa, we found a restaurant less than a few blocks from the Plaza del Castillo and Bar Txoko. It was called Ñam Restaurantes. They were getting ready to clear a few tables under the canopy, which we ended up moving together to seat all of us. I wondered how Jude (Cash and Courtney's son of 14 years) would react to the fiesta. I used the chance to see what he was thinking so far.

"So, Jude, what do you think of Pamplona? Do you like it?" I asked.

"Yeah... it's cool," he said, nodding his head. Jude was shy, but hilarious and clever.

"What's your favorite part so far?"

"Well, I love the kalimotxo."

"Oh, man! You had a taste of the good stuff!" I said. He grinned sheepishly at Cash and Courtney.

"I tried it yesterday at Mussel Bar," said Jude.

"And the run this morning. Were you able to watch from the barrier?"

"Yeah, we had a good view, but I barely even saw the bulls. People just started running and freaking out. It was like a giant wave of people. It was over really quick."

"Do you want to be a bull runner?" I asked. He gave a little shrug and a grin.

Reeling from the pain of my lower extremities, my back, my hands, and my face, I rested up that evening in my hotel room. Later that night, I went down to the lobby at Hotel Yoldi for some bar food—ensaladilla Rusa and croquetas made with cheese and jamon serrano.

Heading into the second run, on Day 24, there was no reason to change my running strategy. I had timed it perfectly the day before, despite being run over. As a runner, it is critical not to waver from your plan the minute something goes wrong. Unfortunately, I see a lot of runners do this. They might have a string of good days running a particular section, on Estafeta, for example. The section of Estafeta comes just after The Curve and is a 300-meter street with a slight incline. There, the bulls are still fast, and if you cannot keep pace, you will find yourself pushed to the side or on the ground. One bad day on Estafeta might be enough to create some self-doubt about your speed and ability to keep up with the bulls. As a result, the pressure and disappointment, combined with the doubt, cause many to try their luck elsewhere. With so few days to run in Pamplona each year, we place a lot of weight on each run. It can generate a bit of panic and overly rash decision-making. However, the name of the game is repetition.

The greatest bull runners—those that find themselves on the horns, and in front of the herd—run the same way every day. If you watch guys like Aitor Aristregui, Pablo Bolo, Juanpe Lecuona, or David Rodriguez, they always start on the same side of the street and in the same spot in the street. Sure, the formation of the herd might change—bunched up, one long line, broken up into small groups, or even a situation where you have lone bulls— but their repetitive actions give way to consistent results. That is the key. Therefore, it is best to plan your run before you start, visualize your goal, and free up your mind to focus on what you cannot control—the bulls and the constant flailing, pushing, shoving, falling, and tripping of other runners.

On the morning of Day 24, I went down to buy another newspaper. I always threw away my paper from the day before, usually because the pages were tearing at the edges, and the whole thing was just falling apart. I preferred a new, crisp, freshly printed paper each time—they smelled great too. There is a bookshop on Santo Domingo where some of the local runners congregate before the run. The owners of the shop—a woman and her husband—stand outside with stacks of various newspaper publishers. I preferred the "Gara" paper, which has been in print since 1999, and is one of the most widely circulated papers in the Basque Country—buying it was a nod to my Basque heritage. After buying the paper, I ducked inside the bookshop. While most runners loitered outside in the street, some went inside for a few quiet moments and to leave their belongings. Over the years, the owners of the shop added some cubbies for us to leave our wallets, keys, and cellphones. It was best to keep your pockets empty during the run. Inside the shop, I left my phone and some change in a cubby, then slowly walked around the book sections. Aitor Aristregui was there. He was pacing back and forth, looking intensely focused.

Aitor, in my opinion, is the best bull runner in Spain. And I am not alone in that belief. In Pamplona, he runs the Telefonica section, which makes up the final 100 meters that lead into the bullfighting arena. He latches onto the first steer he sees, guides it up the street, then delicately slips behind it, finding a bull and sticking his newspaper in front of its snout. Aside from Pamplona, Aitor also runs in towns all across Spain, winning trophies in places such as San Sebastián de los Reyes, where they awarded him the "Best individual run of the whole fiesta." For a guy like that, any bull running event turns him into a local celebrity. Everyone wants to shake his hand or take a photo with him. And while Aitor is a bit of an introvert, if not shy, his greatness as a runner is unmistakable.

"Hey Aitor, it's good to see you," I said.

"Likewise," said Aitor. He was covering his mouth with his

191

newspaper, which he had folded in an accordion-like way. He did this to widen the newspaper and attract the vision of the bulls. My tactic was similar, but I preferred a rolled-up paper, where I extended it out and wagged it like a stick.

"I just got back from the Camino de Santiago. Have you done it before?" I asked, given that Aitor was passionate about the outdoors.

"No, not yet. I want to though. In September, I'm flying to Arizona with some friends. We're going to spend a week in the desert, looking for rattlesnakes and tarantulas."

"Haha! You're crazy man..." Aitor's Instagram account was full of close-encounters with venomous snakes of all varieties. He loved that stuff.

Before I left the bookshop, Bill Hillmann walked in. He was staying with Paula and her parents, one block away from Hotel Yoldi.

"You know what today is, right?" asked Bill, opening his newspaper and flipping through the pages.

"José Escolar," I said.

"Those are the fuckers that gored me on Santo Domingo," said Bill, referring to an incident in 2017.

"Wow, you're right. They were fast that day," I said, as Bill showed me the photos of the bulls in the newspaper.

In 2017, Bill was recording a documentary, and was trying his hand at running different sections of the course. On July 8, 2017, he ran the latter half of Santo Domingo, just before the town hall. There, the bulls are always blazingly fast, and that morning, Bill could not exit the center of the street in time. The bull chasing from behind gored him in his gluteus, lifted him in the air, and dropped him back onto the cobblestones. The goring left a bloody, open wound that took months to heal.

"They're gonna be fast, man," said Bill.

"Where are you gonna run today?" I asked.

"Telefonica. I like it up there. That's my spot," said Bill. He was in great spirits, and he was running exceptionally. Up on Telefonica, he had guided a few bulls into the arena after they had separated from the pack. It was great to see my friends having good runs.

After the brief chat, I was back on the hill of the town hall, ready to give it another go, hoping not to end up face down on the cobbles again. The crowds on Day 24 were worse than Day 23, since it was a Saturday. On the weekends, the French are famous for making the trek to Pamplona. Moments before the run, I took a final inventory of the situation. I looked to each side, gauging the proximity of the other runners, then looked behind me to get a sense of any street blockage. In my head, I was creating a path for me to slip through once I left my spot and started the run.

BANG! The rocket fired off, sending shockwaves through Pamplona and fear through bodies up and down the run route. The herd rounded the corner in the distance, and I could see the steers out front. I took off jogging toward Mercaderes, weaving through the people standing idly in my path. Then, the ground started shaking, people started panicking, and the runners in front of me had faces of terror as they looked back toward the bulls. Approaching The Curve, my head turned back with the motion of a swivel, and I saw a black bull out-front in the lead position—it was hauling ass. I gravitated toward the outside of the turn, hoping to get some action and attract the bull with my newspaper. A split-second later, that same bull plowed through several runners in its way. It was like a one-bull wrecking crew, bulldozing and demolishing anything in its path. Sensing the danger, I clung to the wall and came to a halt, allowing the bull and the rest of the herd to continue stampeding up Estafeta.

After the herd went up the street, the madness settled. At that point, it was about scanning for injured runners, and making sure my friends were OK. When I looked back, I noticed the guy on the ground was my buddy Andrés Romero. He was down just after The Curve, in front of a mural of San Fermín. He appeared fine, no gorings, but the medics were tending to him. Seeing he had a few people with him, I let them be. I caught up with him later on that day. Aside from some bruises and bloody scrapes, he was in good shape, but he planned to sit out the next encierro to get his body and mind right. Andrés and I frequently run The Curve together, not just in Pamplona, but in San Sebastián de los Reyes too. People know San Sebastián de los Reyes, or "Sanse" for short, as the "Little Pamplona" because it hosts the second most popular bull-running event in Spain. You can always spot Andrés in his bumble-bee, black and yellow-colored sports jersey.

Over at Bar Txoko, I chatted with Cash, as we got tipsy drinking our lugumbas.

"Ah, man, I'm sorry you didn't have a good run," said Cash. The feeling of a bad run is the worst. The run is over just after 08:00, and you have to wait almost 24 hours for another shot. On the flip side, a good run will give you an unimaginable high you can ride the whole day, and then some.

"When I looked back and saw the bull ripping through guys behind me, I stayed the hell out of the way," I said.

"That's what I told Courtney when we watched on TV. I told her 'Ander wouldn't do anything stupid,'" said Cash, patting me on the back.

"Ahhh!" I said, grimacing in pain, still hurting from the bruises and scrapes on my back. My feet had not improved either. If anything, they had gotten worse. All the violent movements of juking, running, and pushing off were tearing more skin on the soles of my feet—it was painful. And I could not stay standing idly for very long. But the headaches were not as bad, and the swollen welt on my forehead had gone down a little. However, the most worrying injuries were the tender, lumpy area of my right temple and the lump on the back of my head. The only saving grace was that my hair covered them up.

I spent the afternoon hanging out with Cash and his family. I only saw Cash once a year at most, and despite the pain I was in, there was no way I was going to waste our time together by lying in bed at Hotel Yoldi. So, we drank tinto de verano and smoked some cigars at another foreigner hotspot called Bar Windsor. The bar is in the plaza del Castillo, where they have a canopy with covered seating, providing shade from the hot Navarran sun.

In the evening, I had to work my second and final shift at Peña La Unica. My duties that night were to set the table and serve dinner to about 40 musicians. The worst part about it was starting at 22:00 and finishing at 02:00 the next day. It was far from an ideal shift, especially considering I had to wake up at 05:45 for the running of the bulls. If I was lucky, I would get a little over three hours of sleep. But the shift selection certainly beat working the bar until 06:00, so I licked my wounds and took it.

Venturing into Calle Jarauta was a suicide mission. By 22:00, everyone had just finished eating dinner, and the real party of San Fermín was throttling into full gear. The walk from Hotel Yoldi should have only taken 5-10 minutes, but it was closer to 20-25 by the time I arrived at the clubhouse. Getting through the crowded streets was like threading a needle. The drunkards were oblivious to the courtesy taps and pleas for space to move through, but I managed. The first task was to pick up the hot sandwiches we had called in at a bar two blocks away. Fighting through the madness once again, I picked up the 40 footlong sandwiches and squeezed my way back to the clubhouse. Then, I set the table, including uncorking over a dozen bottles of red wine, 10 bottles of Basque cider, and a couple of cases of Coca-Cola. After that was done, I had to wait. The 40 musicians were part of the procession that followed that evening's bullfight. Once the fight was over, each peña and their txaranga exited the arena through the "Puerta Grande," or the "Big Door," and paraded through the streets of Pamplona. It could last anywhere from two to three hours, given all the stops they made at bars along the way—they had to stay hydrated.

As I waited for the txaranga to arrive at the clubhouse, my legs were killing me. The alcohol had worn off long ago, and I was at my daily limit for acetaminophen—I always followed Aaron's advice. Once the txaranga finally arrived around midnight, there was no place to sit to take the pressure off my feet and my legs. And I could not go far because I was on call in case the txaranga needed anything else. So, occasionally, I went down to the bodega in the basement and sat on the barrels of beer. Eventually, I had a drink or two. A short while later, I had a surprising distraction from all of it. My phone started ringing. It was Bill Hillmann.

"Ander! Ander! Have you seen the Wall Street Journal today!?"

"What? No, I haven't... why?"

"You're on the front page!"

"No way…"

"Dude, I think it's you! I just sent you the photo," said Bill. What he was saying made no sense. If I did not know that Bill was sober, I would have thought he was drunk. But then I opened the photo.

"Oh my God…" I said. "That *is* me…"

"Brother, I can't believe it… you know how many times that paper was sold? How many people saw that photo?" asked Bill. The Wall Street Journal is the second-most circulated paper in the United States and has a significant global footprint as well.

"How did that happen, man? I just… I don't understand," I said, trying to put together a complete sentence. It was a large photo of me on July 7, rounding the corner of The Curve, with the bulls on my tail, and my outstretched arm drawing the bulls with the tip of a newspaper.

"Look how far you've come, Ander. What you went through growing up… now look at you. You're on the cover of the Wall Street Journal," said Bill with a heartfelt tone. I started tearing up. Since 2017, Bill had been with me on this bull running journey of mine. We met at the hospital the morning of his goring. Since then, we have become brothers, united by our passion of Basque and Spanish culture, and that includes, of course, the running of the bulls.

The photo in the newspaper overwhelmed me. But it was not about vanity. It was about how I bridged the gap between the Camino de Santiago and the running of the bulls. To complete the Camino, I had sacrificed my body through injury. No matter how beat-up I got, or how much I had suffered, there was still more. Then, on the first day of the running of the bulls, I came face-to-face with the reaper. My journey in Spain had been eerily similar to Victor Kershaw's series of unfortunate events. However, at the end of *Pain and Gain*, Kershaw miraculously survives the Sun Gym Gang's attempts on his life. The man just kept holding on. And like Kershaw, I got through it all; I survived. Through the grace of God, and that of Mother Mary, I pushed through the injuries and fulfilled my quest of rounding The Curve with the bulls in Pamplona. This realization got the best of my emotions that night at the clubhouse.

Once my shift was over, I took my rickety and pain-ravaged body back to the hotel. That night, on the phone with Bill, staring at the photo of me in the Wall Street Journal, I had enjoyed my moment of glory. But the next day, it was time to offer it to someone else, someone who deserved it more than me, and someone who would not be around to see it: Jeffrey "Thor" Hendricks.

CHAPTER TWENTYONE:

JEFFREY "THOR" HENDRICKS

A few weeks before I ventured off to Spain to begin the Camino, something terrible happened. My friend's son died. He was just two and a half years old. While Josh, my friend, was away on business, his wife, Amanda, and their three children were out for an evening walk. When they crossed a highway, a vehicle came out of nowhere and struck them. All of them sustained minor injuries and were expected to make full recoveries, except for little Thor. He was in critical condition following the crash that sent him flying 25 feet from his stroller and onto the unforgiving highway pavement. Doctors were working around the clock to reduce the brain swelling. It was causing Thor to go into strokes and seizures.

Growing up with Josh, he and his family were strong in their Christian faith. Josh would frequently volunteer at local churches and serve as a beacon of hope to Christian youth. He was selfless in that way. While little Thor was fighting for his life in the hospital, Josh would post daily updates and requests for prayers on his Facebook page. One particular post really stuck with me:

"The Bible does not give permission for anything other than a posture of, 'God, we ask for a miracle. Touch Thor's body and bring him back to full health. But even if you do not, we trust and love You.' This is my prayer today as we place Thor in God's hands."

After 10 days in the ICU, Thor passed away from his injuries. They scheduled Thor's funeral for Sunday, July 9, or Day 25 of my stay in Spain. When I woke up at the hotel, I texted my friend Josh. It hurt that I could not be there with him and his family to celebrate the life of his son. What made it hurt even more was the fact that this was the second time someone close to me was having their funeral while I was in Spain. In 2005, just days after I graduated from high school, I flew from Oregon to Washington, DC. American University had invited me to attend a summer program, which would kick off my undergraduate career before the fall semester. After the program, I had a few weeks to spare, and went to visit my father in the Basque Country. One of my best friends from high school was still back in Oregon. His name was Clinton Grayson. And in the early morning hours of August 14, while I was in the Basque Country, Clinton died in a car accident. He was riding in the passenger seat, heading to meet up with friends in the beachside community of Seaside. The vehicle was speeding around the winding freeway on the way to the coast. The driver lost control, crashing the car into an embankment, ejecting Clinton from the passenger-side window. Paramedics life-flighted him to the nearest hospital, but he died on the way. Clinton was just 18 years old. Even today, nearly 20 years later, it pains me that I did not attend Clinton's funeral. And now, the same was going to happen with Josh's son, Thor, while I was in Pamplona. But since I could not be there, I wanted to honor Thor's memory in some way. And I thought the best way to do that was to dedicate my morning run to him.

"Going to run for your boy," I wrote to Josh. Then, I got dressed and set out for the run route.

Aside from the extra motivation to run well for Thor, the minutes before the run were like most other days. I required more coffee, since I was running on just a few hours of sleep, following my late-night shift at the peña. I ordered two at El Redín, as I caught up with Cash Lawless. He was going to run the second half of Santo Domingo. Preparing for the running of the bulls in Pamplona was especially difficult for Cash. Just five months earlier, he had a close encounter with a bull when we were in Ciudad Rodrigo. Lesser known by foreigners, but revered by the Spanish nationals, is a bull running event that takes place each year in February. It happens in a town called Ciudad Rodrigo, which is in the Salamanca province of western Spain, just 131 km from the Portuguese border. The event is called "Carnaval del Toro," or "Bull Carnaval." It is a celebration before the commencement of Lent—a period of penance and preparation before Easter. And Cash and I had traveled to Ciudad Rodrigo in February, before the Fiesta of San Fermín.

On one afternoon, there was a lone bull in the street. It stood idly in the shadows of a small tunnel. A group of us runners tried to entice the bull to charge forward, but the bull seemed disinterested. Since we were blocking the bull's vision of a clear exit from the tunnel, we moved to the side to see if it would help. A few seconds later, the bull finally lunged forward up the hill and out of the tunnel. Ciudad Rodrigo is not a place for first-timers, it is a place for veteran runners, given the considerably high level of danger. One thing that separates that town from Pamplona is the tendency for lone bulls. Few things are more dangerous in bull running than when a bull finds itself alone, in an unfamiliar place, surrounded by unfamiliar people, and forced to defend its territory. After the bull lunged forward, the runners and I began jogging down the street, picking up momentum to run with the bull. Cash, at the edge of the tunnel, did not realize the group had taken off. Making matters worse for Cash, three steers had caught up with the lone bull, block Cash's sight of the bull. When Cash realized the danger, he sprinted for the nearest barrier, 10 meters away. But it was too late. The Bull made a bee-line for Cash, then pinned him up against the barrier, ramming its head against his legs. Miraculously, Cash hopped over the barrier with the help of the medics while someone momentarily distracted the bull. Zero gorings, just scrapes, bruises, a mighty scare, and an uncomfortable afternoon.

After our coffee at the bar, I picked up a newspaper and left Cash on Santo Domingo. Up on the hill at the town hall, it felt like there were even more people on Sunday than there were on Saturday. I had picked an especially hard day to dedicate to Thor. The bulls running that day were from a ranch called "Cebada Gago." Historically, this ranch has been the most dangerous to run in Pamplona. In 32 appearances, the ranch had produced 59 gorings—the most of all the ranches in Spain. It was going to be an intense morning.

The stampede of runners took off a few seconds earlier than usual, forcing me to start my jog before I could wait for the herd to get closer—the alternative is getting plowed over by a wave of panicked runners. I slowed my pace once I got to Mercaderes, looking back repetitively. At The Curve, an empty pocket opened up, signaling the proximity of the bulls. There was a light brown bull just behind me. I extended my newspaper with my right arm to draw it in, but as soon as I did that, the bull disappeared behind me as it gravitated to my left. In a split-second, I switched the newspaper to my left hand, trying to get the bull to lock on and follow me through the turn. Unfortunately, I took the turn tighter than the bull, which ended up drifting toward the outside of The Curve and into the barrier. By that point, I was completely out of position, having exited to the right side of the street. It was a good run, but I expected more of myself, particularly since I had dedicated it to Thor.

At Bar Txoko, I bought a round of drinks, then checked on the rest of my buddies. When someone is missing, they stick out like a sore thumb. Fortunately, everyone was present and accounted for. Outside the bar, I talked to Jack, a Canadian runner who has had some epic runs over the years on Estafeta.

"You should've kept going. There was nobody else but you… it was all you," said Jack.

"I know…" I said. "I didn't think the bull would drift so far. And then I exited completely." Had I just drifted with the bull, I would have led it up the street for at least 5-10 meters before I needed to get out.

Chugging my lugumba, I had to put my pensive mind on hold, as we had an event to attend on the other side of the square. The Nuevo Casino Principal, a private society founded in 1856, had organized an event for authors who had written about the Fiesta of San Fermín. Since the year 2023 marked 100 years since Ernest Hemingway's first fiesta in Pamplona, the private society wanted to celebrate the occasion. To do so, they invited me, Bill Hillmann, another buddy of mine named Tim Pinks, and a few other authors to their locale in the Plaza del Castillo. Above Café Iruña, Pamplona's oldest cafe, the Nuevo Casino Principal hosts private dances during the running of the bulls. The tradition began over 150 years ago, when men would go run with the bulls, then stop by the locale for churros and chocolate, before going to work in the morning. At one point, members started bringing guitars, accordions, and other instruments to liven up the social gatherings. This led to organized dances, which they still hold to this day. The most famous of the events is called "El Baile de la Alpargata," or "The Dance of the Espadrille." An espadrille is a rope-soled sandal, which is what men used to wear when they ran with the bulls during the 1850s. Cash and the family accompanied us as we entered the large room inside the locale, where camera crews from TV networks had prepared to capture the momentous occasion. The event began by recognizing the authors as they tied an honorary pañuelo around our necks—the Nuevo Casino Principal has their own pañuelo with an embroidered logo. A few members of my Pamplona family had also come to celebrate. They looked on with pride as I took questions from reporters and spoke to cameras, explaining a little about my story.

"A couple of years ago, I published the book, *In the Shadow of My Land*, which was the Spanish translation of my memoir in English. In it, I tell the story of my life in the Basque Country, of how I embraced the Basque and Spanish culture and of how I went from a very sad and hard life to being reborn in Pamplona," I said to the reporter. "You have to take the risk and dare to go in," I said, alluding to Ernest Hemingway's first adventure in Pamplona, back in 1923.

When the event was over at the Nuevo Casino Principal, Cash and the family took a day trip out to San Sebastián. It is only an hour away, and the beaches there are world famous. Running on three hours of sleep, I could have passed out. However, I thought the beach would be a good chance to get out of "Dodge" and recharge my batteries. Perhaps even more than the physical reset, I just needed a mental reset. It had been three intense bull runs, two long shifts at the clubhouse, a rough crash into the cobbles, and hooves to the head and back. This, on top of every other ailing injury I sustained from the Camino. I needed the sandy beaches of San Sebastián.

We all piled into Cash's rental car, which was easier said than done. I squished into the backseat with Cash's brother, TJ, and sister, Chevy. As

ANDER ETXANOBE

luck would have it, all three of us were avid weightlifters, and we were trying to fit into the backseat of a small European sedan. While Cash drove, Courtney and her son, Jude, took the passenger seat. We almost shed tears when we arrived in San Sebastián—the car ride sucked. But the beach, pintxos, red wine, and cheesecake awaited us.

The beach in San Sebastián is called "La Concha," or "The Shell." This is because, from a bird's-eye view, the beach wraps around in a semicircle fashion, resembling a shell. The two mountains on each end create a gateway to the sea, famous for its strong winds. Boats sit idly, anchored up in the harbor. Kids play on floating pool-decks, about 100 meters from the shore. Upon arrival, we found the beaches packed with people. It was the height of summer, and everyone wanted to work on their tan, apparently. Cash, Jude, TJ, and Chevy, being creatures of water, darted for the ocean as soon as we set foot in the sand. Courtney and I stayed back, laid down some towels, and passed out for a few hours. "Go have fun!" we shouted as they sprinted each other to see who could reach the water first. The beach was relaxing, but the trip would not have been complete if we had not visited the basilica.

Tucked away in the back of old town San Sebastián, at the end of Calle Mayor, stands the Basilica of Santa María del Coro. The church sits at the foot of Monte Urgull, which separates the church from the northern coastline. It is an eighteenth-century Baroque-style building, with two towers and a glorious façade in the middle. Just below the clock, there is a statue of Saint Sebastián, who was a persecuted Christian in the third century. They tied him to a tree and shot him with arrows, but he did not die. After being rescued by Saint Irene of Rome, he would later meet his end at the hands of Diocletian, a Roman emperor, who had him clubbed to death. Hundreds of years later, Saint Sebastián would become the namesake of the coastal city of San Sebastián.

When we entered the church, each of us kind of wandered around for a bit. We walked around the large, rectangular shape of the interior, which boasted a semicircular apse, octagonal pillars, and a central vault that measured 27 meters in height. After we took it all in, Cash and I took a seat on a bench, gazing up at the altar. The rest of the family joined us one by one. In the group, I was the only one with Catholic roots, but Cash's family was devoutly Christian. As we sat there, the Fiesta of San Fermín seemed so distant, it all seemed so far away. It was a comforting feeling. Perhaps it was the quiet, calm nature of the basilica. The fiesta is a 24-hour party of non-stop chaos, and although we all loved it, it could also be a bit much. Even when you retreat to your hotel, there is no way to fully escape the noise and the hectic atmosphere. But inside the basilica, it sort of felt like we could breathe again.

Now, more than ever, I was feeling the accumulation of everything: the fatigue, aches, pains, injuries, scrapes, bruises, and mental strain. Perhaps the comforting feeling of sitting on the wooden bench together was just the realization that we were on the verge of burnout—at least I was. People always say that when times are hard, you must "dig deep" to push forward. But the last 25 days in Spain had been a continuous session of "digging deep." And it felt like I had reached the bottom. The figurative shovel clang repetitively against the rock. There was no more to dig. In my heart and soul, I just wanted one glorious run for Thor. Just one.

After the visit to the basilica, we stopped at a nearby restaurant called La Viña. It is famous for its "Basque burnt cheesecake." The major difference between this cheesecake and regular cheesecake is the burnt and caramelized exterior. They also filled the cake with a creamy custard that was just delightful. We ordered everyone extra-large pieces, along with a couple of bottles of Rioja wine. I chuckled to myself about how I had walked past all of those vineyards on the Camino in the La Rioja region. It was nice to be on the other side, enjoying the grapes in the form of a glass of red wine. The cheesecake was a big hit with the group. The tasteful flavor was unique, and unlike anything they had ever tried. However, it was not shocking to experience great food in San Sebastián. After all, San Sebastián has 19 Michelin star restaurants—the highest concentration per square kilometer in all of Europe.

With the wine bottles emptied and the cheesecake devoured, we did something fun. Cash and Courtney's son, Jude, had brought a miniature soccer ball with him. And the great thing about most towns in the Basque Country—big or small—is that they have a "fronton," a court where people play pelota-mano and jai-alai. However, kids will use the court for just about any type of activity. And since we did not have a handball, we used Jude's soccer ball as one on the court. We took turns whacking the ball with our hands, sending it flying up against the wall in front of us, then back down. We would let the ball bounce once, then smash it again. Sometimes the ball would bounce off the front wall, then off the left wall, requiring us to angle our bodies to get a good, clean hit. Within minutes, our hands were puffy and beet red. From the start, I was moving gingerly, limping from side to side to reach the ball. I could not leap, skip, or jump—my feet would not leave the ground. I was in no condition to play handball, and much less a condition to run with the bulls in Pamplona.

We cut the day in San Sebastián short when we realized that TJ and Chevy had tickets to the bullfight that same evening. So, while they went to the bull flight, we stopped over at Cash and Courtney's apartment on Navarrería, near the town hall. Iker and Ane were staying in the same apartment as Cash and Courtney, and they were both there when we walked in. Iker had just come back for a quick break before returning to his bull running tours, and Ane was there taking conference calls on her laptop. They had saved a newspaper clipping for me from the Diario de Noticias, a Navarran newspaper. There was a photo of me running with the bulls with my tongue hanging out. I like to do that when the bulls are close, in those few seconds of intensity. It is a natural reaction. I am not sure why I started doing it, but the tongue almost wags itself. Maybe because I idolized Michael Jordan as a kid and practiced the "tongue-flare" in our driveway. Still, it was a cool moment to share with Cash and the gang, and a special memento to take home with me. Yet, it was an undeniable reminder that I was unsatisfied with my run for Thor.

That evening, after a nice and relaxing trip to the beach, a perfectly timed getaway from Pamplona, I just wanted the whole thing to be over. The taste of the good life was good. It reminded me of being back in Miami, basking in the sunshine of the never-ending summer. It reminded me of those late-night walks down the boardwalk, taking in the glistening, neon lights of Ocean Drive, or how I enjoyed those early morning sunrises with the fiery, peach-colored sky. I wanted to be back under the palm trees, sipping on a cocktail with my feet up. But I knew Thor deserved more than that. And I expected more of myself than that.

Unsatisfied with the partially good run, I woke up with another shot on Day 26. There was another opportunity to make good on my promise to Josh, and to honor his son, Thor. As I washed my face, I kept repeating to myself, "Stay with the bull, stay with the bull." I imagined myself rounding that dangerous corner. As my friend Jack Denault likes to say, "Holding your position out in front of the bull is one of the hardest things to do. It's frightening." Your body, with every ounce of instinct, wants to avoid the danger. You need to wage a battle in your mind to control your body, which is much easier said than done. And one or two seconds can make all the difference. At the same time, the wager you are making is the one with your life. So, wager carefully. As they say, "If you believe you can do something, you probably can. And if you don't believe, you probably can't." That morning, I believed. And I was about to push all of my chips into the center of the table. I was going all in.

The bulls that took part in the run that day were from "Fuente Ymbro," a ranch that had made a resurgence by appearing in the last couple of fiestas in Pamplona. These bulls were big, fast, and tough. Before I went to buy a newspaper, I realized I had no more change, so I asked my friend Will Mulkeen.

"Hey Will, do you think you can spare a couple of euros so I can buy paper?" I asked.

"I'd be honored to pay for your paper," he said, jokingly, not thinking twice as he handed me two euros. I felt embarrassed asking for money like that.

"Thank you so much, Will. I'll pay you back at Bar Txoko," I said.

"Ander, come on. It's two euros. You don't need to pay me back two euros," he said as I laughed. Will had a warm heart. He was always in a good mood, and always ready to party.

On the hill at the town hall, I was preparing to empty the tank—completely. However, the flames inside me were flickering in my frail state. But running well was no longer a hope, an aspiration, or a nice-to-have. It was the only way. And when we find meaning behind the things we do, we will go to extreme lengths to achieve them. Honoring Thor was like adding kerosine to a waning fire. The thought of Thor summoned something deep, something beast-like in me that day. My heart was pounding with the ferocity of church bells, my veins ran cool like the misty air above the Pyrenees, and my spirit roared with the intensity of a thousand lions ready to devour their prey. I was ready. Bouncing from side to side, I tuned out all the noise. And when the clock tower rang from atop the façade of the town hall, I beat my chest with my fist so hard that others around me heard the loud thud. Blessed by my rosary and protected by Mother Mary, both necklaces were tangled up around my neck. I said a quick prayer, and then I was off.

I was moving in slow motion, weaving through the crowd, finding the nooks and open spaces among the other runners. Keeping my position in the center of the street, I began looking back about halfway down Mercaderes. The screams grew louder as the herd approached. Runners fanned off to the sides as the Fuente Ymbro gave chase. I looked back again and saw my buddy, Iker. As soon as he cleared, I saw nothing but bulls out front. That was a runner's dream. There were four fighting bulls leading the way. At the back, they were black, beige, and brown. At the front, with a few meters of distance between the others, was a black and brown bull, charging ahead with a vengeance. He cut through the runners like a buzz saw. "Stay with the bull, stay with the bull," I said to myself. I eased off the gas, holding my viewpoint of the bull a little longer now that he was closer. About 10 meters from The Curve, I took a stride, pushing off with my right foot, then felt a sharp pull—I had torn the fragile, blistery skin on the sole of my foot. But I remained committed and had to keep going. Just 10 more meters, and then 5 more meters. My rosary and Mother Mary necklace dangled inside my shirt. My tongue was wagging in the cool morning air, and beads of sweat dripped down my face. I pushed off with my left foot, lunged my right leg forward, then reached back with my outstretched arm. I drifted into the deep end of The Curve, bringing the lead bull with me smoothly around the corner. This was not my moment. This was Thor's moment. I looked back and stared into the bull's eyes, pointing the paper at the bull, right between the horns. I floated effortlessly above ground with each stride around the corner. The camera lights flickered along the outside barrier as photographers scrambled for the best shot. The bull slobbered at the snout as its hooves collided with the cobbles. I took the bull a few meters further up Estafeta, then cleared out to the right side of the street. My job was done. The rest of the herd plowed forward without a hitch, as I tried to recover my breath. My heart was beating uncontrollably as I tried to grasp what had just happened. I cannot overstate the euphoria I felt in the seconds after that run. There is no drug on earth, no injection available, no drink served that could replicate that feeling.

Reeling from the effort, I limped over to the bookshop, where I had left my phone in a cubby. I had to text Josh. I wanted to share the good news. After the run, my cousin discovered photos of me online, leading the Fuente Ymbro around The Curve. I sent them to Josh. Then he texted back.

"You honored him by facing fear in the face… brought me to tears, man," said Josh. I celebrated with a couple of lugumbas at Bar Txoko, then spent most of the afternoon in bed. I was finished.

CHAPTER TWENTYTWO:

THE END OF THE JOURNEY

Clinton Grayson, my friend, was a dedicated Christian. He attended church regularly with his brother, Tyson. They even went to youth group meetings together, where teenage Christians came together for worship. One of his favorite passages from the bible was from Psalm 139:14. It reads:
"I praise you, for I am fearfully and wonderfully made. Wonderful are your works; that I know very well."
Clinton loved the verse so much that after his passing, his family had it etched on his gravestone. I think about Clinton and that verse often.
By July 10, or Day 26, I had been through half of the bull runs at the 2023 edition of the running of the bulls. Following the aftermath of my "Run for Thor," my friends came to my aid. Cash and his family, even Iker and Ane, all came up to my room at Hotel Yoldi. Aaron and Caroline had since departed back to the United States. Iker came in with a slew of fresh supplies from the pharmacy, ready to put his army medic knowledge to good use. TJ also lent a hand, helping to cut away all the blister skin that had torn from my feet. Together, they doused my feet in 96% alcohol and wrapped everything back up. Jude watched from afar in disgust—he said he could smell the ripped up and blistery skin, but he was a champ, and stayed.
The next day, I introduced Jude to the kid's version of the running of the bulls, where adults roll around wheelbarrows with bull-heads mounted on the front—horns and all. They ran the make-shift bulls up and down Santo Domingo, as hundreds of kids of all ages took their shot at leading the bulls up the street. Jude got front and center with the bulls, leaving no doubt that one day he, too, would take part in the tradition. Amidst the madness of all of those kids, he held firm, kept his spot in the street, and turned his head

back and forth to measure the distance of the bull, just like a great runner. It was a beautiful way to introduce the younger generations to bull running. In the years to come, some of those kids will surely become the next generation of great bull runners—Jude included.

To put it simply, I burned my last match during the fourth run in Pamplona. I was totally and utterly spent. In fact, I did not run very well in those last four days of the fiesta. My timing was off every single day, my positioning was subpar, and I even took a few tumbles when exiting to the side of the street. Despite everything, every morning in Pamplona, I was out there with my newspaper, prepared to face the bulls on the cobblestone streets. I kept at it, regardless of the absence of glory. My friends Bill, Cash, and Iker helped ease the pain of the last stretch of the fiesta. It was a blessing to have them. None of them cared whether I ran well. They were there to support me, and I was there to support them.

During the final run, Day 30 in Spain, we ran with the "Miura" ranch. These bulls are the most prestigious in all of Spain. What sets them apart is their uncharacteristically long and large bodies, their long and wide sets of horns, and their performance in some of the most epic bull fights in the history of bullfighting. The fight that stands out is the one that occurred in 1947. A bullfighter known as "Manolete," born in Córdoba, was fighting a Miura bull in the town of Linares, Spain. The 30-year-old Manolete had already become a legend, having fought around 100 times. He also suffered 11 gorings. And after an illustrious and decorated career, Manolete had announced his intent to retire. But before he hung up his cape for good, he embarked on what would be his last season. During one of his final bullfights, he prepared to make the final blow. And when he went in for the kill with his sword, the Miura bull gored him in his right thigh. The goring severed the femoral artery, which caused massive blood loss. Despite the immediate care of doctors and surgeons, including several blood transfusions, Manolete succumbed to his injuries from the Miura bull, and died later that evening. On the last day of the running of the bulls, we were going to run with the same ranch.

Since 2017, I always wear a white blazer when running with the Miura ranch. The tradition began with some of the earlier American runners, like Matt Carney, Joe Distler, and Tom Gowen, who would wear a white blazer to honor the Miura ranch. And for one reason or another, I too picked up the tradition. The bulls came out hot that day, storming down Mercaderes and cutting sharply through The Curve on the inside of the street. The herd was mostly compact, leaving behind a trail of carnage and destruction. I passed through The Curve a little earlier than most other days, with the bulls still four or five meters behind me. Nearby runners tugged at the tails of my white blazer that flew around as I ran. As I exited The Curve, one runner almost took me down to the ground, pulling down on my blazer in sheer panic. But I withstood the pull and continued. I kept running up Estafeta, holding the center of the street. When I looked back, I saw a steer was out front, providing cover to a string of black bulls on the left. Instantly, I tried maneuvering toward the bulls, but I collided with another runner, which sent me flying to the opposite side of the street, just inches in front of the horns of the steer. Then, my run was officially over.

Following the run, I spotted Iker. He was walking back toward The Curve, with his hand trembling. He had scrapes and cuts all over.

"Iker, what happened?" I asked.

"I went down," said Iker. The hard fall was unlucky. It is difficult to avoid the litany of bodies that line the cobbles after a few bulls have already torn through the street. Still, we were both able to walk away, which meant everything.

Iker and I met up later at the "Runner's Breakfast," a traditional, invite-only meal that began with the greatest Basque and Spanish runners. Americans and other foreigners have also received invitations in the last several decades. Since it was our last big meal together, the rosado wine flowed a little easier, and our glasses became empty more quickly. I even gave Jude my rolled-up newspaper from the run with the Miura ranch, since he wanted one as a souvenir. After we finished eating, Cedric Justice, an old friend of mine, joined us. He was spending the summer in Bilbao and Barcelona, and had hopped on a bus to come enjoy the last day of the fiesta. Cedric and I worked together years ago. When he walked through the door behind me, Jude's face changed completely. I knew it had to be Cedric. Standing at a towering six-feet five-inches, Cedric is a teddy bear of a person, but he stuck out like a sore thumb, and it was awesome. He walked in with his blue hair and black goth attire. It was fun to have him around. One fun fact about Cedric is his love of The Cure. He is such a fan, in fact, that he was once part of a tribute band—he looks just like Robert Smith.

I spent the afternoon with Cedric, Cash and his family, drinking tinto de verano under the canopy at Bar Windsor. There was a street musician with a drum set across from the bar—Cedric could not resist. Being the musician that he is, he went and asked the guy if he could play for a few minutes. I followed him over with my phone, recording every drumbeat. Within moments, there were dozens of festivalgoers surrounding Cedric, all with their phones out recording the blue-haired goth playing the drums—it was a great way to close out the fiesta.

Before we parted ways with everyone, we all went down to the town hall for the closing ceremonies, or as the locals call it, the "Pobre de Mi." The "Poor Me," as it is called in English, drove the masses to the square. The passionate and somber mood spread through the crowd. It was nearing midnight, as the clock on the façade moved ever closer to the end of the fiesta. The square was lit up by candles held in everyone's hands, raised in honor of San Fermín. And before I knew it, the fiesta was over, and I was on a plane heading back to Florida.

On my first day back in Miami Beach, I woke up early from the jet lag. It was 05:45 in the morning. More than ever, it felt strange not having to walk over 40 kilometers, or not having to run in barricaded streets with bulls chasing from behind. It was very weird. But I was already up, so I threw my shoes on and walked three blocks to the beach. I sat down on the sand, about 10 feet from the shore. Still dark outside, I thought back to when I was on the Camino de Santiago. I thought back to those cool morning starts, when I would set out to climb a mountain at 04:30, feeling the fear of how that day would end, whether I would even make it, or whether I would come away injured. I thought about how alone it felt at times, walking by myself out in the hills of Spain. The pain was unlike any I had ever felt before. And I think I learned why.

The fiery-peach-colored sky was rising on the horizon, as I sat on the sandy shores of the beach. The Camino had humbled me through pain, more pain than I had ever expected, but it brought me to my breaking point. And only at that breaking point did I ask God for help. The truth is, God, his angels, and Mother Mary were always there, even before I asked for help. That minor detail will be my fondest memory of the 800km hike through Spain. I will also cherish the pain I felt when I hopped on a train from Santiago and dove headfirst into the running of the bulls in Pamplona. Despite my ailing feet and my injured and fatigued state, I had the faith in God to guide me. Despite being trampled by the bulls and suffering a concussion on the first day, my faith did not waver. Through God, I can achieve anything. He taught me that his presence is constant and never-ending. It is forever.

On my wall in Miami Beach, I have two glass frames that hang side by side: one displays my Compostela, and the other features me running with the bulls on the Wall Street Journal front page. When I look at those two frames, I think of God. At several points in my life, whether it was moving to the Basque Country as a kid, moving back to the United States, or my parents' divorce, I often turned to myself to dig my way out of a hole. And when I did, I think I took more credit than I deserved. God had always had my back. He taught me that through humility. And the vehicle was a 30-day trip to Spain, with a whole lot of pain.

ABOUT THE AUTHOR

Ander is an author and full-time business professional. When he's not writing or advising companies on corporate finance, Ander runs with the bulls in towns across Spain. He is the son of a Basque sheepherder who immigrated to the United States in the 1970s. Ander holds a dual specialization in Finance and International Business from American University in Washington, DC, and the Chartered Financial Analyst (CFA) Designation.